What Happens After The Game

A Memoir

Michelle Reed

Miracle Mindsett LLC

Note

Dedication

To the unwavering beacon that has guided every step of my life's journey, I humbly dedicate these memories, overflowing with profound gratitude, to my Lord and Savior. In this extraordinary voyage that I call life, He is my constant companion, without whom I would cease to exist. His divine presence permeates the core of my being, and I am eternally thankful for this.

I offer my heartfelt appreciation to my cherished family, steadfast friends, invaluable coaches, loyal teammates, wise mentors, trusted advisors, and esteemed associates—each thread intricately woven into the fabric of my existence throughout the diverse stages of my life. You have contributed immeasurable joy, shared laughter, and invaluable lessons, etching countless memories into the tapestry of my story. I wholeheartedly embrace every moment, whether laden with goodness, adversity, or neutrality, for they have all shaped me into who I am today.

With thanks,

Michelle

Acknowledgments

Writing this book has been deeply personal and transformative, and I am indebted to numerous individuals whose support and influence have made this endeavor possible. It is with immense gratitude that I acknowledge the following people:

To my mother, **Marlene J. Reed**, who is my soulmate and lifeline. Your unwavering love and support are the power pack of my entire life. **Handsome Kelly**, my best friend and brother, our bond is irreplaceable. I trust you with my life, and I say that with pride. Words cannot explain how much you mean to me. **Carlene Preston**, thank you for being my friend. You have been riding with me in my happiest and saddest days, and I can never repay you for being you. To **Kesha Worrell**, for your constant encouragement for me to write, write, write, and then publish this book. Your check-ins and guidance have been non-stop, and I appreciate you so much. To **Keith K.L. Belvin**, for the mentorship you have offered me throughout my writing journey. Our brainstorming sessions, idea creations, and accountability calls have been just what I needed to get through this process. **Victor Reed**, my oldest brother. Thank you for believing that time and growth heal. I've always admired you from a child, and time has brought us closer, and I am thankful for that. **Tammy Harrison**, my sister-in-law, thank you for being a part of our family. Your presence and energy bring joy to us all, and your knowledge and support are priceless. To my older brothers, **Jeff and Dee**; to **my nieces and nephews**; and to my **goddaughter, Brook**, I love you. To all of my extended family & friends, all of my teammates & coaches throughout my life, all of the schools I attended & the teachers who were committed to my learning. To the **Heath Family** for always being there every step of the journey. To the **Courtlandt family** for being that extended family. To **Therese Myers**, thank you for the accountability calls and for pulling me out of my shell to start speaking about my experiences more. It goes to show good people come into our lives at the right times and for the right reasons. To **Shonell Bacon** and **Ms. Dorinda**, for your support in helping me edit this book. You have been an important part of this process, and I thank you so much. To **Nike Reed**, those of you who are pet lovers will understand more than anyone the unconditional love a pet offers. You give me a life-saving connection and bond every day. To all who cheered for me in the stands, asked for my autograph, took pictures with me, and shared your words of encouragement. To the parents of all the student-athletes who have trusted my guidance and experiences enough to speak with and mentor your children, thank you. I plan to continue that journey because there are so many more I haven't embraced yet, but I hope to.

To our angels in heaven: **Simone C. Courtlandt, Yvonne Dumpson, Uncle Edward Dumpson Jr., Kim Levy, Grandma Cleo, GrandPop Eddie Dumpson Sr., Tiger, Ms. Johnson, Suzie Q, Ms. Gantt, Ms. Washington, Nikki Washington, Maxine Washington, Aunt Rainie, Uncle Oliver, my godsister Vanessa, Mr. & Mrs. Sommerville, and so many more**, I know you are looking down from Heaven, proud of me and the family. Thanks for the parts of my life you filled with love and purpose. You are forever missed.

I would also like to thank **Noire Publishing House** for their exceptional consulting services. **Sheryl Prince**'s guidance has been invaluable and appreciated.

To anyone I may have missed, please charge it to my fleeting memory and not to my heart.

Contents

Finding My Voice
Celebrating Individuality from Writing

Writing this book brings up a lot of feelings for me. It took me over 10 years to get comfortable with letting people in on the private parts of my life and then four years to become vulnerable enough to work toward publishing it. It is one thing to share my experiences that were already in the public eye, but it was a whole other thing to digging deeper into myself and answering the question "How vulnerable am I able to be?" required a lot of inner work. In addition to that, I had to face hard truths about myself because if I was going to put things out there, I had to keep it one hundred with how I showed up in every experience. I had to take complete ownership of the hard truths in order to grow through this book. I was taking responsibility for everything, even the things beyond my control.

I understand more about cause and effect and how much of where I was mentally played a part in my present life. My connection with self helps me to this point. Understanding my relationship with myself and the love I have for all of who I am is so important.

One activity I have pursued since I was a little girl aided me in putting my experiences onto paper and learning and growing through those experiences: journaling. I honestly think I found my love for journaling and writing when I was in elementary school, and one of my teachers made me write "I will not talk without permission in class" 50 times. At first, it felt like torture, but ultimately, it became practice. I got to work on my spelling and my handwriting. At home, I was always doodling on paper, acting like I was a teacher, and working on my letters. So why was this any different? I got tired of the repetitive wording, but the only time it really affected me was when it cut into my recreation time. I didn't have these assignments too often because I followed instructions well, but there were times when I would get a little fresh at the mouth.

After school, I would go home and write my letters from A to Z, line by line, over and over again to work on my penmanship. Line one all A's, line two all B's, all the way to Z. Then I started playing with words. When we had spelling words to study, I would write them over and over again. This helped me learn the words quicker, and they stuck. When I took my test, I could visualize the words as if I were writing them out. This worked well for me, I aced every spelling test, getting one or two wrong here and there. I usually got those wrong because I would rush, be anxious, miss a letter, or get confused by the order of "i" and "e" in words like "achieve" and put "ei."

I found myself writing more and more as a way to express myself and show my emotions. Being the baby in the house, I heard and saw a lot but didn't always understand it all. These were times when I would open up my loose-leaf notebooks or composition books and write whatever was on my mind. I always wrote before going to bed, and when I was in class and got bored with the lessons, I would doze off into writing about being a star athlete one day.

The older I got, the more I wrote. To this day, I have journals about my life in different storage areas in my house. Sometimes, I would find them during my spring cleanings and reminisce. Some go as far back as junior high (JHS), but most were from my high school, college, and adult years. When I reflect now on my journals, I look at where my thought patterns were then and how much they have changed, if they have changed at all. One thing my journaling shows me is how much I tend to write compared to how much I tend to say. I learned that my true self comes through my writing. As a reader, you can feel the emotions and gain more of an insight into how I am feeling way more than I could give you in a speech. I feel heard when I write, and I feel understood.

To this day, journaling helps me get clarity on my thoughts and feelings in ways that I can go back and reflect on at another time. It teaches me about why I write, what drives me to write, who I tend to write about, and if I've learned anything. From my writings, I got to see what experiences and habits I repeated, what excited me, what made me sad, how I communicated, and what areas I was consistent and inconsistent in. I learned about my fears and my challenges. I learned what drives me and what shuts me down. I got to see how I view love and when I was afraid of it.

Journaling is powerful for so many reasons. It's more than learning about my emotional intelligence; it shows me the patterns of my thoughts. It has taught me to be honest with myself because what I am writing is a no-judgment zone all my own. If I cannot write and be honest with myself, then what does that behavior say about my life as a whole? Journaling gives me a reason to be real and truthful with myself. This is my time, my safe space, my reality, my truth, and my reflections. Be it real or made up, it's for me to understand and relate to.

And through this book, what I have come to understand about myself I share with you, and it is my hope that you can glean something important from my story so that you, too, can learn and grow in your journey of self-discovery and personal success.

Healing Wounds & Crafting a New Mindset

Affirmation: I Am Naturally Brilliant, Marvelous, & Phenomenal.

When I first started writing this book, it was with a victim's mindset. I blamed this one and that one for how things played out in my life. My childhood was impacted by so many experiences that the effects resonated into my adult life. I had not yet acquired coping skills to mold these experiences into wisdom, strength, and a refined version of myself. Yes, some experiences were painful, but the woman in me now understands that in order for me to be who I am meant to be, I have to stop blaming others, pointing fingers, and living in those experiences. I realized I had to grow the hell up. It doesn't mean my past should be forgotten and people should easily be forgiven. It means my past cannot continue to hold me back from what I want my present to be.

There are people I need to speak with to address some things I need to get off my chest. In order for me to be genuine and real with you, the reader, I have to be willing to face who I was then and hear their part in that experience. It's not about what their perception of me was but more about resolve for me. Even if the conversation ends with us not seeing eye to eye, I am ok with the process that happened. The idea is to speak on it, not live in it anymore, and to move past what has me stuck like a stubborn stain that will not wash away no matter how many times I tried. No, I am not referencing every relationship. I am referencing those strong ones that started as friends and family-ship, developed a love, but flatlined for reasons that resulted in absence.

This book and process isn't about going back and developing or demeaning them. It is about self-love and recognizing what is important and what must happen so I can continue with my life's journey. To revoke the negativity of the past and concentrate on the creation of a path of positivity. I'm not trying to change the past nor reenact any scenes to make them look or feel different. Absolutely not. It is time to face those experiences head-on, embracing the messages I didn't get back then, and to rediscover them now so that I can share meaningful experiences with you.

I will introduce to you all facets of myself by peeling away my layers to expose the marvelous and phenomenal woman that I am in all of my imperfections. Some experiences will come off in victimized forms only because I never sat down to understand the lesson. I want to put you in my mind, body, and spirit and then share with you the outcomes, be it a Cinderella ending or a continued work in progress. Trust and believe, there is still a lot of growing that I have to do, and some things need addressing to move on from it.

I have actions that haunt me and take up space in my mind because those wrongs cannot be made right. I prayed and gave those situations to my Savior and asked for his forgiveness. As you travel with me on this journey, know that I speak from the heart, and write each chapter from a place of growth and hope. I hope that what I share with you is conveyed in the best way possible for you to connect with and understand even if you don't agree with it.

This book needs to be written not just for the healing of the little girl in me but also for to the brilliant woman I am destined to be. This book is for everyone who identifies with daily struggles, entrapment in webs of despair, and the victory that emerges when self-truth, love, and strength are found. I had received these things, but I needed to take the blinders off, heal from within, take responsibility for my life, and forgive myself for what I didn't know but had to live through. The great part about life is it's a constant and necessary journey of experiences. My past does not define who I am, but it influences who I am on a personal level and how I view my possibilities. The goal is always to see things from many perspectives and to understand how to respond with what I am confronted with. My past shaped who I am and gave me the capacity to grow and change along the way. My ability to understand and change within helped me pave the way for who I am in the present.

I choose to utilize my experiences as part of my blueprint toward being better, dreaming bigger, shaping my culture, and celebrating one victory at a time. I let my stinking thinking set me back for too many years. In order to grow authentically, I had to break bondages of the past.

My commitment to myself is to practice getting right—not perfect but right.

Right starts with having a healthy mindset, body, and spirit.

It comes with healing and forgiveness to self, so let me say, *Michelle K. Reed, I forgive you, girl, and I love you even more. I know to serve me well I must let the knowing begin.*

Family, Community, and the Inner Child

All of us have a story to tell, a story that illustrates how we've come to be who we are, and if we spend enough time reflecting on the trajectory of our lives, we'd come to realize that our TODAY is connected directly to how we were raised, what we were (and weren't) taught, and how these early experiences affected, for better or worse, our words and actions. And if we dig deeper than that, we'd come to understand what helped us and what failed us and what choices we can make now for a better tomorrow.

Creating a Lasting Legacy by Tailoring My Why

As a little Black girl raised in 40 Projects in South Jamaica, Queens, I knew there was more to my life than the brick buildings we lived in; the brick buildings I went to school in; and the drugs, death, and crime that was surrounding my neighborhood. I came from a single-parent home with my mother raising me and my three older brothers. At that time, no one could convince me we were considered a low-income poor family because we always had everything we needed. We had food, clothes, toys, TV, music, furniture, a clean apartment, heat, a/c, hot and cold water, washer and dryer, and all the essentials we needed to stay clean and smelling good every day. Even with the shooting and killings in the neighborhood, I felt safe and was looked after by everyone. This was truly a time where the village helped raise the kids. Police officers that walked the beat knew us by our names, played stickball with us and, if they saw us, made sure we knew they had an eye on us.

In my community, we were taught by adults and our teachers that our actions mattered, and they were concerned about the choices we made. It was because of that love and protection that I engaged in sports. People recognized my talents early and encouraged me to participate in activities that shined a light on my gifts. They let me know early that I had the ability to make it out of the hood and make something of my life. I didn't really understand what "out the hood" looked and felt like, but the older I got, the more sense it made. The more I engaged in sports, the bigger the world got beyond the projects

I lived in. What was on TV was often told to us that it wasn't real, but it helped me fantasize of what could be. There were predominantly white actors showing on our black and white TV, but it still painted clear pictures of houses with stairs and the kids having their own rooms, a family car, taking family trips, singing songs together, eating dinner together, looking happy and jolly. Yeah, my family often sat down and ate together, played music that we sang and danced to and that made our home full of laughter and fun. So, they just weren't winning on TV; we were winning in my house, too. At least for a while but let me not jump the gun.

I was a regular little Black girl who loved school, loved sports, and loved playing with my friends. I didn't know what a dysfunctional household was or that much was wrong because my mother protected me from whatever she could to keep my possibilities of making it out the hood real.

I want this book to tell the story about the little Black girl who defied odds, made it out the hood, and stretched herself so far that she achieved more than what the world painted for her. I want this book to speak to the journey, the lessons, the fights, the setbacks, the poor choices, the wins, the confrontations, the fears, the days I quit and the days I regained my strength and lived to fight another day. I want this book to speak about my brokenness and how I learned to turn those bruises into a legacy that will outlive me.

I knew I needed to write this book when I started feeling down on myself and forgot about where I started, what I achieved, and how much more that is still left for me to do. Those days when I heard parents wondering how they could help their kids fulfill their dream, I realized they didn't know who they could turn to or trust. Those student-athletes who have dreams of making millions playing the sports that they love but feel they can't do it because the people around them keep telling them they can't. This book is for those athletes who don't know that their talents are their brands and that the moment they acknowledge their gifts and accept their true selves they will become marketable and get to tell the world how to do things on their terms. This book is for the little girl whose family stole her dreams and made her feel like she wouldn't amount to anything because they didn't live up to their potential... But then, then that person comes along and lets her know that her opportunities are endless, and if she dreams it, she can achieve it. This book is for those who just need to learn the mental capacity of athletes—what we go through internally and how sometimes the sport is our cry for help, and we run to it because it doesn't judge us, and we can be true versions of ourselves when we are engaged in it. This book is for that community leader whose voice and presence is needed to use their influence and power to bring options, opportunities, and funding to the disenfranchised; to be the help communities need so impacts can be felt where we live and dwell not because of our skin color but because we deserve to have great lives, too.

I wrote this book because it is the right time for me to share what I inherited from the people who led me to my truth, through my struggles, and reminded me every day that my dream is yet realized, but I will make it. I want to give back to others as much as I can of what was given to me in the shape of HOPE. That's exactly what I incorporated in this book. I may have been born and raised in the projects, but I am not, nor was I ever, anyone's project, and you aren't either. You get to set your course, believe in your vision, and generate your own reality. You get to choose because you have a choice. What you will read isn't experiences I read from someone else and am now summing it up for you. These are my real-life moments of triumph and victory, and how the walk I am on today is still being realized. It may be a culture shock for some, and no surprise to others, but through tears and laughter, pain, and passion, I am here, and there is no limit to my prophecy. I didn't, nor do I have to, settle for what others say I am worth. With knowledge and execution, I get to make the rules, and you do, too.

I know I can reach more people with a book than I ever could talking in classrooms or in small groups. I needed to write this book to start the healing process for young ladies at the community level, and then expand to the national levels. I needed to write this book to get this wisdom into the rooms I wasn't physically in and to the parents who I know wants to hear it, but I couldn't reach. I know there are a lot of girls out there with dreams of playing junior high, senior high, college, and pro basketball and are committed to their future. But you should know the journey and the hard work that goes into achieving such success. You should also know that not everyone succeeds, just like not everyone fails.

It isn't so much about what I made and how I made it but more about how much of what I experienced you can learn from and use so that you don't go blind into pursuing YOUR dream. Everyone must learn from someone; what better people to learn from than those like myself who already lived it. Use what you can, make it yours, and blaze your own trail. Take my pains and my pleasures, not just my wins. Nothing comes easy, and no one's path will ever be without conflict or struggle.

You will inherit some bad habits from family members that you will need to heal from. Unfortunately, we are taught things meant for others but get passed onto us. But you must learn how to recognize these things and heal past them so that they don't become setbacks for you. You will live a phase where you blame yourself because of what you didn't know, but when you know better, you do better or continue to be ruined. So, walk with me, heal with me, become hungry for greatness, bet on yourself, and break generational curses and make it start with you. I needed a guide, you need a guide, I am the walk and the talk. I have gone from the projects to the WNBA, to creating conversations and sharing my experiences to inspire others. Why? Because I am qualified to do it.

Give yourself permission to create your voice. I hope my voice provides you with a spark of inspiration to allow your mind, body, spirit, *and* voice to shine.

Growth is an internal job, so commit every day to loving you. I promise you that in this book you will find something to connect with and take with you. Take what you will. You're welcome!

Let's Go. Welcome to *What Happens After The Game* with Michelle Reed.

Playful Curiosities

Affirmation: The most important part of who I am is my inner child.

My childhood consisted of 80-, 90-, and 100-degree days in Jamaica, Queens, NY, which meant we got out the monkey wrench and turned on the fire hydrant to cool off. Usually, the streets were blocked off by cars in the neighborhood because so many of us were playing in the hydrant and having water fights. When the block was open, some drivers passed through and left their windows down, almost daring us to wet them. The daredevils who chose that route found themselves soaked and upset. Some would get out of their cars and chase us, but oftentimes, there were too many of us for them to get too bold. It never stopped them from cursing us out or throwing up their middle fingers as they drove off wet and mad. We were in the hood. How dare they think we cared! Between the groups of us in the water, the adults in with us or off sitting on the stoops, we rolled deep when the hydrant was on. The fun was contagious. If you were outside, you got wet, period! There were times when family members came home from work, and we got them, too. It was that type of fun. My childhood was…

- hanging with the boys, sometimes with a few girls in the mix
- going to Margarita Pizza Shop on Jamaica Ave. once a week or going to McDonald's on Linden & Sutphin

- being at JHS I.S. 8 Park an hour and a half before school every day to play open run with the guys
- going to Jamaica Ave. Coliseum to hangout or shop for new gear
- going to Green Acres with friends and hanging out in the mall or at the movies
- going to Midway Movie Theater, paying for one movie, and distracting the security guards or ticket agents to sneak others inside
- going with my brothers to DJ parties, battles, and basketball games
- going to the skating rink on Jamaica Ave.
- breakdancing on cardboard boxes with my crew in front of our building
- playing kickball, handball, softball, and punch ball games with our parents and other adults in the neighborhood
- watching people who were not from 40 P get chased out
- having NYPD officers take us to pro baseball and basketball games
- being looked after by everyone in the community—beef with an outsider meant that person had a beef with the whole neighborhood
- drawing hopscotch and skelly boards on the ground with chalk
- buying push-up ice cream pops to use the tops to put either clay or melted candle wax in the tops to make the top glide better while playing skelly
- my brother putting his speakers in his bedroom window and playing music for everyone to gather and dance to
- hanging out in the hallway when it rained too hard
- playing video games at each other's house
- knocking on people's doors and running

- dressing up for Halloween, getting candy, then going on the roof of our building to throw eggs at people and cars
- roller skating up and down the block
- riding our bikes everywhere we went
- gathering in 40 Park for the Park jams my brother and his friends gave
- waving at DMC from Run DMC when he drove past us after school in junior high
- meeting up and coming rappers when they came to my brothers' parties and park jams
- building club houses in the back of our buildings to hang out
- jumping in and out of my brother's bedroom window to go to the store for him without our mother knowing
- playing sports in snow storms because we didn't want to stay in the house
- having snowball fights as a community
- trying to fit into size 9 adidas when I wore a size 7 just to be like my older brother and everyone laughing at me when I walked into the park
- being a kid with no worries in the world

My childhood was fun, adventurous, and memorable.

40 Projects
One Five Nine Street

I was born in South Jamaica Houses, a public housing project. We knew it as 40 Projects because of neighborhood Public School 40, which is the elementary school that most kids in the community went to. 40 Projects consisted of 27 buildings, but we grew up in what was called "the squares," three connecting buildings, *squares*, which had adjacent apartments directly across from each other. We lived in the middle of the three squares. Our square held the neighborhood flag pole which draped the American Flag until bad weather came and blew it away. That flagpole was our pitcher's mound, safe base in tag, a place we sat to hang out, and even our target when we wanted to practice throwing rocks. When we described where we lived and how to find us, that flagpole was the indicator.

This was one of two apartments we lived at in my years of living in 40 Projects. This address symbolized where family, fun, laughter, friendships, gatherings, and love were born. It also symbolized sadness, death, disappointment, and destruction. The biggest takeaway for me was my most fondest memories of my family being a family. It was also the place where my oldest brother almost lost his life, more on that later.

I had the kind of mom who worked a 9 to 5, came home, checked our homework, and made dinner for us. We all sat at the table or on the living couch and ate together, showered at a certain time, and went to bed by a certain time. She was extremely active in the community for

16

over 60 years. She was PTA president, volunteer, activists, and community leader. She was the first person elected officials came to when they wanted to win a seat. They knew who had the people's ear and how she could help them get votes. I don't know how many times we walked up and down the neighborhood getting people to sign petitions and register to vote. It felt like she was running, that's how dedicated she was.

Some of her good friends were leaders within the community and police officers who always came to the neighborhood to take us to baseball and basketball games. They even joined us during our kickball, baseball, basketball, tag, and many other games we played. That's when police knew the community, and if they caught you doing something, they took you to your house and handed you to your parents. They even made it their business to constantly come around to check and make sure the trouble makers were doing right and mentored them. It was just a different and pleasant time to be raised. True epitome of a village raising each other. We didn't have too many after school programs like now. We did have the Police Athletic League (PAL), and they brought the sports and games to you, along with the officers. Riding in a police van wasn't uncommon because they would pick us up and drop us off all the time, either from school to school or to and from events. A great family friend to this day Detective Stevens and Detective Keith Williams (killed in the line of duty) came around often. They were two officers who used to bring me to and from the PAL in the neighborhood from basketball workouts.

Not only did 40 Projects represent love and my start of identifying myself as a female athlete, but this part of my life also showed me how to survive and mature in an era I was supposed to grow up amongst the negative statistics.

The community would introduce me to my first play-play boyfriend, so many best friends and friends, and god sisters/brother and babysitters who had such positive impacts on my life (Cynthia, Cheryl, Hope, Vanessa, Lamont, and Bobby). It blessed me with being named after my godmother Cathy, who spelled her name with a C; I spelled mine with a K. It introduced me to twins Cher and Gerard, the greatest childhood friends ever. It allowed me to be raised as a young pup by loving babysitters Ms. Brown, Ms. Leebow, Ms. Johnson, Aunt Rainy, Ms. Heath, and Mrs. Carson. It taught me about life way before life began to happen.

40 Projects was like the TV show *Cheers*: "Sometimes, you wanna go where everybody knows your name." Everybody knew my name. Everybody knew my family's name. Everybody knew what we represented. That comes with both the good and the bad. For me, that acknowledgment meant protection, it represented a village raising a child, and it meant comradery. It also meant belonging!

Unfortunately, 40 Projects also meant death. It knocked on my family's door really hard when my brother's best friend and my fourth brother (as we called him) Mike was shot and killed. Mike was everything to our family. He and my oldest brother were like what they called bookends; you rarely saw one without the other. His passing is stamped in my mind for so many reasons, two main ones being I almost lost two brothers that day, and as a result of Mike passing away, my oldest brother, in anger, crashed his hand through a five-inch thick glass of our apartment building's front door. The pain he endured in that moment to cause him to do that was unimaginable to me. I've never witnessed so much blood in my life—glass and blood throughout the hallway leading into our apartment, glass stuck in his arm and blood shooting out like a mini water fountain, learning later that my brother could have lost his life that night too if he hadn't arrived at the hospital in the time he because of the glass puncturing his veins and the increased loss of blood. What saved him was the fact that someone was aware of the need to restrict the blood circulation in his arm, which ultimately saved him.

As a child, I saw my first dead body up close and personal in front of the outreach community. I witnessed the crack-cocaine epidemic take over the 40 Projects' community like a bandit. I witnessed some of our family friends die because of this powerful drug and drug life. I also witnessed friends and family become so addicted that they were unrecognizable. I witnessed my very family become victims of the epidemic not by death, but by the decisions that were made to be a part of a lifestyle that had only two doors at that time, death and/or prison. Beyond those decisions were an additional four choices, you either used drugs, sold drugs, went to jail because of drugs or succumbed to drugs.

My family structure changed from one of togetherness to one in which we made constant trips to courthouses and prisons for visitations. Change moved into my family because the choices my brothers made challenged us and the home I knew of love and happiness became damaged. The family gatherings and family dinners faded into the night. The family bond we struggled to keep above raging waters drowned—never to be seen again.

Magoony Land
One Six 0 Street

At age nine, my family moved to Magoony Land; it was on the opposite end of the neighborhood and was considered the boring part of 40 Projects. My mother moved us here because we were in a two-bedroom apartment, and she wanted me, being the only girl, to have my own room. At first, it was awesome. It was literally right across the street from my elementary school and the neighborhood park. This was heaven for me. I could cross the street and play basketball, baseball, handball, swing on the swings, and anything else we wanted to do in the park to have fun.

This move had so many pluses, but we had no idea of the minus lurking in the dark. Many of the habits that my brothers picked up from The Squares followed us and amplified. Their lifestyle made adjusting to this move very complicated because the choice they made to deal drugs was now causing heartache among the family. Two of my brothers had many stents in and out of jail for years. My oldest brother Vic, however, was cut from a different cloth. As a DJ, he took the art of using our mother's vinyl records and turned it into a masterpiece of art. He blended her albums and mixed songs together that you didn't even know would sound good together. He would put his speakers in the window sill inside or set up a speaker outside right under our first-floor window, allowing everyone to hear and dance. He became known as Grand Master Vic the Master of the Blends. He was, and still is, one of the greatest DJ's that ever did it—call me biased, but The Greatest whoever did it. At 7, I was going with him to his DJ battles and parties. His most infamous battle was against DJ Jazzy Jeff, better known as Will Smith's DJ. That battle was crazy because a new style of DJing was formed called the "transformers" sound. My brother mastered that sound. He used to DJ with handcuffs on, blindfolds, behind his back, with his chin, and all. I and a few of his friends were the only people who watched him prepare for these battles for hours, and so the night of the battle, I was geeked because I wanted everyone to witness what I knew was coming.

When I tell you my brother pulled out all the stops on Jazzy Jeff— poor dude never saw it coming. The crowd went crazy. Each round, my brother bought something different that no one had ever seen before but was trying to duplicate after that night. My brother was and is more than a household name; he is a legend. He rolled with the likes of Nas, The Lost Boys, LL Cool J, Frick & Frack, Salt-N-Pepa, Usher, Run-D.M.C. and Jam Master Jay, and so many others. My brother was and still is a trend setter, and I am so proud of him.

Moving to Magoony Land was supposed to bring us a new and better way of life and it did to an extent, but it brought so much drama and it changed the course of our family. One thing I did witness that would uplift me is my mother's strength. I watched her battle for her kids even when they were wrong. I witnessed her further her agenda of becoming a positive staple in the community regardless of how much others bashed her because her sons were dealing on the streets. I watched her become more active in the schools to help make the streets and school safer and have more options so that children could make better choices than my brothers had. After school programs didn't exist the way they do now. Back in the '70s and '80s, we only had the PAL, and most of those were outdoors programs during the summer and catered more to help working parents have a place for their kids to go that was safe. As years progressed from the 90's on, more money funneled into after-school programs, but in the 90s, it was a slow process. Indoor facilities were rare and not as accessible as they are now. So, kids in low-income communities followed the trend, and at that time, the trend was how to make big money and hopefully make it out the hood. In The Squares, we celebrate every holiday, every birthday, graduation, mother's day, you name it. In Magoony Land after year two of living there, celebration became less and less, mainly because my brothers were in and out of trouble. Holidays, birthdays, and special events went from a celebration of five to a table of two with me and my mom. Absenteeism took on a new level in my home. Almost to a numbing feeling that to this date remains. What I missed most was the bond I developed with my brothers as a child. Year by year, that bond faded away, and I replaced the absence with basketball. It became my outlet *and* a replacement for my brothers. The streets took my brothers, and basketball was my escape and my savior.

40 Projects, despite the challenges presented, still managed to represent the friendships built, the respect built, and most important, the shape of who I was becoming and the footprints I would then add and leave the world with through my experiences. It taught me resilience, how to withstand challenges, and how to go after my dreams. The main takeaway was how having the right people in my life saved my life. Living my life in a bubble of protection shielded me from becoming a subject to my environment. God had a bigger plan for me, and the power of good people within my community and outside of it made that possible for me.

I will never take away my childhood as a young Black girl growing up in 40 because it prepared me for a far bigger world beyond those brick buildings. The 8-year-old tomboy, as I was called, could never see nor imagine without the lens of God the bigger picture of my future life and my desire to be a great basketball player.

A Mother's Strength Can Never Be Measured, Just Admired

My mother came from humble beginnings. She shared an unbreakable bond with my uncle Eddie, often describing them as "thick as thieves." He was her protector and someone she looked up to. Although she was the oldest, he would always claim to be the big brother. He possessed an innate ability to capture the hearts of those around him, becoming the beloved source of laughter through his impeccable Bill Cosby imitations and humorous anecdotes. My uncle often carried around a card, supposedly from the mayor, giving him permission to pass gas wherever and whenever he wanted, an embodiment of his carefree spirit. He had such a great sense of humor. Whenever my uncle entered a space, his presence radiated a contagious energy that illuminated the atmosphere, a personality my brother Jeff inherited.

On the other hand, my mother was to the point, outspoken, sassy, and confident in her voice, demonstrating her natural flare of leadership. Her long strides of confidence when she walked were characterized by an air of self-assuredness. With a strong-willed disposition and a willingness to vocalize her opinions, she endeared herself to her community. Her influence was such that declining her requests was a challenging feat, particularly in matters concerning her children and the well-being of her community.

In tandem, my mother and uncle emerged from modest origins to carve distinct places for themselves in the world. Their intertwined stories reflect the essence of humility, strength, and the impact one can make through willpower, unique qualities, and contributions beyond themselves.

Growing up, my mother had the desire to become a nurse, a dream she conveyed to her teachers as she consistently vocalized throughout high school. My mother and uncle were raised primarily by their mother Cleo. She kept a tidy home and kids clean and fed but had a revelry and indulgence in entertaining and drinking alcohol. The risk of her drinking sometimes posed challenges to the lives of my mother and uncle. In some instances, sending them to school hungry and wearing clothes that weren't always clean. Due to her drinking, they moved around a lot from relatives, friends, and boyfriends not really finding stability at stretches of time and often overstaying their welcome. While the support of their extended family was valuable, the environments they found themselves in were not always secure. Amidst grandma Cleo's social interactions, the atmosphere would occasionally turn into chaos, particularly when alcohol was involved. What might have begun as minor disagreements had the potential to escalate into more serious confrontations. The unfortunate result was that my mother and uncle had to live through these unsettling incidents, creating environments far from the stability they desperately needed.

During these times, kids didn't party in the same room as adults, so they heard things but stayed in the other rooms. When my grandmother would drink, her sister would step in to ensure the well-being of my mother and uncle. They felt safe in her care until the point when my grandmother had to undergo surgery to remove a tumor. During her hospitalization, my mother and uncle went to stay with their aunt. Things were fine for a few days until their aunt's husband started getting aggressive toward my uncle and put him out. Her brother Eddie was sent to stay with his father (referred to as Grandpop Eddie Sr.), and this left my mother alone due to limited space at my grandfather's house. After my uncle Eddie pled to bring my mother to stay with them, they were reunited but not for long. My grandfather's girlfriend complained about the crowded house and cramped space, which ultimately led to my grandfather sending my mother to stay with one of her uncles, an uncle who would make inappropriate advances toward her. After running away from the situation the moment it started, she found herself back at my grandfather's house where she and my uncle found relief in sharing what happened to her. Thankfully, my grandfather welcomed her back in, where she remained until their mother was discharged from the hospital. My uncle had to stay with his father, while my mother returned to live in a studio basement apartment house with her mother. They would continue to bounce from place to place, but she was just happy to be with her mother because she loved her mother so much, and although she drank a lot, she felt safe. With the living situations far from ideal, in comparison to what she already experienced, being with her mother outweighed every external experience.

She hated the separation from her brother, however. He was her protector, he made sure nothing happened to her. If she could rely on anyone, it was him. Despite being a grade apart, they attended separate schools, only because of who they were living with. High school was tough on her because she had buck teeth, and a tall and slender frame, and was often teased because of it. With her athletic ability, she sprouted even taller by her senior year, standing out even more from her classmates. My uncle would often go to her school and fight off the bullies, but he couldn't always protect her. Even though he intervened against bullies, she would often be verbally abused by other students during school and sometimes chased home. Her most difficult moments arose when hunger gnawed at her during classes, dressed in unwashed attire due to her mother's prolonged revelry and alcohol indulgence. Much of her day was spent aiding teachers, a strategy to sidestep the ridicule of her peers. Over time, she formed strong bonds with these educators, who often provided her with meals and fresh clothing.

By her senior year of high school, she set a plan that once she graduated, she would become a nurse, find a stable place to live, and stand on her own. Vowing to have her own family one day, and make sure to protect them from family members who just weren't doing right by her. For years she watched them cater to her brother while abandoning her. They knew her mother's habits and knew she would slip up when she drank, but yet left her to figure things out herself. She often wondered why she was treated that way. Why were they so hard on her, especially as a child? She just wanted to feel safe, have a place to live, go to school, and be with her brother. Their playing favorites drew her and her brother closer but didn't make her feel loved growing up. Most of this abandonment came from her father's side because they were the most visible and she couldn't help but believe telling her brother about the attempts made by their uncle had a lot to do with how they were treating her. It seemed they were blaming her for speaking up instead of protecting her.

A week after my brother Dee was born in 1962, my grandmother gathered one evening with a relative, both drinking heavily. While partying, she was in an altercation that resulted in her being hit over the head with a hammer. Never recovering from the trauma she suffered, she died from her injuries. Her death hit my mother and uncle hard, and it left them motherless. Here she was 21 years old, with two young boys, and a husband. Growing into her role as a nurse and watching her mother enjoy being a grandmother only to endure such tragedy. This rocked my mother's world. Regardless of their unstable environment growing up, she had a special bond with her mother. She removed herself from her father's side of the family, never forgetting how they took her brother in and left her out there many times alone.

What Happens After The Game

When she graduated from high school, my mother felt she had been given the fresh start she needed to build her own life. She was tired of running from family members who had a terrible habit of touching young girls, a father who loved her, but chose his girlfriends over protecting her, and choosing to walk away from other relatives who watched her struggle as a child and teen, and just turned the other way.

The strength she built from that made her a fighter. As empty and lonely as she felt not having her family around, she found family in her job as a nurse at Queens General Hospital. She forged bonds and friendships with the doctors and other nurses she worked with. She created a special bond with Reed, whom she would go on an marry, have three boys, and build a steady home with until he was killed in a car accident soon after Jeff was born in 1966.

She was now a single mother of three young boys at a time when boys needed their father more than ever. She would take pride in her kids' schools, their activities, and her community, as she volunteered to help bring jobs, opportunities, and resources to 40 Projects where she lived. She would spend her life offering her time to help and improve others' lives. Working alongside elected officials, she helped them find their voices and place in seats they would hold to represent the development. They all knew her influence and often went to her first when they wanted to connect with the community. Her main focus was for them to improve all of their living conditions, fund and offer programs for the youth, and create jobs. Her involvement in the community landed her a job with New York City Housing Authority, which is the largest public housing authority in North America. Now, she held a position within the dwelling she lived. This gave her a bigger voice and even more of say of what comes and goes in 40 Projects. She helped whoever asked, even those who resented her.

Her strong personality got things done, but her bossiness sometimes rubbed the adults wrong. The kids within the community loved and respected her. She had their backs and they had hers. Her days was working full-time for her and her family, and her evenings were spent at her kids' school engaged with the Parent Teacher Association. She did this from the time my oldest brother Vic started school, up until I graduated from junior high school. For over 60 years, she served others in mostly a voluntary position.

I watched my mother put her blood, sweat, and tears in that community. Even beyond her retirement in 2002 after over 25 years of service, she continued volunteering within the community, using her resources to help the residents as the Resident Association President, a position that meant so much to her and hurt her heart when she was voted out. It wasn't about the fact that she was voted out, it was how it was done, and who it was done by. Things sit differently when the very people you committed years of unpaid services to use disrespect to hold a seat and act upon a service that can be done by anyone, whether you have a title or not. If you are committed to a cause, action can be taken regardless. I had to watch her pain from these actions, and it made me see a place we called "home" differently. Home wasn't just the buildings and apartments we lived in; it was the people. When people change, so does the picture that once was a beautiful canvas. I feel the Jamaica Playground should be named after her for her over 60 years of service. Will someone step up and honor her while she can still see it? I will continue to pray over it because she deserves it, and I am not just saying it because she's my mother.

Thank you, Marlene J. Reed, for what you've done for 40 Projects. You are worthy of praise.

Overlapping Forms of Oppression

Winter 1988.

11 a.m.

I was in my bedroom, and Mom was in the kitchen.

Like an explosion, a crescendo of chaos swelled from everywhere all at once: screams, sirens, cars screeching, doors slamming, yelling, and the shouting of police officers in person and over their radios blared from the outside..

I ran into the kitchen, my mother looked at me and said, "That sounds like Dee."

We both ran to the front door and were met with three officers beating on my brother. I mean they were whaling on him with their fists, guns, and sticks. My mother's first instinct was to leap to the defense of her son while at the same time yelling, "Get off my son, get off my son."

One of the officers came up for air long enough to lunge toward us, push my mother back into the house and crossed our doorway to jump in my mother's face telling her to "Get the fuck in the house," he yelled it several times before turning his attention back to beating on my brother.

Before we knew it, a flood of officers came from outside, rushing up the stairs and started piling on top of the officers already beating on my brother; they wanted to get in their punches, too. There were so many of them in the small hallway that at some point, they were all beating on one another.

Because my mother and I continued watching, one officer raised his fist in an attempt to hit her, and I grabbed her back. Another officer charged into the hallway and threw the other off balance and onto the pile. Anyone who knows my mother knew she wasn't going to close that door even if it meant they took her, too. With my mother being a big advocate in the community, one of the officers recognized her and made attempts to defuse the situation, which may have saved my brother's life, possibly ours, too.

When they finally, one by one, started peeling off the top of my brother, we didn't know whether he was dead or alive. With the officers all standing around him, we saw that he was handcuffed the whole time. I will never forget how two officers picked him up enough to drag him down the stairs like he was a rag doll; my brother was 6'4", 250-plus pounds solid.

I ran to the living room window and watched them throw him in the back of a squad car. My brother wasn't moving, and all I could do was cry. I felt so helpless. My mother went into action mode and started writing down badge numbers. They wouldn't let her out of our apartment door, so she wrote down whoever was in the hallway and ran to the living window to get whoever she could see. Something she always told us to do; if nothing else, get those badge numbers.

Dozens of officers filled the sidewalks and the street. The entire block of 160th Street between 109th & 110th was filled with police cars from corner to corner. I had never seen anything like this before, not even in one of the many police raids they made in the building. There were officers standing around laughing while others were hyping each other up, acting like they just won a boxing match. Little did most of them know they were pummeling their fellow officers, charges they tried to later put on my brother, but they didn't stick.

All of this was related to the NYPD's manhunt for any and every one they felt could aid their investigation of finding the people involved in a police officer murdered in the Queens area. They were pulling over cars, doing illegal searches, and harassing whoever they felt like. We would be in the park playing ball or walking from school, and they would look at us as if to dare us to react in a way that would give them a reason to bother us, early teenagers. Their goal was to intimidate any and every one until they got who they were looking for, making it very uncomfortable to exist in our own neighborhood. This was considered a high profile case, and it was on every news outlet and on the front page of every newspaper. I think over 3,300 arrests were made, averaging about 13 a day. Each message echoed how they weren't going to stop until they got everyone involved, and that made for very aggressive actions in our communities. They wanted to be triggered and wanted an excuse to whip on or arrest somebody, anybody.

The way they violated and unnecessarily terrorized our community was frightening and, needless to say, illegal, but they got away with it. My mother called every precinct in Queens trying to find my brother, to see how he was doing, what he was being charged for and we could not find him. Either she was met with someone rude on the other end or told he wasn't in their custody. Not until she called people she knew would she finally be told where he was and if he was alive, ok, and getting medical attention.

We kept wondering what brought all that on. We knew those answers wouldn't come until we spoke to him. Why did it take so many officers for one person? What did he do? We later found out that their reasoning was that "he fit the description of the suspect," which was a common excuse used to justify their actions for just about everyone. Their reason for the arrest and our hallway being filled with police was due to a code 10-15 call that went out over the police scanners. A code 10-15 in NY meant "a prisoner in custody." Apparently, this code attracted not just the local precincts but many precincts throughout Queens, and when that call was made, a lot of angry cops responded with revenge on their mind.

That Saturday morning was my brother's day to be targeted, attacked from behind, and beaten. This was the 1980s, and here we are in 2023, and this type of abuse of power still exists but is now being captured on camera in real time. Back then, there were no cameras at our fingertips. So, it was your word against theirs and obviously the abuse of the badge still exists today.

It is not all cops, but they all are put in one basket of badges. There is no reason why, at 15 years old, I had to suffer such trauma. My family was terrorized and had to live with such a horrifying experience. Yet we are one of millions of families who have these stories to tell and have constant reminders of such incidents most of the time when we turn on our TVs.

It is hard to heal the wounds of these acts because it is so in our face and a constant reality no matter where you live. There are so many injustices to list here, and it has not let up. They keep talking about training and providing tools to improve policing, but that seems to be rhetoric for the media to pitch us. For those who do stand by their words and initiate change, kudos to you, but even they are often met with resistance and retaliation in implementing change.

Why is the talk of change always met after a life is taken? To Protect And Serve shouldn't come with the right to abuse the law. Human decency is not a clause in job description, it is a way of life. If you are not a part of the solution, then you are the problem. How many more innocent lives must be examples before "real change" is not an option but a requirement? Video or no video, until the root of why this misconduct continues to exist and is ultimately properly unpacked to defuse its issues, things will not get better. Let's not normalize this behavior by saying "another one." Let's not let them condition us to think that we must adjust to their mistreatment as ok. It is not ok. It is not acceptable. It will never be normal behavior. I grew up with police officers within the Police Athletic League being positive reflections within my community. Unfortunately, that image has been tainted. I won't put them all in one basket, but it's very difficult not to when the nonsense just won't end. To all the good cops who go above and beyond to do the right thing, thank you. We cannot leave your goodwill unrecognized. We need your presence, and we hope you can speak out when we are not being protected from your own.

My heart goes out to every family and life who is forced into these experiences. The direct effect is some, but the impact we all bear witness, too. Let's not guard our hearts so much that we choose to ignore and forget to show empathy. Can we learn how to coexist in a world that is becoming hard to function in? We have to because if we don't, then the misguided wins. Every day we leave home and make it back safely is a blessing and should be met with gratitude.

Acting like these things don't exist will not make the trauma easier to deal with. We all have a voice and take up space in this world. How we reserve that space speaks to how we accept right and wrong. I hear all the time about *generational wealth*, but let's not neglect generational *health*.

God protects and heals our hearts.

A Meaningful Life Beyond a Father's Absence

I remember when my mother asked me if I was attracted to women because my father wasn't around. I found that to be a strange question at the time, However, I also knew it was her way of trying to understand my decision to date women. Addressing that question and making it clear from the gate, my lack of relationship with my father played no part, but his absence did have a big impact on how I viewed men. If anything, my lack of trust in the male figure played more of a role because I constantly asked myself, "What is wrong with me?" Unfortunately, the memories with my father are not positive.

No unconditional love stories to share and no moments in the park shooting hoops preparing for my first date. Memories are built on lies, deceit, abandonment, and the devalued feelings of not being enough for him to embrace the child he brought into the world.

I remember vividly the evening my mother came into my bedroom and said she had someone she wanted me to meet. I was about eleven or twelve years old, and it was early evening, close to the time for a bath and bedtime to get ready for school the next day. My mother walked me into our living and on the couch sat a handsome older man dressed nice, clean shaven, and with a nice smile. My mother went on to introduce him as my father. She gave us a formal introduction, and I can remember crying and saying, "Hi, Daddy."

What Happens After The Game

He gave me a big hug and a kiss on the cheek. The three of us sat on the couch, him to my right and my mother to my left. The conversation was geared around the fact that I loved playing sports, loved school, him being a Muslim, and that I had other siblings that he would love to take me to meet one day. I was so excited that I actually had sisters and younger brothers. He had this way of verifying me as one of his kids. He had me extend my right hand out and spread my fingers. If the right pinky extended further apart from the ring finger, which he stated all of his kids had, that would confirm it all. As shady as I now see that statement of validity was needed, it was also his form of ignorant confirmation. For any doubt he may have had about me being his child, my resemblance of him and the pinky solidified the facts. My mother wasn't the sleeping around type, so for him to need any such confirmation was a testament to the type of man he was. My mother just happened to fall prey to his good looks and charm for the short time they spent together.

The need for confirmation could be looked at as an insult, but I was going to leave that thought behind. That day, I thought, was going to be the start of having a relationship with my father, but it actually led down a path, from 9 to early twenties, of countless hurt, disappointment, and lies that kept us from being father and daughter. He only partially fulfilled his promise to familiarize me with my siblings and other relatives. He introduced me to my aunt and one of my sisters soon after our initial introduction. I only saw him by chance when my friends would inform me that he was in the area visiting other people. As a little girl, seeing my father in those moments, I was so happy. The happiness soon faded as I wondered why I wasn't good enough for him to spend time with me. His appearances were never directly related to me. I will, however, say thank you for lending me and my friend David his car while he was visiting his friends. This gave David the chance to teach me how to drive so that I could get my learner's permit when I was 16. Ironically, this would be last time I would set eyes on him until I had dinner with him and some of my siblings who wished me well as I prepared to leave the country to play pro ball in Croatia.

As much damage as the pain and abandonment after meeting him caused me as a child and as an adult, I no longer have angry feelings toward him. I've learned to understand that God has his reasons for his seasons. I worked hard on getting myself past the hurt. God may have removed him when he did because there were things I was not supposed to experience with him so as to not block the path He had for me. I did and still do have issues with allowing people to get close to me and oftentimes stick around hurtful situations longer than I should, thinking if I do enough of something they would love me just enough for us to be right. I have been trying to fill childhood voids in my mature relationships. This just made my emotional walls thicker and higher, blocking as much pain as possible. Yet I cause more self-affliction to myself and others from immature methods of dealing with triggers. I sacrificed myself in so many situations for love and happiness externally, but internally, the young child was in so much pain hoping to be loved by everyone I thought should love me. If that meant staying in a relationship I knew I wasn't happy in or there was no emotional attachment, I endured more than I should have, sacrificing to please another person, even if it meant I did without. Unaware that I needed to heal, I still allowed people in. I just know I was hurting. If people I was friends with, intimate with, or in relationships with, offered me enough of themselves to help me feel loved and appreciated in those moments, I welcomed it. At least until I put my protective walls up.

I had problems trusting every man after my experience with my father. The funny thing is 95% of my basketball coaches over the years were male coaches, and many had great intentions. However, with as much good intentions as they had with me as a person and player, they were the ones I had the biggest barriers with. I was not able to make strong connections with them as a player should with their coach. This was especially true with those who would say they had my best interest at heart. Those were the ones I feared most and knew how to keep them at bay. Oftentimes, this was the reason our relationships weren't healthier. It was easier to just be the athlete and player than it was to be transparent and vulnerable.

I've learned to forgive my father enough to accept the one and only happy birthday phone call from him on my 44th birthday. It took 44 years for me to get that one Happy Birthday, and that came because one of my father's best friends ran into my mother, and from their conversation, he reached out to my father, who in turn, reached out to my mother, then ultimately me. The good part about the timing of receiving this call was that I allowed myself to let go of the years of hurt he caused while I was still learning to trust and get past my abandonment issues so that I could love and be loved beyond fear and limits. The images of me sitting in a window for hours waiting for my father to come pick me up on numerous occasions only to never show carried with me through life. I would look at people defensively instead of with love and good intentions. Having fought for years to obtain love from a father who is incapable of giving me that left scars that I have trouble healing. For me, losing people and relationships was a numbing feeling that couldn't and didn't feel any worse than that feeling I experienced with him. My psychic shield would lead me to always have emotional self-control and not let people close enough to instill such heartbreak again. I'm not saying no one has gotten close enough to my heart to allow me to safely feel because a few have. There was a good stretch of time when I would purposely sabotage situations if I felt my heart getting too involved. As a protective measure, I would give myself a reason to pull away and want to just be friends. For most of my teens through my mid-thirties, I would tell myself if my own father couldn't love me or didn't love me, how could someone else, especially a man. I blamed myself until I began to understand that I am not responsible for the actions or inaction of another person. I continued to be a people pleaser, putting others before myself, which was unhealthy, just so I could receive love.

While in the process of healing through this circumstance, I wrote my father a letter.

Dear Father,

I needed a dad! I needed your love. I needed to know I was enough for you. I needed to not hurt so much as a child that it followed me into my adulthood. I wish you could have done better, been better, projected better. Not only for you to me but so that you could have been a part of the celebrations that came with the gifts God instilled in me to be great. The fact that there are a total of eight of us, that I know of, that you brought into the world, I guess you missed the memo that with each of us came a responsibility for you to protect and love us. I can't speak for any of them, but from my perspective, I don't know if I would have hurt less having you around or not. You missed so much. You ignored so much. I wonder if you regret any of it.

I am grateful to know that my siblings exist. To even know their names is great. It's unfortunate that I didn't get to know each of them as I should have and them me. For the ones I did meet and got to share conversations with, I am truly happy about. However, the blessing of us speaking, from time to time, sharing our moments, and ending the call with I love you is enough for me to be grateful. I admit, with them, too, I fear the closeness. I fear that I will not be enough. Yet it is not their fault nor mine. By the grace of God and prayer, I leave space in my life and heart for each of them.

I pray that God has mercy on you. As much as my mother wishes I could have a relationship with you, I beg to differ. I just don't have the patience to try to rekindle what was never positive at a time in my life where self-love is my priority. I forgive you because I need to, for myself. My priority is living each day knowing that I am enough and worthy of all the things your actions caused me to doubt. I love my mother so much for being my mother and my father. She couldn't protect me from the hurt you caused, but she loved me even more because of it.

I learned to hide these emotions through playing basketball, at least I thought I was anyway. That's the funny thing about basketball. It was my magic pill for so much happiness and pain until I retired from dribbling it. I was able to control the mechanics of that ball for a long time, providing myself a shield from all the hurt. Never did I learn that the pain I was shielding myself from, all those years, would be exactly what I needed to heal from, after the game.

So, what happens after the game to the little girl that needed the healthy part of her father?

She's healing and seeing life exactly the way God intended it, taking the blame off of herself and forgiving you. That forgiveness is for me, not for you. The biggest lesson I learned from your heartbreak and abandonment is that you are not responsible for my happiness and self-love. No one is but me. I wish I had learned that earlier; I wouldn't have carried that pain and resentment into my adult life. It's never right to believe someone else is responsible for one's own happiness. It is unrealistic and impossible. Once I discovered the basis of that and began working on myself, life opened up. That release is real. So is the life that awaits the deserved love I am so actively ready to embrace. I know my worth. I know my value. I know what I am deserving of. I am just sorry it took so many years for the little girl in me to heal and let the woman in me embrace the life she deserves with the people she deserves.

Signed: Healing Heart-Making My Future Better Than My Past!

Male Expectations

My father was absent the majority of my life and had a habit of disappointing me. Just like me, my brothers grew up without a dad. Their father was, unfortunately, killed in a car crash when they were very young. Although they were deprived of the man they needed to guide them to adulthood, my mother filled that void. With our big age gap, I placed the expectation on them to be my supporting advocates. They honestly didn't have the ability to pass that on to me. Taking nothing away from my mother and her teachings and parenting, no woman can teach boys to be men. Therefore, because they missed it, I did, too.

All of these years, I held on to the fact that they were supposed to be there for me: in the seats at my games, supporting my event, being my loudest cheerleaders. I witnessed them give that to each other but often wondered why the cheers for me were silent and the applause was missing.

When they lost their dad, they had our mom and each other. By the time I came along, they were in their early teens and focused on their friends, and that is how their ideology of manhood developed. My image of boys and men formed through interactions and observations of my brothers whom I knew, yet they could only be what they knew, and what they knew taught me a different lesson. I learned from a woman how to be a woman. I learned from them how to be a tomboy. Neither of us knew how to create bonds beyond our needs of understanding of who we were individually. From my oldest brother down to me, our identities came from our gifts. Vic had his music, friends, and girls. Jeff had basketball and girls. Dee had his softball and his love for money. I had sports, friends, and small nuggets from each of them. Our single mother had to adapt to each of our personalities on her own at times while making sure we had a roof over our head, clothes on our backs, and food on the table, which were her highest priorities. My brothers had to become sitters for me when they wanted to be young teens, but they learned that process from trial and error and winging it, just like my mother did. They did their best with what they knew, as did my mother. I looked to each of them to fulfill the roles of Mom, Dad, big brothers, friend, supporters, and my mentors. In retrospect, they just didn't have all the tools because the dads I was looking for in them, they lost, too. How could they move from boys to men to Dad when they, too, missed out on such an important person?

So, have I been unfair in holding onto the facts I held inside that they weren't there for me, my career, my achievements, and my celebratory moments? Have I been harvesting things inside that I needed so badly from them but didn't understand that they, too, missed out on the very things a dad was supposed to give to us all? Is my anger and disappointment solely the fault and blame of my dad for not being who he was supposed to be for me but left me to think and believe his shortcomings were supposed to be picked up by my brothers? My brothers and I lost out on that need of a healthy male figure to provide those ingredients only a dad or dad figure can give. The tears I shed are not just for myself but also for my brothers, too. They couldn't give me what they didn't have themselves. For that alone, I should begin to heal and forgive them. I have to heal past my need for them and the times of my life they missed. As kids, we shouldn't own those responsibilities; however, our choices are our own when we become adults. That, I will not bail them out on. I needed my brothers to make the right decisions for their sister, and I can never excuse the choices they could have made as adults to be my audience, to be my crowd, to be my season ticket holders, to be my brothers, just like I wanted to be their sister. I held hurt in my heart since junior high because my brothers missed moments I wanted to share with them.

However, on this day of Feb 19, 2021, I forgive.

The Impact of Family on Identity

From very early in my career, I lacked my family's support. Having a family of four, one would think someone would always be available to support them, but *no*. Very seldom did I have an immediate family member come to my games. I understood why my mom would miss so many games; she was the breadwinner. She had to work. She worked in Manhattan, which required a bus ride to the train and a train commute well over an hour to and from every day. Her commute consisted of the 2nd stop on the F train to the last stop. She took random days off to support me, but back then, there weren't many sick or vacation days for her to take to keep up with my schedule. Miss too many and it hits your pockets. I understood her hustle but missed her presence.

I do feel, however, that my brothers should have stepped up. They weren't in school and had plenty of time. It just wasn't important to them. I was disappointed so many times by their promises to come. I would keep looking in the stands, hoping to see them. My brother Jeff came to a handful of games in my three years of junior high. It was better than none. Unfortunately, my other two brothers were no-shows. The hardest part about having to experience this was they always supporting each other and always supported their friends. To come home from games and see that they didn't come because they were home sleeping was the most hurtful feeling in the world. It was always an excuse or an "I'm sorry, the next one." That next one was never fulfilled.

During this time period, I watched my second and third older brothers go in and out of jail. Like a revolving door, when one would come home, the other would go in. Despite the lack of support from them, I would go see them each time. For a time, Queens Courthouse and Rikers Island became part of our families routine of visiting them—until I eventually chose not to make those trips anymore. For one I hated watching them go behind those doors, two I hated walking through those gates to see them, I hated the nights of tears I had after those visits, and I just couldn't endure it anymore. I wanted better for them, and I wanted it even more for myself. Plus, to make those trips for them to come home and not be there for me like I was showing up for them, I just couldn't do it. I wanted to feel important too and if they would constantly choose their lifestyle and friends over family, then I wanted no parts of the pain that came with that experience anymore. I would randomly write, but over time, that paused for me, too.

Junior high was an amazing time for me and my basketball journey, which made it even harder to understand why my family wasn't a part of the excitement. Whenever we had games, it seemed like the whole neighborhood came. Our home games were packed, standing room only. We had undefeated seasons. Our team was the squad to beat. We were the team everyone wanted to play on but hated. I had a crew of big brothers. It was so unfortunate that the most exciting years of what was to come for me was missed by the ones I love the most.

This trend carried right into high school. My mother came to the majority of my weekend and holiday games. But once again, my brothers were no-shows. I stand corrected, my oldest brother came to one of my high school home games. At this level, I made the city's newspaper every game, earned All-American honors, PSAL City & State Championships, and still, it was just me and my mom. I felt like an outcast, like I wasn't good enough or that they weren't proud of me. I know I was doing something great because everyone around me was so proud of me and made sure I knew it. I just couldn't understand why people on the street came before family, especially when Mom didn't raise us like that. Yet I was always supportive of them. I went to pretty much everything they did that I was able to go to. I had so many friends that the only time I missed their presence was when it was game time because that's when everyone from the neighborhood showed, but them, well in junior high anyway. I had hoped that high school would be different—it wasn't.

Neither was college. Of my four years of college, my family only attended one game. That was the WKU vs. Rutgers game during the 1993-94 season, 1st Round of the NCAA Tournament. To me, there was no reason for my family not to travel to some of my games. Everyone would brag about me when I came home for breaks, but they were never proud enough to take time out to be in the stands to support me or even call to see how my games went. These experiences created a feeling of abandonment that would further develop me into a person who felt if my family could abandon me, why should others be any different? To combat that, I created a block to keep people from getting too close and hurting me. If that meant me being in the wrong, then so be it. I was cool at meeting people and even making and keeping friends, but when it came to expectations I had none. I would isolate myself to protect my feelings and from being too emotional. I always had this feeling of when people are going to leave or when they will disappoint me. I equated love with abandonment. First it was my father, then it was my brothers.

Not until later in my adult life did I acknowledge that part of me needed healing. The road leading to the healing was a rocky one. It consisted of me learning who Michelle was at the beginning of my self-discovery. To identify with who I am to the core without attaching my emotions to anyone but me, I had to face a lot of loss and hurt, including the self-inflicted, me being hurt and me hurting others. Being unpredictable to people and sometimes being hard to get along with. Definitely, not easy to get close to and love. In relationships, I would let you love me enough for us to have a good time, but I would like them enough to stay in control of my emotions. There was some room for feelings, but not enough space to trust it to not let me down. That would take some serious commitment, and those walls seldom came down. I think I have been in love twice my whole life. Those feelings sneaked in, in my early 20s and my mid-30s. I'm not saying I didn't care or have feelings for those I committed myself to. What I am saying is I cared enough to walk away unscathed. Wonderful people they were, it had nothing to do with them, yet, everything to do with me, my abandonment issues, and me not feeling worthy of being loved.

I still have my triggers; however, I have more recognition of it to control how I react. I believe it always will be. It was easier to like than to love. I got to control that feeling and walk away when I wanted with emotional attachments I can get over in a short amount of time. That way of life was lonely, is lonely. It's emotional. It's draining. I wanted to be likable, I wanted to have the sisterhoods and the bonds, but I didn't know how. Fear of losing and being abandoned followed me much of my life. I didn't know how to embrace difficult friendships that needed more resolution and compromise than it did confrontation and defense mechanisms. I was terrible at keeping in touch with people. I got so engulfed in the game that I didn't know how to balance it. I didn't understand the importance of keeping those good people in my life even beyond the times I spent with them because everywhere I went I just met more people. I was comfortable with saying I knew them, and we hung out, but I would have loved to continue the friendship with many of them because it was worth it. I didn't know how to make myself available for that, and the wall I had up in general made that behavior ok for me. Was it self-sabotage? I didn't know it then, but yes, it was. And I didn't have the awareness and know-how to change it. I just knew it was safe, and it was my shield. I didn't know who to ask for help or how to ask for help. I just held it all in for years.

During my late junior to senior year of college, depression set in heavy for me. I knew of the word and what it meant, but I never equated it to me, and I surely didn't know the signs or how to dig myself out of it. My mother was battling colon cancer and had two surgeries. My junior year, I watched and cheered and cried as my teammates approached graduation and their families came to their Senior Night game. Senior Night comprised of all the seniors on the team being recognized one last time, and we celebrated them, with their families by their sides, during our last home game. During halftime, the senior players were announced, their families walked them out, and they were given a replica of their basketball jersey, flowers, and hugs by the coaching staff, school admins, and their families. The coaches shared kind words and the game resumed.

In my senior year, I dreaded this day. If I could have crawled under a rock and hide and gotten away with it, I would have done it. So that whole summer before the start of my senior year I feared this day when it would come. The season started, and I feared it. I had players on my team from other countries and their families came to games. I had a family that could be at a game with just an hour-and-forty-five-minute plane ride but never came. So, you can imagine when I pictured this day I saw myself standing alone. One alumni family member saw sadness on my face one day and asked me what was wrong, and I felt comfortable enough with her to be honest at that moment. To hear her say, "We will be your family on this day if you want us to" meant everything to me, but it wasn't the reality I deserved. After years of asking and hoping for support from my family, I was scared of being disappointed yet again on this day.

How did I handle it? I went into darkness. I held in my anger, I isolated myself from everyone, and I went into a funk. I took trips to

Cincinnati on weekends, hung out with friends, relaxed, and escaped from all the horror. After returning one weekend after a short break, I had a 22-point game, and a few weeks later, I went to my coach's office and told him I wanted to quit the team. You can only imagine the shock and disappointment on his face. I was a starter, set to have a breakout season. I worked hard over the summer to get my body ready for the new responsibilities coming my way. In a few weeks, we'd be in the Bahamas for our winter tournament, I had a new car, I moved out of the dorms and into an apartment with my teammate, I was nine credit hours away from earning my degree, the ABL Professional Women's Basketball League in the states was being created, so after graduation, I was definitely heading there. They were paying players great money, and here I was ready to walk away from it all.

My coach told me to take a few days to think about my decision. He had me see the program's therapist. She was great, but she didn't help. I didn't give her a chance to. I didn't stick around long enough to allow her magic to work. My teammates tried talking me out of it. One of my teammates cried, I mean cried her eyes out, asking me over and over again not to leave. She was so amazing. I didn't want to disappoint her. I didn't want to disappoint any of my teammates, alumni, student body, nor coaching staff. I didn't want to disappoint myself; however, at that moment, things were so dark for me, nobody mattered, not even myself.

Reporters came to the practices and asked me all kinds of questions because I still attended practice but stayed in street clothes. They wrote a full spread article about me not practicing and hearing that I might be leaving the team. How did they find that out? You would think because it was Bowling Green, KY, a small town, it wouldn't be newsworthy; however, that's exactly why it was—our every move was watched at all times. It only took one person to talk, and everybody knew your business. Honestly, that didn't help because I didn't privately have time to sit with the decision I was about to make. The noise made me want to escape even more. I'm not blaming them; it was just my space at the time. A few days later, I made the decision to walk away from it all. I packed up my belongings, had some friends from Ohio come help me move, and away I went to someplace unknown all because I was afraid of getting rejected and abandoned by my family on senior night. The thoughts of having to walk mid court with a family that wasn't my own ate at me something terrible. I could not do it. After years of disappointment, nothing was going to convince me that this one time would be different.

That lack of family support still beats at my door, but I have tools now to help me remember my worth, remember what I need, deserve. Having support is a *huge* thing for me. I will not negotiate it with anyone, as it is a definite deal breaking.

Emotional Leaps and Landings

This chapter is important to me for two big reasons. One, I went my entire basketball career, from junior high through the pros, with very little family support. I know the effects and the mental hurt this causes. I cannot go further without clarifying that my mother was a single parent and had to hold down the home. I understood that. She made it to my games when she could from junior high to senior high on her off days and weekends, and I thank her so much for that. It felt absolutely amazing having her presence there for me. She didn't get to see me play while I was in Kentucky at Sullivan College, and she saw me play in-person once at Western Kentucky and once in the WNBA against the NY Liberty. I wish there were more opportunities, but unfortunately, that was it. When I moved back to NY in 1997, she supported me at the local tournaments I played in and played parts in basketball events I hosted for the community.

Two, I keep hearing this same story line being shared among athletes when they speak of their journeys, and I would be remiss if I did not talk about this. I don't want to focus too much on the pain this causes, but I want to emphasize the importance of athletes healing from our traumas. It is something that sticks with us forever, and I feel how we gain the tools to help us begin the healing process is so important. I hope by the end of this chapter I've helped other athletes in some way and educated families about the important role their presence is in our careers. I'm sure non-athletes can find solace in this, too. It's an important topic, and it needs to be brought to the forefront as the dialogue continues.

Let me start with this. Healing and moving forward from lack of family support is possible. It will take the right support and guidance. It will take time. There are ways to cope with it and still find success within your career. I am no therapist, but I am speaking from a place of experience and from a place of doing the healing work every day. I'm sharing tools I've used and the methods I am still using to heal past the hurt to get to who I am outside of the absence.

The first step to healing the past of not having family support is understanding and accepting the reality of the situation in front of you. It is very difficult to come to terms with the fact that you are walking a journey without your loved ones, and it will never make sense to you why. No explanation will discount the absence, yet it becomes a self-healing process that has to happen for us to move through life as healthily and as fearlessly as possible. The process is necessary to alleviate the feelings of being disappointed and those triggering feelings of being abandoned and betrayed by the very people who say they love you. The hardest but most important thing to do is train our thoughts to get past what isn't there and concentrate on what physically is. Absolutely easier said than done but very necessary. It is all about controlling our thoughts and emotions, deciding what we choose to give feelings and emotions to, and training ourselves to shift into more positive thoughts when triggers come up, and they will come up.

Let me explain my process. Learning who I am was the beginning of my self-discovery. As I stated earlier, healing would start with me being able to identify with who I am to the core. It was not only necessary; it was also my mission. It was vital to honestly answer the hard questions and face the even harder truths beyond the fear and self-judgments that came up. All of my life, I was taught to study the lives and journeys of others to gain insight into who they were and the impacts their existence had on society. Ironically, no one has ever said that the most important person I needed to know and study was me. I do have to spend the rest of my life with myself, so why wouldn't I commit more energy into knowing me inside and out? Forget comparing my life to others. My true life's work exists with understanding the phenomenal person I am with my flaws and all. I get to decide what that looks and feels like, in addition to learning to be comfortable with my authentic self.

Life for me isn't about being envious of what others have and what I don't; it's about embracing self and wiring my life to reflect that. I love to see others win and be successful because their wins and losses are defined by their journey, just like mine are defined by mine. How I move is aligned toward who I want to be, the choices I make, the efforts I put into fulfilling my dreams, and the values I believe in. I literally had to learn how to control my overthinking and improve my level of execution to live a courageous life built off of the internal work I do daily. I had to own and accept that no one is responsible for my life and happiness but me. Those bold thoughts and moves allow me to accept all of who I am and use that to lead my life with confidence and not malice.

It was painful to face my flaws, let down my defenses, and be me, but it revealed a lot about the good, bad, and downright awful that I was confronted with. The confrontation revealed areas in my life that I needed to seriously work on. The hard work was allowing all of it to come up, and as it arose, I had to face it, examine it, and accept that this was who I was showing up as every day. My weaknesses and setbacks are no longer my crutch. I learned every day what drove me before and what drives me now because these things are ever changing. I get to learn what motivates me and how to assess why. My desire for growth is my why. It's the catalyst for the impact I want to have and the legacy I want to leave. Once I noticed the distractions within my life, I began asking the right questions. Once I started spending time with myself, those questions started revealing answers.

Learning how to move toward a clearer purpose became my quest, and it wasn't about money. I discovered it to be about doing what motivates me and how that attracts the money. Success for someone else isn't my success. It looks and feels differently for everyone, and understanding that uniqueness helped with my breakthrough, which also happens differently for us all. My right answer is my honest answer, and that was when I realized I had to fix my Why's and be aware of the problems so I can reach the solutions. I control my fate, and the benefits of that are creating positive habits that lead to a great mindset for life. I needed to understand me, my triggers, and when I did that, the face staring back at me in the mirror started to look different. The constant question I ask in that mirror is, "Am I living who I want to be in this world, and do I feel great about her?" Bottom line is what determines if I win in life is me. It always has been, and it always will be. I had to take the soul journey with myself because if I didn't, my life would have spiraled downward to a place I don't even want to imagine.

To walk through the healing, we must find new support systems, one that will match and exceed the feelings we want. We know for sure we want to feel loved, appreciated, celebrated, acknowledged, and validated for doing what we love and for what we are achieving. Identifying what we want gives us the starting point. Now this is where we do the work. Now it's time to find safe people to surround ourselves with and that can provide us these very things we yearn for. It will never make up for the feelings we desire to come from our loved ones, but what we cannot do is make other people do what they are not capable or willing to do. Just like anything in life, we can only control ourselves. The things we cannot control we must learn to let go of. For me it required me asking myself, "How can I cope without the support I am not getting from my loved ones?"

Outside of doing the very things you love, it may require you to take up hobbies and interests that take you toward the direction of your passion and purpose. This may be the very thing needed to find your identity outside of the absence of your loved ones. Take back control of your life and become the inspiration you seek internally and externally. Build up your self-satisfaction and heal from the inside out. Remember the healing process will take time, and you control how much time. It is ok to speak with a therapist for help and support. Oftentimes, speaking to someone who is not close to the situation can shed light on how to navigate and cope with the process. That on top of a great therapist or counselor helps take the pressure off of you trying to figure it out alone.

Start imagining your life in that happy place you believe you would have had if your loved ones were around. One thing that is true—they will never know the impact they have on your life until you speak on it. At some point, it is good to speak up and do so from a place that will not hurt you if their actions don't change after you've shared your feelings. This is where you go in with the mindset that whether they support you afterward or not, you will be ok, and you will go on with your life in the healthiest and most productive attitude.

The bottom line is they don't define who we are, and it doesn't limit our potential. It's about you overcoming this challenge that overwhelmed us for far too long, and now it is time to take our power back. Go on to achieve great things with your life and find success around the areas of your life that fill you up. Build the life you want and the way you vision it with or without them.

One thing I did was convince myself that if my loved ones will do this to me everyone will. That isn't true. It took me years to change this stinking thinking. I made it hard to genuinely love others and let people too close to my heart because I believed it was only a matter of time before they too became that pain point. My relationships came with a wall that never came down. It allowed me to care, even love, but crossing that deep love line, well, that was another story. I cheated myself and them out of who I had the desire to be, but I chose to play it safe. It was simpler for me to keep people at a distance than it was to let them in, and if I felt someone getting too close, I would sabotage it by finding something wrong and convincing myself it was enough to limit how much I cared. A very sad and disturbing way to live. It was easy to play by those rules as a basketball player because I had a busy life and was always on the go. It didn't hit me hard until after I retired and wanted to trade long-distance relationships for closer ones. I struggled with opening up because I did it the same way for so long and got used to it being tainted that way. I'm embarrassed to admit that of all my committed relationships, only one person got close enough for me to stay with and love her for almost five years because she gave me the one thing I lacked since junior high: unconditional love and support without me asking for it. I let her in, and she provided me with that safe space I never had. That relationship helped me see more about who I was, and that was a turning point for me. Mo was my awakening.

The best advice I can give family members and friends is to be there. Show support. Be that love we need and want to help us through. We will give it back in more ways than you can ever imagine because we know how important it is to receive. We just want your love, and we want to give it, too.

To my healers, acknowledge your feelings. Understand and accept them in the healthiest ways you can. Go through those emotional feelings of sadness, anger, and abandonment but don't live in it like I and so many others do. Feel your emotions and then accept them and grow through them. Many times, people are removed from our path because they would have disrupted where we were meant to go.

Build a strong support system. Your family or loved ones may not be present, but it doesn't mean you have to walk your journey alone. Love On Yourself! Self-care is everything! Do things that elevate your mind, body, and spirit and do it with the people who are willing to be on the ride up with you. If you need to find closure, then start from a place of forgiveness, graduate to understanding, and then acknowledge your reality and get up and get on that forward march. It's ok to reflect on these feelings enough to learn the lesson and live to love another day as the strong and amazing person you are. Become a healer for someone else. Use your experiences as a way to motivate yourself and others to know that the healing process is possible and doable.

Take care of yourself because *no one* can do that better than you. You Got This!

Shifting Seasons

This is a very difficult chapter for me to write, yet it is a meaningful one. My mother is 81 years young and will be celebrating her 82nd birthday in a couple of months. Growing up, I watched her for years leave every day for work and walk to the Q25/34 bus stop, which was about 20 or so NYC blocks before she retired. Wind, sleet, or snow, she trucked it. If the weather got too bad, she would catch the Q111 or Q113 bus on Guy R. Brewer to her bus, which took her to her job in Pomonok Houses. She played softball games with us and played handball and paddleball at work during lunch, weather permitting. That's why watching her age scares me because the active life she had is being replaced with osteoporosis, which gives her trouble walking and losing her balance. As she ages, she's developing onset dementia and having trouble with her vision.

My mother is a strong woman and stood strong through many challenges in her life, and when faced with a near-death experience, she bounced back and lived to tell another story. She bore and raised three sons. She became a widow. After suffering through two miscarriages, she, having had her tubes tied previously, became pregnant with me, her miracle baby. To this day, she tells me that I was *meant* to be here, that the plan for my life was written before I was born, and that how I entered the world was a true testament to how I would survive in the world.

My mother survived colon cancer twice; the first procedure almost took her life because the doctors left gauze in her stomach, which caused internal bleeding and had her in agony. Thank God my brother Vic visited her and stayed the night because after years of them not speaking his presence that evening saved her life. If he had not come to visit, she would have bled out and died in her bed. The irony of his visit was that he and my mother hadn't spoken for a few years due to a disagreement they had. This day, he chose to stop by to see her and decided to stay the night. Because he was there, he was able to get her to the hospital in time to save her life.

I've watched my mother all of my life be strong and powerful in her own right. There was nothing she couldn't deal with, and she always came out the victor no matter how much of a fight it was. She lost her mother when she was about 22, her father around 47, and her only brother at 62. She endured all the challenges that came with these experiences, even when her own relatives turned their backs on her and left her at a young age to fend for herself while taking in her brother.

That's why watching her now is so jarring, as she now has to rely on help with things she did independently all of her life. Her memory coming in and out is the hardest for her because she would be mid-sentence and forget her thoughts. She knows what she wants to say but can't find the words to finish. She remembers things from the past clearer than she does new or recent information. She still has her wit about her and her sassiness, but watching her struggle like this reminds me that my mother is changing and aging.

With this change comes a new level of patience for me. I often have to catch myself getting frustrated from constantly having to repeat myself, and listening to her fuss at us for what she did but don't remember saying or doing, which often turns into her getting mad with us about it. What is the scariest is when she talks about people of her past who have passed on showing up in her dreams. On top of that, she brings up not being here long. For years, my mother used to make comments about us missing her when she was gone, her tactic to try to win an argument. But hearing her say it now hits differently. As I look at her now frail frame, along with all the other changes, I work consciously on just listening more rather than getting frustrated because… it just hits differently now.

My mother is old school for real. Her memories of her doctors are when they used to call and check on her. It's been well over twenty years since that type of doctor-patient etiquette existed, but she still feels it should be done, and she's not all the way wrong. Because she doesn't get these services, she tends to complain about her doctors. I keep telling her gone are the days when doctors gave such courtesy calls, but she's set in her ways of thinking and there is nothing anyone can do about that. What frustrates me is their lack of services gives her cause to often cancel her appointments. I always confirm her appointments, but she will secretly cancel them. No matter how I try to explain to her she is only hurting herself, she still wants what she wants. At this point, I stop debating with her to attend her appointments unless I know it is vital to her health. Majority of the time, when I am taking her, she will go, but if my oldest brother takes her odds are 50/50 if she goes. She will sometimes create stories to make me think they canceled knowing I have access to her doctors and her charts. Therefore, I know if she went or not or if they canceled or if she did.

This is the part of her health that gets scary because although my mother is aging, she is still feisty, and if she doesn't want to do something, she isn't going to do it. I know the importance of her keeping these appointments, but to her, she is not going in spite of their lack of being attentive to her, punishing them, so she thinks. While she feels she deserves a call from the doctors themselves, the reality is it is not happening. One thing I've learned, you can't tell a stubborn

Aquarian to do something she already has her mind made up to do. My mother is that type of person, and that demanding side often backfires on her.

I'm scared for her because she makes decisions out of emotions and does not think about the consequences of those decisions, especially when it comes to her health. These canceled appointments always lead to her feeling like people wronged her when she wronged herself.

If you are dealing with an aging parent, trust me when I say you have to learn to communicate with them in a place of teaching a child, especially when they are dealing with dementia. It's teaching and listening from a constant place of patience and love. It is not easy. There is no cure for it. Overpowering their needs does not help. You have to educate yourself to understand what the disease does to their mind and body. Then there's learning how to cope with the changes you are witnessing. It's hard to witness. It's a level of reality that we will never be ready for. Understand that this phase hurts them more than it does us because they are slowly losing their independence and feel like they are burdens on us. Even if we feel that way, we must try not to show it. I struggled with this every day. There are some days when I just cannot handle it all because it comes with emotions and actions that are hard for me. It is a challenge we can never fully be prepared for. There will be days when things run smoothly, and there are days when it is so hard. You will attempt to avoid certain situations just to keep from dealing with the reality of the situation. But if you are anything like me, guilt sets in, and you do what you have to do to make sure they are ok. I constantly thank God for the experience because I still have time with her and know that if she leaves me, I will not be the same person. It's one thing to know she is in her home, and I can go visit or call her whenever I want. It will be a whole other thing when that presence is no longer accessible. That is a reality I will never be prepared for. No matter how life goes for us, I will never be prepared for the day God calls her home. I deal with whatever I have to because I love every ounce of her.

I plan to be loving and to be kind. I will let her vent, babble, fuss, and complain as much as she needs to get to her smile. I forever commit myself to being my mother's miracle baby.

It's Time to Heal

Dear Family,

Let me start by saying, I LOVE YOU! Family feuds and generational drama can be incredibly destructive forces that have the power to tear families apart and create rifts that last for years, decades, or lifetimes. These conflicts often have deep roots, and they are fueled by a wide range of issues, not short of money; power; jealousy; hurt feelings; lack of communication; resentment; misunderstandings; and differences in values, beliefs, and lifestyles.

Lifelong family feuds and generational drama is emotionally draining and have caused rifts and divisions within our families that have lasted far too long. One of the most challenging aspects of us dealing with our lifelong family stuff is the sense of powerlessness that it has created. It feels as though the conflict is beyond our control, and because so much time has lapsed, it feels as if there is nothing that can be done to resolve it.

This is especially frustrating because these feuds tend to trickle down and involve multiple generations, as the issues at hand may seem so deeply entrenched and intractable.

Sadly enough, I can say that unresolved issues have separated our family at the core at the expense of loving each other. No matter how much time passes or how many people we lose, nothing connects a feuding family like the loss of life. Then there are times when not even death can mature a mind that's been running for so long that people rather keep on their track shoes.

What Happens After The Game

Our family wasn't and still aren't the best at communicating. It can be difficult to navigate family relationships when communication is not strong. Without effective communication, our misunderstandings and conflicts existed for years with hurt feelings and strained or non-existing relationships.

I often pray that we are all able to sit down and talk freely from a place of peace and empathy. Everyone has experiences with meanings to share, reasons for their feelings, and the need to be heard. But the walk to the table comes with everyone's ability to listen with open ears, hearts, and no vengeful spirits. Speak to hear and not to respond, dominate, or bully. Respond from a place that echoes what you heard and our willingness to accept the truths of others whether we agree or not. To understand that everything said we may not agree with, but it is the speaker's truth. No one can be faulted for how they feel regardless of the opinions of others.

Yes, some things will hurt, but if we establish at the beginning we are speaking from a place of love and keep love in the words we use, respect and consideration will be exercised.

No matter how difficult or complex our family's differences may seem, it is always possible to work toward resolution and reconciliation. It will take time, patience, and a willingness to listen and to understand the perspectives of others, but with effort and determination, it is possible to heal the wounds of the past and move forward in a more positive direction.

Identifying the underlying causes of these yearslong conflicts is important. It will require digging deep and replaying events and experiences that have tainted relationships between some or all of us. It will involve acknowledging and taking responsibility for any hurt caused or actions that contributed to the strife. Yet, when emotions flare, we all have to be willing to approach things from a place of resolve and try not to animate the situation any further than it's already measured.

It will take a lot of compassion and understanding. It is ok to feel angry and hurt when emotions are triggered, but it is important to try to see things from the perspectives of others and to recognize that everyone involved is likely struggling in their own way. I hope, however, it plays out that we are kind to each other and have empathy toward each other's truth. It's important that we can create an environment in which healing and resolution are more likely to be the outcome. This is important for us to heal through so the generations behind us learn and practice what we are able to do together. You have to admit, this is more about them than it is us. Who are we if we are not before the ones that carry our legacies?

Ultimately, I hope, no, I pray that if ever the day(s) come, we all will sit before each other and work on resolving some lifelong family feuds with a combination of honesty, openness, and our willingness to work together toward common goals that we can set together and hold each other accountable for. It absolutely will not be easy, but the effort is well worth it, as the rewards of a more harmonious and close-knit family are immeasurable.

Ballin':

B-Ball Days

For a large part of my life, my existence was intrinsically tied to my love of basketball. This particular facet of my journey presented me with my greatest highs as I experienced my first true tastes of leadership, confidence, goal setting, adaptability, and discipline. My sports journey would also present me with some of my most painful lows as lessons learned during my childhood would affect my beliefs in myself and in others.

The "It" Factor

I was told that as a child, I had that "IT" factor. I was capable of intense visualization at a very young age. I grasped new concepts with minimal instructions and sometimes by observation alone. At five years old, I began teaching myself how to dribble a basketball just by watching my brothers. At six years old, I taught myself how to ride my oldest brothers twelve-speed bike, the one with the pole across the top. I knew how to maneuver myself under the bar so I could pedal and control the handlebars at the same time. It turned into a neighborhood attraction. I learned how to run track watching my godsisters at their track practices. When my oldest brother Vic "GMV" gave me a chance at his DJ turn tables, I grasped that, too, with very little guidance from him. It took only few lessons for me to learn how to hit, catch, and play baseball. I instinctively knew to run to consecutive bases as a child rather than like most other kids who would go from home plate straight to first then to third or into the outfield.

I practiced relentlessly to shoot that basketball until that ball hit the backboard, then eventually the hoop. It took some work to actually start making baskets, but I kept at it. The fun part was my brothers and their friends putting me on their shoulders to help me feel what it was like for the ball to go through the hoop. The first make caused me to fall in love with learning to keep making them.

I was often bored in school because I learned things fast. I believe that came from me having older family members who left their books around the house, and I was always mimicking whatever they did, from playing with their race tracks, G.I. Joe action figures, and board and card games. My mother only had to show me twice how to tie my shoes at 2 years old, and I had it on lock. The only thing I couldn't do well was wear a dress because I always wanted to play sports. I was born with the ability to do things well, almost anything I put my mind to I made it happen. While I was terrible at pitching and hitting, I was excellent at playing the field and running when I did manage to hit a fast-ball pitch. I could not time the speed of that ball very well, so I stayed in my lane and played softball which turned out to be my second love, with basketball, of course, being my first.

I often amazed people at how quick and talented I was. That was how I elevated so fast playing sports because starting young I always played with people older than me no matter how skilled they were. I had the need to always keep challenging myself to try and be exceptional. I never was a follower. I did things I enjoyed with the people I enjoyed doing them with. Whether it was running track, playing basketball, baseball/softball, football/flag football, kickball, volleyball, handball, I did it with enthusiasm and to have fun. I didn't have to think, I just had fun. I wanted to learn everything about every sport. That's why my game grew so rapidly in basketball because I learned to play all five positions. I learned early that playing every position kept me on the court. In softball, I played all positions: infield, outfield, and pitcher. I didn't care for being the catcher, I passed on that one. All that squatting was not for me. I wanted the highly active parts of the game. I was that kid. I enjoyed the thrill of competition, running, throwing, catching, jumping, kicking, all that. I won countless medals and trophies every year at school Olympic days, competing in every single activity the school and community had to offer. To this day, my mother still has most of those trophies and medals from every grade level.

I was a unique child. I stood out from all the girls, and I was never average. I was gifted, and those gifts would take me places little girls like me in the '70s and '80s didn't know existed. I was born with the ability to be great at whatever I set my mind to, and it gave me the upper hand in life. It helped me build character and hone characteristics that many couldn't, wouldn't, and didn't understand.

Oh, but they would.

My athleticism definitely came from DNA. I grew up in an athletic family. It stems all the way back to my great uncle Billy "Showboat" Dumpson who was a professional basketball player with the original Harlem Globetrotters in the 1960s. My mom was athletic and played sports, and all three of my older brothers were athletic, too, so I was destined in this world to carry the torch. Many in my family had interests in basketball or baseball; however, I dabbled in every sport that existed. Athleticism and sports flowed within the blood that coursed through my entire family. So much so that at the young age of five, I knew that playing sports would be my thing. Never did I imagine how much and how far it would take me. I couldn't help but keep inside me the fascinating feeling of that bolt of lightning that jolted through my body whenever I got that orange ball to go through the net. Oh, what a feeling! I knew at that moment that basketball was the game for me. They created a monster by giving me those moments to shine. Not only was I practicing my dribble constantly, but I started teaching myself how to throw the ball as high as I could while in the house, so that the next time they picked me up, I was going to make it each time.

Yeah, I thought, *I can do this, and I will.*

I continued watching my brothers play on the courts behind our apartment building, I practiced with my brother, Jeff, and I played with the boys in school and in the community.

What Happens After The Game

From age 5 to 12, my game was developed by playing in the park with my friends. Rain, sleet, or snow, we played. We were so committed that if our basketball didn't have air in it, until we found an air pin, we shot with a flat basketball or played taps. If we had no ball, we would have challenges to see who could jump the highest and "reach or smack the boards" as we called it. This is a big reason why I had the jumping ability I grew to have as my career developed.

One basketball—it only took one basketball to appear on the court, and almost instantly, the entire crew was outside. Most of the time, it started with the first person who finished their homework. Once homework was done or the person who owned a ball showed up, the ones who didn't have a ball would come running. It was magnetic.

This momentum carried me through elementary school. Once I got into junior high, I experienced my biggest adjustment as I moved into organized team play. I was the only girl on an all-boys basketball team, and I was practicing with high school and college girls, in addition to playing with older guys in the parks. I always played up, as playing with people better and older than me challenged and groomed me at the same time. Win or lose, I showed up every day to compete. I didn't care if the competition was older, taller, stronger, or more physical. I played with them all and held my own. I loved playing against the guys. They didn't have any mercy on me, and I didn't ask for any. They treated me like one of the guys on the court, and I accepted the challenge every time. Playing with the guys made the game so easy and effortless when I played against girls. I would often get bored playing with girls because the game just wasn't as competitive, even though I practiced with high school and college girls when I was in junior high. My game was elevated when I played against boys; they brought out talents in me that took my game to another level. Although I appreciated the challenges from the guys, the more I attended the practices with the girls at August Martin High School, the more I began to sharpen my skills and mindset for the game. That was needed regardless of who I played with and against.

I was first introduced to August Martin through Faye. Faye lived in a house around the corner from me and often came to 40 Park to workout. 40 Park was a local playground that was right across the street from my building. I would literally walk out my building, cross the street, and I was in the park.

I didn't know college basketball existed for women until I started practicing with these girls. This was primarily because many of the girls that graduated from Martin attended college on scholarship and often came back during college breaks, and when they returned, they would come to the gym and run with us. This was a reunion for them to see each other after being away at school, and it helped them stay in shape as well.

Playing with these college ballers opened the possibility that I could continue my passion to play by going to college, too. Playing with them also brought me back to when I played with the guys in the park. They were tall, strong, and competitive. They had many styles of top-level competition for the game. Like playing the guys, they had no mercy on me, and again, I didn't back down. I was more intimidated by their strong personalities than I was their game. I had nothing in common with them besides the game, so once off the court, my time with them ended. I wasn't much interested in their college experience because I was trying to get through junior high. By this time, women's basketball was gaining momentum with the media. Title IX was put in place, and women's basketball began to seek the same relevance as men's sports thanks to organizations like the Women's Sports Foundation, which fought for equality in sports for both men and women athletes across the board. The momentum carried me through my high school experience. That sunny day in 40 Park set me on a path that I didn't know existed for me.

What Happens After The Game

Faye, Coach Asch, Coach DA, all of the girls from August Martin HS Angels, those I played with, and those who came back and played with us were instrumental in my athletic development. Every single one of them helped me in my transition from the girl who started playing with boys all the way to the young adult who attended JUCO on basketball scholarship, graduated with an associate degree in business, named to the Kodak Women's All-American basketball team, and made team MVP on a squad that went 34-1. Then, that same young woman would become a recipient of a full scholarship to a top-10 Division I program, win a Sun Belt Conference Championship, earn player of the week honors, play in the NCAA Sweet 16, and ultimately earning her bachelor's degree. And the blessings would continue as I was afforded the opportunity to travel the world to play the game I loved professionally in Europe and in the WNBA.

Not only did these experiences shape my game, but they also shaped my life.

The Foundation of the Game

Basketball isn't a sport. It's artistry, a lifestyle. It's a culture and a positive social network with the tools to teach everything an athlete needs to thrive in life, on and off the court. It consists of all the key ingredients in a group setting, such as teamwork, communication, bonding, comradery, and connection. I learned responsibility, time management, self-awareness, work ethic, determination, drive, and commitment all from this game. After falling in love with basketball from watching my brother, Jeff, dominate the game, I would sit and imagine what it would be like to master absolute control of the ball, and people enjoyed watching me do it. Developing myself as a basketball player came easy for me. Because I loved it. When you love what you are doing, it never feels like work. I struggled more with finding my identity off the court than I did on the court. On the court, I saw everything I wanted to be. Women's basketball wasn't televised in the '70s, '80s, and for me, it really gained wings in the '90s. I would watch the NBA on TV, all the time. I admired the likes of Jordan, Magic, Bird, Wilt, Dr. J, and Earl the Pearl. I even admired the greats that would soon come, like Chris Mullin, Mark Jackson, and a few others, because they played with my brother, Jeff. Jeff had all kinds of college scouts approaching him to play for their school. I didn't understand the capacity of the basketball scholarships they offered him. I remember when the late great John Thompson of Georgetown "Hoyas" University was ready to sign my brother immediately. I mean this man really wanted my brother on his campus! As famous and respected as he was then, I thought for so long that he was an NBA coach because when his name was mentioned, people performed, and he was the coach to be recruited by. Seeing all of this was exciting to me. Every time I watched my brother and his friends play or watch an NBA game, I would later grab the ball and work on dribbling between my legs, passing, and shooting, and this started before I could make my shots reach the rim. At five years old, sports became my best friend, but basketball became my love.

There wasn't a day I did not have a ball and was dribbling. I practiced the rookie moves, like trying to dribble the ball between my legs with a high kick in the air and having the ball roll away. When I see little kids learning for the first time and displaying the same practice technique, it reminds me of how I started, and a big smile forms on my face. Playing basketball has taught me valuable lessons, such as teamwork, discipline, and resilience. Additionally, basketball taught me the importance of sportsmanship, time management, respect for diversity, and adaptability, which were all sources of creating the well-rounded person in me on and off the court.

The **leader** in me learned to step up, while **good sportsmanship** instilled respect and humility. Developing my **confidence** improved my skills and influenced how I showed up on and off the court. As I built upon my **aspirations**, it translated into effective **goal setting**, focus, and achievement. **Managing my time** taught me to balance academics, basketball, and life's commitments to meet all of my **responsibilities**. My **adaptability** allowed me to strategically adjust, make split-second decisions, and learn from experiences. Having my body **ready to physically compete** and being a **good teammate** are always keys to success in sports, but **discipline** and **structure** in my beloved sport helped me excel in both playing and in life. These skills enrich my life, fostering **mental resilience** and **interpersonal skills** that still benefit me to this day.

Making of a Basketball Prodigy

Over the years, I was committed to perfecting various basketball skills in the areas of becoming a strong ball handler, a solid consistent shooter, and a strong passer and finisher around the basket. At Grossley Junior High School/I.S. 8, I worked a lot on my jump shot, ball handling, passing, and speed. I wanted to keep up with the boys being that I was playing on an all-boys team. Because many of them were taller than me, I focused on nailing the shot, using my ball handling skills to get around them, and finding my open teammates. I developed quickly playing with boys because of their physical skills compared to girls. They gave me a competitive edge I needed and used to beat out my female competitors. In junior high, there were players ranging from 5'5" to 6'4", and I was a good 5'6", maybe 5'7". I had to work extra hard on every area of my game to stay the course. Physically, they were always stronger, but I used the skills I developed over the years to keep up. I was often underestimated by other teams until they saw me play, especially when they saw that I wasn't intimidated by them. My coach was often protective of me and wanted me to play it safe and stand around the perimeter and shoot, but his fear was just that, his fears. I didn't have those same fears, so going at players and taking it to the hoop developed his confidence in me and me of myself. Playing three years on my JHS boys' team made transitioning to high school competition simple. To me, no one was tougher to play against than the guys I grew up playing with and against, and it was time to test the waters.

The Rise of "Baby Jordan"
High School: Sophomore Year 1988-89

The work ethic I was creating as a basketball player had me a step ahead of a lot of female players and I used that to my advantage. I dedicated hours every day to evolve my game making myself a well-rounded and exciting player to watch. I had to be creative playing amongst the guys all of these years and I developed the confidence to go with it. Building on that earned me the name "Baby Jordan" in JHS and it carried over into high school. I earned the name because I studied his moves so much, I would take what I studied, practice and execute them during games. I would often finish my shots saying "Jordan." I worked on my turn around-fade away jumper like he had, and I had it down packed. The same confidence I developed in JHS I took with me to August Martin High School.

I walked into August Martin High School in 1988, a 5'9" sophomore filled with both excitement and nervousness. Leaving behind the all-boys championship team at I.S. 8 and joining the Martin Angels, who were ranked 17th in the country, was a significant transition in my basketball career to date. Having played on boys' teams, I was unsure of what to expect when I stepped into the uniform and on the court consisting of an all-girls. While I had the opportunity to practice with these ladies during my junior high school years, the actual experience of playing exclusively with them and other females only would be quite different.

First, I had to get the jitters out of my body. I was being introduced to a brand-new school, where the only people I would know at the start would be my teammates. This was a total-180 from home, where I knew everyone, and everyone knew me. That feeling of starting over again was nerve-racking, but I have to admit being on the team didn't leave me on the island alone. Martin was big for its basketball and football teams. Being part of the Martin Angels meant everyone would know who we were as a team. After all, the Angels were the Public School Athletic League (P.S.A.L.) Girls Varsity City and State Champs. Whether that was a good or bad thing would be explored as I went through the journey. The first experience I had was whether people saw me as a lesbian female because that was a connection tied to some of the players on the team. Regardless of our individual preferences, we were all labeled somehow in some way. It was something I had to learn to adjust to being that I was not a lesbian. I had no problem with anyone regardless of who they liked, I just wanted to be respected for who was and nothing more. It wasn't my place to convince others, honestly I just didn't have that kind of time. My primary focus was on my classes and getting used to this level of school work. I knew what to expect in Jr. High, High School, well this was something different. I noticed right off the back how different the teachers were. Some had that "I don't care you're an athlete" attitude. Others had that "love that you're here to join our winning team" attitude. And there were still others who fell in the middle of feeling overworked and underpaid and just cared about getting through the day. I felt right away who cared and who cared less. School safety and the custodians were everything. They were for us 100% and looked out for us constantly. Made sure we were good and where we were supposed to be. We had a couple who looked out when we wanted to sneak out to KFC for lunch and let us back in. Our lunch periods were held in school. You couldn't leave campus during school hours without permission. NYC schools weren't about leaving and coming back, you had lunch in the cafeteria during your scheduled time like everyone else. Our relationship with school staff was different than most students because we saw them all year around. While other students were on break and home for the holidays, we were usually in the gym practicing because Coach Joel Ascher had us in the gym all the time—rain, sleet, and snow. That spoke to the team's winning history and legacy. Because we practically lived in the gym, we got to know all the school staff, from maintenance to security to administrators; they all knew us on a first-name basis. They got to know us and spend time with us on the regular.

When it came to balling, the first few months of practice were challenging, and I couldn't help but notice the stark differences in playing styles and dynamics between this team and my junior high teams. It took some time to feel familiar with playing on all-girls squads. I was used to the physicality and intense competitiveness against boys that made me push limits and honed my skills to help grow into a standout player. It took time for me to adjust to the different approach of the girls' game, because it was challenging for me mentally and physically. I noticed immediately how much more athletic I was compared to other girls. I jumped higher, I ran faster, and my style of play was more competitive. I didn't realize how slow of a pace it actually was between the two. This would work in my favor because that allowed me to adjust easily to playing with my upper class teammates. My first hurdle was the mental adjustment. What took some of my other teammates time to adjust, I was ready to compete no matter the skill level. Yet, the biggest mental adjustment was the pace and aggressiveness I missed. Each practice presented a unique challenge, yet our team was talented enough to meet a challenge head-on and bust through it. Not only did I play against boys in junior high, but I also played against grown men in the parks for years, so I wasn't scared to go up against anyone. I had a thirst for playing against players better than me because it developed my game like crazy mentally and physically. What I did need to adjust was my patience. I often felt restless, eager to push the tempo, and execute with the speed I had developed playing with my JHS team. This change taught me to focus on reading the game, understanding my teammates' strengths, and finding the right times to use the pace I was used to, to my advantage. It was to control the game from a leadership viewpoint because of my ability to play at a higher level. I worked on balancing it all. It was about me being led and being ready to lead when called on. To offer this as a sophomore was a role I not only embraced but was ready to shine when called on. When I exercised patience, I quickly realized that the Angels wasn't just another girls' team, we were competitive and skilled, and during games, these girls were just as competitive. I didn't mind coming off the bench because as an observer I had impact, and I was still being called on to play in every game.

Despite my best efforts to embrace the change, I often found myself getting bored during some games. The level of competition wasn't always as intense because we were often better than our competitors, blowing teams out by 50, 60 plus points a game. Most times after our games I looked forward to heading right to the parks to play pickup ball with my homies to burn off energy I didn't during games. They help keep my game sharp and exciting. The feeling of pushing myself to the limit and facing stronger opponents was something I loved and missed dearly. I will say again, our Martin team was no joke. Our squad had a game consisting of some of the most top talent in NYC. We had a six-footer that towered over our competition, point guards that handled the rock, and power forwards with a game that I would pick over any player in the state. I am humble when I say we were tough to beat. We were in the Public School Athletic League (P.S.A.L.) Class A Division, which was the top in the city. Coming into my sophomore year, Martin Angels won multiple city and state championships. In their 1987-1988 season, they went 24-2 and won the P.S.A.L. City Championship against Murry Bergtraum High School and won a state championship title. So, coming in, I had big shoes to fill, and I was up for the challenge.

What Happens After The Game

As a player, I brought my finesse, the razzle-dazzle, and the excitement. My creative moves to the basket and my ability to jump high caught the attention of my teammates, coaches, opponents, spectators, and the local newspapers. It wasn't long before I earned the nickname "Baby Jordan" at the high school level, a moniker I wore with pride. Being compared to the legendary Michael Jordan at this level was even more exciting than JHS and served as a constant reminder of the expectations and potential I carried on the court. I grew to be an even bigger Jordan fan. I wore only Jordan sneakers to play in, I wore baby blue North Carolina basketball shorts under my uniform just like he did, and I watched his video "Come Fly with Me" before every high school game. I studied his videos so much I even had his walk down when I played. I practiced his moves and shooting style, using them to build my game around. I went to sleep staring at Jordan because my bedroom door and walls had Jordan posters taped everywhere. My favorite move ever by Jordan is when he took off from the free throw line, floating in the air, palming the ball in his right hand to dunk, but switched the ball to his left, and laid it in. THE BEST MOVE EVER! I didn't try that move until a rec game in Ohio years later. I amazed myself. But back on topic, I didn't have that kind of hang time in high school, but what I did master during pre-game warm-ups was taking off a step over the free throw line, gliding down the lane, finger-rolling the ball in the basket, and smacking the backboard after making the layup. Yes. You heard that right! I hung in that air long enough to finger-roll the layup and smack that backboard on the finish! Tell me, how many female basketball players have you witnessed do that?! It was funny because other players would try to do it, and it was a sad scene to watch. I developed my work ethic around customizing what Jordan mastered and making it my own.

As my game advanced, so did the players I studied. I still loved Jordan, but I began to study Magic Johnson, too. I used to watch him with my brother Jeff years ago, but now I was really paying closer attention to his game. My finesse for passing the ball came from watching both my brother and Magic Johnson: the no-look pass, behind-the-back pass, using my peripheral vision to see where my teammates were without turning my head to find them. Many people used to tell me I had eyes in the back of my head. My college coach used to tell my teammates to keep their eyes on me when I drove to the basket if they didn't want a broken nose because I had the ability to make passes that no one would think were in my field of vision. Developing these skills helped develop my game big time.

As a sophomore, I got to quickly experience the different levels of talent throughout the city. The first big crowd I played at was the Annual Doc Turner East Coast Classic Tournament held at The City College of New York. We had nice crowds at our home games, but at CCNY, the bleachers were stacked high with thousands of basketball fans on both the girls and boys side. This was the very first time I actually walked into the gym and was extremely nervous. The thought of playing in front of this many people had me paralyzed. There was a boys game being played when we walked into the gym, and it was loud. As we walked in, people stared at us and pointed. I had no idea why, which made me even more nervous. I just looked around at all the screaming fans and just wanted us to hurry up and find the locker room. All that was running through my mind was "if I had jitters now, how was I going to get through warmups and the game." I had to get it together. My coach saw the nervousness on face and tapped my shoulder with his big strong hand.

"Are you alright?" he asked.

What Happens After The Game

I nodded vigorously, but inside I was saying nope. This was what big time high school ball was about, this is what I signed up for, and I couldn't clam up now. I wasn't the only one feeling it though; my other teammates who were experiencing this atmosphere for the first time felt the jitters, too. We went from laughing and joking in the car ride to the gym to freezing up like little kids arriving at a new school for the first time. The upper-class players knew what to expect; they just had to bring us up to speed. They walked with confidence, and we walked in ready to wet our paints. Plus, we were the team to beat, and that explained the finger pointing. Where I'm from, when people are pointing, it's time to be ready for anything. It wasn't that though, thank God. Our squad was ready to play, ready to prove why we were the best team in NYC. And that is how my sophomore year went. A bunch of first time wow moments and ice breakers. Game by game our hard work we put into training all year around was paying off, as we consistently blew out teams game after game. Although my sophomore year was my adjustment year, I got better every step of the way. There were junior and senior-level players who were having breakout seasons and I came prepared when called. I was happy to be in the constant rotation as a rookie coming in. I wanted more playing time, and I knew coming in it was a process, but I also knew I was ready. I was happy with averaging 12 points this season coming off the bench as a rookie. Yes, I had some growing to do and I showed I was ready way before I attended the school. Just like I had to wait my turn in junior high, this year was no different. The great part about this year is I got to ride the wave of victory. We finished the season 24-2 and won another City Title against John Jay High School (21-2), earning our seat in Glen Fall, NY for the State Federation and where we won the State Title beating out Troy.

That's how strong the Martin Angels were. Back-to-Back City and State Titles. What I also loved about attending Martin was Asch also coached the softball team during the Spring which was pretty much filled with the girls basketball team and a few other students. Outside of basketball, playing softball was my second love. I was just as good at it as I was playing basketball. I played every position except the back catcher. All that squatting wasn't for me. I loved to play outfield because I had a strong arm. I was able to throw people out at home plate from the outfield. Me and my teammate Vee went hard in both sports. Our athleticism mirrored each other. We fed off each other's talent. I loved playing with Vee, she brought out the best in me. All of my teammates did, but with Vee it was like playing with the guys, and I loved it. We both played all the other positions to keep from getting bored. Softball was the neighborhood game growing up. I learned by playing with my mother, my brothers, and all of their friends. If we weren't on the basketball courts when the weather was nice, we were on the baseball field. Depending on who showed up to play determined where I played, and I didn't care I loved the game. I was strong on both offense and defense. When I was younger as a joke the outfield would move in close when I got up to bat until that one day I slugged it over their heads, from then on I developed as a power hitter. When I got up to bat people backed up, and when they did I switched it up and hit close to the in-field. Versatility is key. I loved it.

After experiencing a successful basketball season, I found that the positive momentum extended beyond the court and into my academic year. Despite facing new and challenging class loads, I managed to finish with a B average. The discipline and determination I cultivated on the basketball team translated into my studies as I adopted new study skills and habits. It wasn't easy and it took many late nights playing catch up from procrastinating on my studies. I wasn't a morning person, so after struggling with going to bed at 1 a.m. and 2 a.m. in the morning and having to get up at 6 a.m. I started learning quickly how what worked in Jr High wasn't going to fly in high school. I gradually learned how to manage my time effectively so I didn't slip academically. I didn't master balancing my life, but I was a dedicated student which was required to be a dedicated athlete. I knew sports wouldn't happen if I slipped in my grades, so I found a happy median that got me through, but with the most challenging of classes yet to come in my junior year, I had to make some adjustments to stay balanced and eligible.

Hoop Dreams: The 1989-90 Junior Year

The momentum from our successful basketball season carried into the summer of 1989, marking a turning point in my basketball career. Basking in the glory of clinching both the City and State Championships really bookmarked our goals going into the 1989-90 basketball season. Now that school was out, we had ample time to dedicate to training and developing our skills even more. This was the time of year when many of the Alumni Angels returned from college and would often come to Martin to practice with us. This was great for our growth as high school players because we got to feel what it was like playing against Division I College players. They came in going at us just as they did during their seasons. I personally loved it. When I first went up against some of them when I was in junior high school, I was a bit nervous because I didn't know what to expect. However, once I got on the court, I went at them, and they came at me. It felt just like playing at the park back in the day. They often returned every year during their breaks to stay in shape, and that helped us, too. Amidst the excitement and anticipation, our summer had two particular events on the horizon adding to our summer plans—attending basketball camps.

Having attended both Cathy Rush and the B/C All-Stars basketball camps the year before, I was looking forward to attending again this summer. This would be my second appearance and I was eager to go. I felt a newfound confidence that set this year apart from any previous experiences. With a full year of high school basketball under my belt and a successful season at that, I knew I was developing as a player, and that growth did not go unnoticed. Going to these camps played a significant part in molding my game. These camps to me represented invaluable opportunities to refine my skills and understanding of the game. Recognizing these intensive training sessions were crucial steps toward elevating my game to the next level, which was exactly what I aimed for going into my junior year. One of the most thrilling aspects of these camps was the opportunities we had to compete against so many talents from all across the country and being coached by some of the top coaches and mentors in college basketball. These week-long sessions focused on both individual group workouts, challenging us to push our limits and enhance our techniques every day. Moreover, these camps offer us a taste of independence as we venture away from home. We learned to take responsibility for our actions and decisions, following the schedules set for us. Our days started early, at 7 a.m., and were filled with breakfast, morning workout, lunch, and evening workouts including dinner, which lasted until 5 p.m. or 6 p.m. The hot summer sun accompanied our outdoor play, while indoor activities were balanced out within our daily schedule to prevent heat exhaustion.

The camp facilities were impressive, boasting multiple full-size outdoor basketball courts and several main courts and individual baskets indoors. Every single day, college coaches filled the sidelines and bleachers, meticulously jotting down notes on players they were interested in recruiting. I have to admit, during my sophomore year, my primary focus was on having fun, meeting new people, and playing. I really didn't learn how important these camps really were until I started witnessing former players graduate with free basketball scholarships which showed the true significance of these camps. As I matured as a young teenager, receiving numerous interest letters in the mail throughout the year, the gravity of these opportunities became clear to me. They showed the potential the sport had on my future, fueling my determination to get better for the upcoming season and succeed at the college level when that time comes.

Coach Asch and DA made sure we had every opportunity possible. Their commitment to our success was evident as they took charge of all the camp preparations, organized our travel to and from the camps, and attended to our needs throughout the year. Their dedication and passion for the game and to us had no bounds, they went above and beyond to ensure the best for each and every one of us. In their eyes, if you had the passion to play basketball, you were a valuable member of the team. It didn't matter if you were a novice player taking your first dribble or a highly skilled athlete, they made sure you received the guidance and support you needed. Attending these camps were an integral part of that process, where we had the resources to grow individually and collectively on and off the court. It was about growing as young ladies to become proficient you ladies in everything that we did.

As much as we loved playing, we enjoyed our free time beyond the official camp hours, and we had a blast. After training, we would often have water fights, bonding around the dorms and hanging out in each other's rooms. We occasionally snuck out of our rooms to play harmless pranks on each other when we were supposed to be in bed. One unforgettable night at Cathy Rush camp, we called ourselves being sneaky in the middle of the night banging on players' doors, acting like we were camp directors, and laughing as we heard them scurry to get in bed and pretend being asleep. In our mad dash back to our rooms, we ran right into our coach Asch who often kept a watchful eye on the campus along with other coaches. After pulling off a few pranks, we went to open the door of another teammate's room to run back to our dorm room and were startled by Asch approaching the door. In shock, we slammed the door shut and went to hide, hoping he didn't see who opened the door. He instantly started knocking on the door, shattering our hopes that he didn't see us. This was the first time we ever got caught, and we just kept saying he's going to take us home. We got a good talking to for our mischief. It scared us because we didn't know what to expect, but he knew it was us goofing off. It didn't stop us from trying once again to be adventurous the next night; we worked to devise better planned pranks. These moments were priceless, strengthening the bonds among us and giving us good stories to share in the future. We made some great new friends during those weeks. We wouldn't see many of them again throughout the years, but we would often come across articles and write ups highlighting some of their progress. These camps really honed in on developing us mentally and physically for the game while teaching us real life skills, too.

Besides catching the attention of coaches who came to scout our high school games, these camps proved to be exceptional platforms that made us visible to colleges across the nation with women's basketball teams. Scouts for every skill level were present, and hard work did not go noticed. My performances at these camps yielded excellent results, as evidenced by the abundance of college interest letters that flooded my mailbox before the school year even began. Many of the coaches were shocked to discover that I was only coming off of my sophomore year and wasted no time in showing interest in me early. As my Junior year approached, I found myself holding hundreds of letters from colleges from all over the country. It really was an amazing year, filled with opportunities, newspaper write-ups as the dominant player to watch, and promises for the future. What a year!

What Happens After The Game

As the summer of 1989 came to a close and the start of my junior year, the 1989-90 season, loomed on the horizon, a sense of anticipation and excitement filled me up. As my nickname, "Baby Jordan," began gaining more traction among my peers and those in the media, my plan was to live up to the hype. It made me feel good that my style of play was exciting for the spectators. I was moving out of the shadows of the game and becoming one of New York City players to watch. I was now grabbing the rim at 5'-9", close to actually dunking the ball. I worked hard on my game and got even more creative with my moves to the basket. This was a pivotal year for both my basketball career and academic pursuits, and I was eager to embrace every moment of it. The experiences of attending basketball camps during the summer, coupled with training, and the overwhelming interest from college coaches, had fueled an even deeper passion for the game. I was determined to take all that I had learned and apply it all to elevate my skills to new heights. The thought of stepping into a new leadership role alongside my teammates, who had become like family to me, was exhilarating. We have come a long way as a cohesive group, and the special bond we were building both on and off the court made the upcoming season truly special. We spent a lot of time together all year around and as much as we sometimes got on each other's nerves, we loved each other even more. The prospect of embarking on another season with them, aiming for even greater achievements, filled me with determination. Academically, I felt motivated to improve upon the lessons learned from my sophomore year. The realization that my academic performance held a higher level of importance hit me hard, especially the significance of maintaining high grades and demonstrating my commitment to my studies. Having the opportunity to attend pretty much any college I wanted made me realize that my performance in the classroom was bigger than just my basketball career but the opportunity I have in front of me to attend college for free. That is big. Chances like this don't land on the front of everyone and I knew I had something special happening for me here. All thanks to my mother blessing me with her YES to Faye's introduction to her coaches and the belief possessed by those two coaches in me, I found myself at the center of something truly special. I was in all of the NYC papers for what I had already achieved in basketball, but I was featured in many articles in which writers spoke about how excited they were to see what I was going to bring this year.

And I was ready.

I coasted through my sophomore year, and that wasn't going to fly in my junior year. As the challenges grew more intense, I found myself juggling the demands of being a student-athlete, dealing with more rigorous classes, attending both weekday and weekend practices and games, it filled my schedule to the brim. The weight of responsibilities started to take a toll, leaving me feeling constantly exhausted. I realized with each level of advancement brought with it a heightened sense of responsibility and accountability. I soon realized that finding balance was increasingly challenging. The time I spent playing the game was exhilarating, but it left little time for anything else, leaving me with a narrow window for my academic commitments. My days seemed a blur as I rushed from school to practice, and then back home to tackle those books. As my workload increased, I felt the pressure mounting and it had no end in sight. Assignments, projects, and tests seemed to pile up quickly, leaving me feeling overwhelmed and stretched thin. Despite my best efforts, I couldn't let up, and falling behind in any area wasn't an option. Each day presented new challenges, and I was focused on navigating through these demands step and at time. I had a big year ahead and I had to mentally be ready for it all.

What Happens After The Game

I fell ill early in the year having a stomach virus leaving me out and unable to participate in both school and basketball for almost two months. The virus was relentless, it kept me weak and unable to keep any food and liquids down. This was so frustrating for me and very scary. It was physically uncomfortable and mentally draining, as I yearned to return to the court but was confined to bed rest. My absence from the game and the team weighed heavily on me, and I felt a sense of loss and helplessness. The setback taught me the importance of taking care of my body and having the resilience to fight through it. It was a humbling experience, reminding me of how fragile our bodies are and the unpredictability of life. With the support of my family, teammates, teachers, and coaches, I managed to stay positive and focused on my recovery. Teachers sent my school work home for me to complete so I didn't fall behind, and they helped me so much. This was one of the blessings of playing sports and our coaching being active within the school. The conversations my mother had with the principal and my coach helped me stay up to speed. I am so grateful for everyone who played a part in that process. I found strength from watching my Michael Jordan videos, and the NBA games of which I watch the live games on tv and those I had recorded. I was determined to get back on my feet and reclaim my place on that basketball court. I tried many times to convince my mother I was ready to return to school only to be denied. As the weeks passed and my health started improving, I began to slowly ease back into eating, gaining my strength back, and getting the clearance to return back to school and basketball activities from my doctor. I lost 25 pounds during this time, so I had to rebuild my mind and body. It was a process, but I worked my way back rebuilding my stamina and regaining my confidence. As much as I wanted to rush my return, I understood that healing took time, and patience was important. The last thing I wanted was to end up in that situation again or worse. Although I did my school work from home, once I returned to school I felt the workload increase and the pressure mounting on me to catch up with where the class was in the physical. It stretched me, but I got through it better than I did before I went out. My formula was "No A's and B's, No Play." Simple and to the point. I realized that I needed to be intentional with my efforts moving forward so I made conscious efforts to prioritize my responsibilities. Developing the habit of creating detailed plans and organizing my time better, it became my go-to, as I started meticulously writing down my scheduled activities for studying, basketball practice, games, meals, and rest. As I brought structure to my daily routine, managing everything became a far more manageable task. Learning to make the most of every moment became crucial. I learned the importance of self-care and getting proper rest. Sleep was something I lacked, and I prioritized slowing down to recharge for my physical and mental well-being, which was key. Taking care of myself ultimately translated into better focus and performance both on and off the court.

One of the first steps I took upon returning was communicating with my coaches and teachers. I let them know about the demands of my time and the toll it took on my body, and we discussed strategies to strike a balance. Having their support and understanding played a significant role, as they worked with me to find solutions that accommodated both my academic and athletic commitments. It was hard to study during the times we traveled to and from games because we were all packed in our coach's station wagon. We rolled two in the front seat with him, sometimes four or five in the middle row, and another four or five in the rear. This was us all year around. He made sure if we wanted a ride we had it. He would travel daily with us stacked, picking up and dropping us off after every practice and game throughout the years. From the first day I met him, this was his routine without complaint. Asch commitment to us was unwavering.

Therefore, our commitment to him was just the same. He showed up for us, so we showed up for him.

As the season approached, I was more confident in the upcoming season. Now that I had a full year under my belt, I knew what to expect and was ready for what was to come. The Daily News and New York Newsday papers wrote numerous articles about players and teams to watch for the upcoming season. Along with a couple of my teammates, I was the only junior amongst the majority seniors as a key and exciting player to watch this year. Coming off the bench in my sophomore year prepared me for the new leadership role I was ready to embrace as a starter in my junior year. I worked for it and now I got it. We remained that run-and-gun team and we planned to continue the momentum from last year. We hardly ran any plays because once we had possession of the ball we were racing full speed up the court for quick baskets. Our team was in very good shape conditioning wise because we played all year around. We would often go to the school's weight room to strengthen our bodies, but for the most part, our skills came from how we dominated on the court.

Most of our P.S.A.L. Class A season games were very easy, mostly blowouts. As Bill Travers, in a 1990 *Daily News* article wrote, "August Martin's girls basketball team is like Freddie Krueger in the *Nightmare on Elm Street* movies, the nightmare that just won't go away. This year is no different." We went up against Queens teams like Franklin K. Lane, John Adams, Hillcrest, Beach Channel, Andrew Jackson, Thomas Edison, Far Rockaway, Flushing High, Francis Lewis, John Bowne, Richmond Hill, Townsend Harris, Martin Van Buren, and a few others I may have left out. We used games we played outside of NYC, in areas like New Jersey and Pennsylvania where we played Paterson East Side, Coolidge, University City of Philadelphia to name a few, which helped prepare us for those upcoming really competitive games we will face in P.S.A.L. Playoffs and Championship rounds. Those were the games we looked forward to the most because the competition was often better, and it allowed us to step up our game to another level. It was evident that we had big shoes to fill during our season and we were building off of the chemistry and teamwork we started developing from the summer months. Thankfully because our coaches put us in competitive tournaments like the Doc Turner Annual Christmas events and those scheduled Jersey games, it kept us humble. We knew what was ahead of us beyond the regular season, so we made sure to be ready. All of those weekday and weekend practices prepared us for key moments to come. We knew teams like South Shore, Murry Bergtraum, John Jay, and Paul Robeson High Schools were gunning for us and we had to be ready. We were familiar with these teams and many of the players from going up against them during the off-season as well and we knew they could ball. And all of them wanted the City and State Titles of which we held, and we had the target on our backs.

As usual, our practice kicked off with our winning routines. Every practice Coach Asch would call me down to do my individual shooting workouts. He started from day one when I was junior high school instilling in me the art of proper shooting form. He emphasized the importance of fundamental techniques, guiding me to spreading my fingers, keeping my elbow in, and ensuring a smooth follow-through on every shot. Starting with my dominant right hand, keeping my left hand behind my back, and focusing on shooting with precision and accuracy ensuring that I grasped the core principles progressing as we went. His patient and consistent guidance allowed me to grasp the essence of a well-executed shot, setting the stage for my continuous growth as a skilled shooter. We often put up 50 shots from ten different spots on the court, counting makes and misses from each spot. The goal was always to improve every day with a goal of trying to always finish above 50% makes over misses. Anything above 50% was good, however, the real accuracy came as I got into the range of 70-85% consistently at a minimum, with the aim to shoot higher of course. We always ended with free throws. It started with making 25 before I could stop, increasing to making 50. He had this routine with several of the girls on the team. This was our routine every single practice. On the weekends he would often add extra because we had more practice time. He always stressed warming up by taking shots closest to the rim and then working my way out. Develop my rhythm and routine and stay consistent. To this day, it stands true. When I teach players, I pass down what worked so well for me. This improved my shooting game big time. He made my shot what it grew to be. When we would scrimmage in practices I would be in such a good rhythm from this routine that my jumper was pure water. Because of him, I had proper form, follow-through, and that rotation on my shot that every great shooter works toward. My routines started with his ability to exercise patience, consistency, and commitment and it paid off big time. Last year I averaged 12 points coming off the bench, this season I plan to double that.

In the weeks leading up to the start of the basketball season, I began putting in extra work to fine-tune my skills by playing with the guys in the park. I would leave practice at school, to hit up the park, getting up as many shots and as much conditioning as I could. For conditioning, we ran full in the park, and I would run extra line sprints. I would often workout with my childhood friends Greg, Michael, James, Ronnie, and Melvin. So once the season started, no one player we played against phased me. Because these guys were my hitters on the court, I needed this from them because they kept me ready. Our basketball regular season was a breeze, we would often have to make five passes before we would score because by halftime the score would already be over 50 - 60 points. This was exciting for the younger players on the team. They would often want us to run up the score so they could play the second half of the game. There was no relaxing though because we knew teams like Paul Robeson and South Shore star players were putting up big numbers and having good seasons. We were confident we would meet one of them for the ship at the Garden. Finishing the season 24-1.

1990 Madison Square Garden Championship Game

Here we were again. It's March 1990, and we were arriving at Madison Square Garden, once again, for the championship game. This year, we were actually playing at the main arena after an absence of 26 years. We were on the big stage that the greats of the NBA played on. It was one thing going to a Knicks game and watching them play, but now we got to grace the stage with our talent. Our game was the second to be played that evening, so by the time we were up, the arena was filled with thousands of screaming fans for both the girls' and boys' games. This feeling was surreal. Walking into the stadium from the rear entry, up the elevators, and through the tunnels to the locker room. Reading the names of the Knicks players on the lockers. We made it. The feeling was a lot different from last year because we played at the Theater. As we took our team pictures in uniform and for the newspapers, this was the moment we suited up for. The reporters interviewed a few of us about the season and the game, but to be honest, I had such jitters, I can't remember what I said. As we prepared to take the court after the final horn from the boys game before us, butterflies filled my stomach. We lined up and ran through the tunnel, making it to the hardwood court, under the hot arena lights, I instantly felt beads of sweat start to fill my forehead. The sound of the ball having that hollow sound as it hit the floor, the rim seeming extremely higher than normal, listening to the student section filled with students from our school, this all felt amazing. I looked for my mother in the stands who was sitting with the other parents behind the bench. I took my first layup on the layup line and finally got loose after my third and fourth shot. After a few jump shots I found my spots on the floor and feeling even more those hot lights beaming down on me, I was ready to play. The clock ran down the final seconds before the start of the game, our coach called us over to the bench, and within seconds that loud horn sounded indicating that it was game time. We huddled, did our team chant, and then lined up for the announcer to read off the names of each one of us. The ref blew the whistle, we met center court, and it was game time. I instantly went into a zone. Suddenly the crowd's roar went silent, and all I could hear was my breathing and the ball hitting the hardwood floors. Up went the first shot, first two points on the board and the crowd was going crazy. We came out guns blazing, plans on keeping our title. I was coming off the season averaging about 18 points a game and it was time to go to South Shore with all we had. They had a six-footer in K. Artis who was averaging over 27 points a game and had a 72 point game during their regular season. We knew she was the most dominant player on the team and had to concentrate on stopping her. Our strategy was to put our best defender on her, which was E. Ross, and defensively WE made it very hard for K to control the game by exhausting her physically. We knew if we stopped her, we had the game in the bag. We defeated South Shore 69-39. This win sends us to the State Federation Tournament in Poughkeepsie, NY to compete for another Class A state title. We would unfortunately accept defeat from Shenendehowa of Clifton Park who would go on to lose to Christ the King for the State Title. This ended our back-to-back State Titles, but we maintained our legacy by claiming the back-to-back City Title. I was the only junior named to the Daily News Public High School All-Stars First Team along with two of my senior teammates. As mentioned in the *Daily News*, "The only junior on the first team. But well worth the pick. She'll be heavily recruited next year. She's 5-10, can jump out of her sneakers, she's quick, she handles well, and she possesses some pretty incredible moves to the hoop. She averaged 18 points a game for the Angels and will be their leader in '91."

Flashback to 1990-91: Senior School Year

Coming off of the previous school year and basketball season, Summer 1990 was symbolic to last year. Working out with the team, attending basketball camps, and this year I embarked on getting a Summer job. Being that Popeyes was down the street from the school, I applied for a position there. I was hired and lasted about a month before leaving. I was bored to pieces and all they had me making was biscuits. Although I worked only three or four hours three days out of the week, I just didn't like it. I enjoyed the free food I got, but I just wasn't stimulated by the work. So, I applied at the Key Food that was directly across the street. I lasted there for about two months and left because of the basketball season. I learned early the difference between the love I had for the game and the love I didn't have for working a job at that time. I knew, if I was going to do meaningful work, it was best I get a job that involved sports and allowed me to utilize my creativity. I appreciated making my own money and getting some experience working, but that wasn't where it was for me. I honestly just wanted to play ball and go to school. I didn't have to work, I was spoiled, my mother made sure I had what I wanted, and my brothers would give me money for ironing their clothes or just because. I was good with that. My busy sports and school schedule made it hard for me to have energy to work. I was trying to step into my independence but wasn't quite ready yet. As the school year approached my mother wanted me to focus on my books anyway.

What Happens After The Game

As the school year started, academically I had taken all of my core classes and was just taking electives to remain on the schedule to stay eligible for the season. My key focus was on a couple of regents that I needed to graduate. I took them at the beginning of the year to get them out of the way. As team practice started, so did the conversations around what college I wanted to attend, and I had no idea. At this point there were hundreds to choose from. As I sift through my milk crates of letters I really couldn't decide by invites which one to choose. I started talking to my mother, coaches, and some players about my choices. St. John's University, Western Kentucky University, Iowa, University of Kentucky, Tennessee, Old Dominion, Coppin State, Nebraska, Georgia, and many more were on the list. If I wanted to stay close to home St. John's would have been my choice, but I enjoyed venturing away from home, so I moved them to the bottom of my list. Old Dominion, Western Kentucky and Coppin State had Martin Angels players already on the roster, so I wanted to hear more of their experiences. St. John University was very interested, the Assistant Coach Ms. Haywood came to my house for a visit and was a native New Yorker who followed my high school career. University of Iowa's Head Coach C. Vivian Stringer made a visit to my house, met with me and my mother and I really liked her. She was down to earth, and kept it real about how interested she was in bringing me to Iowa. I met Pat Summitt of Tennessee several times at our basketball camps and had many offers from her program. I took a visit to Coppin State in Baltimore and liked the coach and the campus, but I wanted to attend a school where I could blaze a new trail. I really was leaning toward considering Iowa. I was a little discouraged when I saw where it was on the map and how it was in the middle of nowhere. I wanted a fresh start, but I didn't want to be that isolated. Needless to say, I struggled with choosing.

In the meantime, the basketball season was going full speed. We were beating everyone in our division and were on a good pace with the first half of the season until we met up against Paul Robeson High School at the Annual Doc Turner Christmas Tournament at City College of NY (CCNY) in December of 1990. This was again the tournament to be invited to and many teams wanted to play. Martin held the winning record for the tournament over the last five years, and this year we hoped to claim number six. Robeson High School had two great players in Kendra and Jennie. Kendra's and my game was often compared to each other throughout New York and the newspapers, so going into this game, I already knew this matchup was going to be intense and one to be talked about for years to come. I did my regular routine of watching "Come Fly with Me," Michael Jordan's video, as I did before every game and twice before big games. I also watched it one time before bed and again before I left the house.

This game started out on fire. We traded basket for basket with Robeson, and they matched our faced past style. As expected Kendra and I went head to head battling it out. The gym was filled with nearly 3,000 screaming basketball fans, and it was so loud in that gym it was difficult to communicate with each other and our coach at times. The game came down to the wire. We had the lead 70-69 before sending Kendra to the free throw line to shoot a one-and-one with 15 seconds on the clock, in which she made both, putting them up 71-70. With two seconds on the clock, I missed the jump shot that would have sealed the win for us. Like Kendra I had the hot hand, but when I needed that shot to fall, it bounced off the rim. I finished the game with 32 points, and Robeson beat us with two people. Kendra scored 41 points and Jennie scored 30. Combined, they scored their entire team's 71 points. We didn't know this until after the game. We knew their teammates kept feeding them the ball, but not until we read the stats sheets after the game did we see we got beat by two people. The papers called them "double trouble," and they were right. We all feed off of the energy of the crowd. It was really a great game. I would say the best high school game of my career by far.

After the game, I felt good about how we played but really wanted to bring the title home. I put it all out there on the floor. I brought my "A" game, but it was that last shot that didn't fall. After that game I really hoped to meet up for a rematch with them. They definitely had the ability to make it to the ship. That Sunday, it was a cold Winter day, but I grabbed my basketball and went across the street to the park and started shooting until my arms got tired. That shot not falling played over and over again in my head. I knew I couldn't change the outcome of the game, but I wanted to be ready if ever that last second shot came my way again. I wanted to take that shot, I asked to take it, and my team had faith in me to make it, I just wish the outcome was better. That game highlighted the rest of the season. Game after game led to the buildup of making it back to Madison Square Garden for the championship. I wanted to end my high school senior year on top and I wanted it for my teammates and school. I was averaging over 20 plus points a game, and we had to face John Jay at Hunter College playing against Pietra, another great sophomore guard in the PSAL semifinals. This girl lit us up. When I tell you it seemed as if every shot she took went in is not an understatement. She scored 27 points on us, leading her team to a 71-65 victory and a trip to the Championship game at the Garden. We played them close down to the wire until the ref started calling against us. The game went back and forth all the way until the last 1:07 remaining in the game tied at 65-65. I had four fouls of which two were bogus, I leaped over everyone to grab a defensive rebound, touching absolutely no one in the act, and the referee called an offensive foul on me which fouled me out of the game. The way they were calling the game down the wire was horrible. I knew when it counted the most they were going to foul me out. It was obvious by the way they were calling the game they favored John Jay. Don't get me wrong, they had some talent, but it was obvious how slanted the calls were favoring John Jay. We experienced it on the court and the crowd saw it from the stands. With me out, it hurt the team and John Jay put the game away. My 20-plus points and 11 rebounds weren't enough to carry us into a win which would have given us an opportunity to get that rematch versus Paul Robeson at the Garden after that Christmas Tournament loss, but that opportunity never came. I was bitter for a while after that game. I give props to the talents we faced, but we saw the season playing out differently. I didn't want my year to be one that didn't have a city or state championship. Of all the seasons that meant the most, it was this one. I was named to the Exceptional Seniors Team which was made of the top All-Star Seniors throughout the city of New York. I was named P.S.A.L. Player of the Year, The New York Daily News First Team All-American Team for the second year in a row and named to The Newsday All-City Team.

Now that the season was over, I found myself faced with the decision of selecting the college to which I would accept a basketball scholarship. With my concentration entirely on my classes, I had to stay disciplined with my studies as tests and term papers approached, all while dealing with the disappointment of how the season ended. The days that were once filled with classes, practices, and games were now reduced to just attending classes. I didn't know didn't know how to fill all this free time I now had. For a few weeks I shut my body down, I went straight home from school, showered, watched tv, and went to bed. I was taking easy classes, so besides assignments, there wasn't much to study for. Yet, I still made finishing the year strong my priority. Although basketball is what always drove me to work hard in school, now that the season is done, I wanted to maintain the same commitment as if we were still in season. Waking up in the mornings for school was always a nightmare for me, but now, without basketball being a part of my daily routine, it felt entirely different. I realized I needed to approach each day with the same level of passion and dedication I had for the game. I was determined not to develop poor habits as I prepared for college. Times like this was teaching me to see life through a mature lens, especially in the most sensitive times. I learned to appreciate the season for the success that it was and not let the outcome overshadow what we achieved as individuals and as a team. While we functioned as a cohesive unit on the court, as this was my senior year and last season, things felt different as I walked the halls of school. I couldn't ignore the countless hours sacrificed for this pivotal moment of moving beyond high school. Part of me didn't want it to end, yet, another part was eager to see what new opportunities the world had in store for me.

As I was coming to terms with the disappointment of our season ending without championships, another blow struck. My guidance counselor had made a crucial mistake in my class schedule. She failed to schedule me for a History regents exam that was only offered once a year, and as a result, I wouldn't be able to graduate on time with the rest of the 1991 graduating class. They offered me the opportunity to walk for graduation, but I declined because I knew without passing the regents exam, I wouldn't receive my actual Diploma. Adding insult to injury, I had to enroll in a couple of minor classes in September and then take the History regents when it was offered in October/November. This error cost me the opportunity to sign with a Division I college with a Full-Athletic Scholarship. I was livid. Though I eventually received clearance when I passed the regents, my Diploma would be dated for January of 1992, and I was still figuring out the impact this had on my college plans. I found myself sinking into a funk, feeling like there was no way out of this predicament. My mother and coaches were aware of the situation from the previous school year, and I was desperately hoping that my coaches could help me find a solution to these two pressing questions: Was I still going to college? What colleges were still interested? Just when things seemed uncertain, Don Andelsman, the man with the master plan, sprang into action and secured a spot for me at Sullivan College Junior College in Lexington, KY. It was a school I had never heard of before, and I knew next to nothing about Kentucky. DA shared with me that Sullivan College had an impressive ranking of No. 4 in the nation in women's junior college basketball and secured a spot in the top 20 teams of the National Junior College Athletic Association. They offered me a partial scholarship to join the Executives. The scholarship covered all of my tuition, books, and fees, and part of the scholarship paid for my housing. To cover the remaining portion of housing, my mother took out a student loan without hesitation.. Both DA and my mother stepped up when others went silent, ensuring that this opportunity became a reality for me. Without visiting the campus or having much knowledge about what was awaiting me, everything unfolded swiftly. I had to trust that this was the right decision for me, and I held onto the hope that it would all work out for the best.

My mother and I were introduced to the coaches of Sullivan over the phone. After several conversations with Head Coach Laura Litter and Assistant Coach Corbett Grigsby regarding the opportunity, they walked us through the loan process. Once everything was completed with my high school, they sent me my flight itinerary. I was about to become a Sullivan Executive, and I owe a great deal of credit and thanks to DA for making it all possible. He was the only one who stepped up and made this happen when there seemed to be no way. It felt like I was on an island by myself, but he reminded me that I wasn't alone. He assured me from day one that he would get me into college if I wanted to attend, and he was a man of his word. I am filled with gratitude for all he has done for me throughout my career. Now, with everything I had been through, I finally felt prepared to embrace whatever awaited me in the unknown.

The challenges I faced during this whole ordeal proved that having the right people in my corner to work through the process is valuable. The lessons' life lessons stretched far beyond the boundaries of high school. These were real-life experiences knocking at my door early, and I worked through how to adapt. Growing up in the hood, I knew how circumstances happened beyond my control, but understanding who to lean on during tough times became crucial. I gained an appreciation for both the significant and seemingly insignificant aspects of life. It taught me how to confront dark days by finding strength and resilience in the eye of adversity. This was just the beginning of my journey into adulthood, and I understand that life's lessons know no age. The ability to persevere can develop at any point in life, it's how we embrace them, grow from them, and use them as stepping stones toward developing ourselves personally, gaining confidence along the way.

Building Champions

A Salute to Coach Asch

Junior and senior high were very critical periods in my life, as I began to learn essential skills and form connections with people that would last a lifetime. One of those people is Joel Ascher, my high school basketball coach; he played an influential role in shaping how some of those connections began forming for me, and I have the utmost gratitude to him for being a positive image and having a significant impact on my life.

Asch was more than a coach; he was a mentor and role model who taught me valuable life lessons beyond basketball. He showed me how to be disciplined, work hard, and persevere through challenges. His dedication and commitment to his students and players inspires not just me, but everyone he came in contact with on and off the court.

Asch gave me options and opportunities that I never thought were possible. He recognized my potential when I was in the 7th grade after being introduced to him by a neighborhood friend, Faye. Faye was a trailblazer herself. She was the one who opened the door for me as a female basketball player at Grossley JHS 8 (I.S. 8) where she was the first female to play on the all-boys' basketball team. I came in right behind her, becoming the second.

Asch provided me with opportunities from junior high to develop and highlight my skills and improve as a player and student. More importantly, he encouraged me to focus on my education and not just basketball. As a coach, he made sure we wanted for nothing. Whatever opportunities were available to us to be successful in school and basketball he made sure we had them.

During junior high, I practiced with the high school girls on the weekends, and during the summers, I practiced during the week along with attending the Cathy Rush and the B/C AllStars sleepover basketball camps Asch to us all too. These camps were popular and had players from all kinds of schools and skill levels. It attracted the top college coaches in the nation. These coaches were there to see us run through a bunch of skill assessment drills half the day, and the rest of the day, they watched us scrimmage each other. There were hundreds of girls at these camps of every nationality. We had so much fun at these camps between meeting new people, and spending time away from and we got to be adventurous. There were many nights where we were supposed to sleep but instead were sneaking out playing pranks and cracking jokes. It was the best time of year for me during these away camps. My first time at this camp was after my 7th-grade year, and I never slept away from home before. I was excited and nervous at the same time. The experience was my first real venture out of NY and without my mother. My mother never liked me staying overnight anywhere, but she saw the excitement coming from me and let me go. It was the best experience ever. These camps had us staying in dorms or cabins, sharing the rooms with our teammates and other players. Our days started as early as 7 a.m. for breakfast and lasted until 5, sometimes 6 p.m. This was all basketball besides the lunch and dinner meal breaks. These practices and camps made me a better player on my JHS team and developed me even quicker going into high school. From eighth grade to my senior year of high school, I received interest letters to every Division I and II college in the nation. I literally had hundreds of letters from schools I never heard of coming to my house weekly every year. I wish I had kept them. I didn't realize how important those were as keepsakes.

You did that for me, Asch. You helped me create those memories and opportunities.

Because of your influence, I was able to graduate high school and pursue my college education on basketball scholarships. You helped me understand the value of education and how it would help me achieve my dreams. You provided me with the support and guidance I needed to navigate through high school and be ready for my college experience. You help me see the power in sharing your gift with others and using that gift to lift people toward their purpose doing what I am passionate about. We won city and state championships. We broke barriers and records together. You consistently only ask that I get my education and make something of my life.

Our connection was off and on after I went to college. I hoped to hear and see you in the stands like I did in high school, but it was understandable that after you helped mold my group, there were others who needed your time and attention. I missed that male figure going through my college experience, but I knew wherever you were you were cheering for me. It was always good to see you when I came home during break and see how you were still making things happen for the girls who were under your leadership.

You taught me through your actions that I mattered. It is because of your commitment to all of your girls that my career and education had a vision. I want to be what you were to us, in ways of giving pieces of yourself to make sure we were able to dream, have options, and were guided correctly. How you showed up for me is how I hope to show up for female athletes, but in my own unique way. You help me become the winner, the champion, an option, of importance, educated—where I would see the world and create my own lane.

During COVID-19 on April 29, 2020, I got the call that you had passed away. Because of the pandemic, we were not able to get together and grieve your loss in the ways we have wanted. This made the grieving process very challenging. We wanted to support your family and honor your legacy the way you deserved but could not, so we had to honor your memory in our own way by releasing balloons virtually and speaking our words into the heavens for you to hear. On Feb 24, 2023, we honored you by coming together on your birthday. You were honored by players both near and far, your friends and coaches that shared some beautiful stories in your honor. This night brought us closer to each other and to you. We individually and collectively honored you and did it with love and appreciation.

It is important for us to give you that. That we honor you properly and tell you thank you. You would have been proud of the work put into honoring your memory with photos, videos, and articles of remembrance of the time we all spent with you together. You left us with a lot to treasure and pass on to others. Your legacy will live with us forever, and your work can never be erased nor forgotten. Your impact continues to be felt, even in your absence.

Rest in Peace, Coach.

Thank you for what you did for my dream.

2 Steps Back, 4 Steps Forward
A Tribute to Coach DA

It *was* a really great time.

It was my senior year, and I was literally taking what I called "just because" classes to fulfill required hours to graduate. Excitement ran all through me, and all I was left to do was pick the Division I college I wanted to spend the next four years at while on a free basketball scholarship, tell the school, and set up a signing date. After an evening of sifting through hundreds of letters and schools, I couldn't make a decision. The thought of going away for school was the ultimate excitement, but picking a school was so hard. I spoke with friends, family, teammates, and coaches, and I was still torn.

Until I didn't have to make the choice at all. With graduation a few weeks away, I met my guidance counselor, and she advised me of an error she made in my schedule. She didn't notice I had not taken the social studies regents required by NYC Board of Education. This test was given earlier in the year and wouldn't be given again until the next academic year. I'm sure you can imagine the shock on my face upon hearing this. Just the night before, I was sorting through college letters and narrowing down my final decision, and now, I was being told I could walk with my class, but my diploma would not be real. The more she talked, the more she pissed me off because, on top of that, I would have to attend a summer math class because, once again, she did not recommend it in my current program.

What Happens After The Game

Tears welled up in my eyes. Gone were thoughts of college selection and signing dates. I was going to summer school, and then I would have to return the following September, register for classes I didn't need, and get a damn good tutor to make sure I passed the regents so I could complete my diploma. How did I go, so fast, from thinking I worked so hard on my grades and basketball to get to the point of graduating and accepting a full ride to college to feeling embarrassed and thinking my life was going backward? How could this happen? This wasn't my fault, so why couldn't something be done to schedule the exam during this current school year so that my life could proceed as planned?

After the meeting with the counselor, I left school and went home. I cried for days. I had no desire to be around anyone and flat out wanted to beat my counselor's ass. Did she not understand how her poor guidance really set back my life?

Once this news got out to the coaches who were offering me full rides, my home phone got quiet. Then to top it off, I had to cram for SAT and ACT and pass them, or I would face sitting out my first academic year of any Division I four-year college I selected. When I tell you this year just kept getting better. Now I was taking a summer class, getting tutored for both the social studies regents and now the SAT and ACT. Mentally, I was done. It took everyone around me to keep me encouraged. I had confidence I could pass them all, but my biggest and most needed question was what college would accept me mid-year. Filled with embarrassment and hurt, I didn't go to graduation, and I didn't go to prom. I did get to relish winning New York Newsday 1st Team All-American, making the Exceptional Seniors All-Star Team, and receiving honors from the Public School Athletic League (PSAL).

This was the first time in my career I had to face real life heads-on. In doing so, I not only learned that giving up on myself is the sure way to failure, but I also learned that giving up is not an option, no matter how bad things may seem. Yes, I passed the summer requirement; yes, I aced the social studies regents; but I did terrible on the SAT and ACT. If it wasn't for getting my name, address, and date of birth right, I probably would have walked out of that exam room with a perfect score of 100. With the exception the reading and comprehension sections, the math sections were so foreign to me. Sad to say a public school education didn't prepare me to pass either of those tests. Although I had a tutor, I struggled with that section during those sessions, too. I didn't feel confident going into the exam because of that section, but I paid for it; therefore, I went to make the attempt. The highlight of that testing experience was what came next.

My high school Assistant Coach Don Andelsman reached out to Sullivan College, a junior college (JUCO) in Lexington, Sullivan was willing to offer me a partial scholarship to join their team. In JUCO, I didn't need to pass the ACT or SAT exam to be active on the basketball roster, which was music to my ears. If I chose a DI school, based on NCAA eligibility rules, I would have sat out my freshman year and not traveled with the team. I could practice but not play and travel. I played all of my life, so I knew I didn't have the discipline to sit out that long. I liked school, but I didn't love it. I say that to say, playing basketball kept my grades up. It was my motivation. Knowing if my grades slip I wouldn't play meant "don't let my grades slip."

Going through and getting through meant everything during this time. Having people in my corner meant everything. However, not giving up on myself when challenges struck meant so much more because those challenges *did* strike, and I was able to push through each of them. From this experience, I spent the rest of my life double- and triple-checking everything. I left nothing for chance and never settled for leaving my life in the hands of others. Asking for help is one thing, but expecting others to check all the boxes for me without knowing the details is just not an option for me. The fear of not having control scares the hell out of me. I've learned the hard way that stressing over things I cannot control does more harm than good. I also learned to exercise and develop my leadership skills and to pay extra attention to details.

Although my high school experience taught me many hard-earned lessons, it encouraged me most to go after whatever my heart desire. I set my mind and treat each experience with gratitude and hopefulness.

Although I didn't graduate on time as scheduled, I did graduate.

Although I didn't sign to a DI program as planned upon the original graduation date, I did go on to Sullivan College, played on a great team, finished the year as an All-American, and completed my two-year associate degree in business administration in a year and a half.

Although my life didn't fall within my exact timeline, I did ultimately sign to Western Kentucky University, a top 10 DI basketball program in the country, on a full basketball scholarship, and graduated with my bachelor's degree. The dream still came true in bigger and better lights. I learned that things don't always happen the way I plan, but they happen even better when they do.

Refining My Game:
The Collegiate Years, 1991-1995

Welcome to Lexington, KY, 1991-1993

The fall of 1991, I was leaving high school behind. As amazing as those years were, it was time to step into a new venture as I prepared to leave for Lexington, KY. As I packed for college, I was filled with nervousness. I had no idea what to pack, but when in doubt I loaded up on sweat suits and sneakers, with a few dress up outfits. Whatever I didn't take, my mother would send later if I needed it. I didn't know what to expect because this would be my very first flight. I had my CD player, with my favorite CDs, and plenty of extra batteries. This would help me relax. I didn't have to worry too much about playing for a few months because I would be joining the "Executives" mid-season as a spectator and student. Sitting out the current season allowed me to retain full eligibility for the 1992-93 basketball season. With Sullivan operating on the quarter system, each quarter lasted eleven weeks; this made my transition into the school very easier. Moreover, attending JUCO allowed me the opportunity to earn an associate degree within two years.

I left my Jamaica, Queens home, heading to LaGuardia Airport joined by my mother, my boyfriend Marvin, and a friend of my mothers who drove us to the airport. This would be my first time leaving home for an extended period of time, which brought a mix of excitement and nervousness of the unknown. As I sat in the back seat of the car with

Marvin, he held me tight as my mother chatted about something from the front seat. My mind was so all over the place I couldn't focus on what she was talking about. As we got close to the airport, Marvin began to hold me tighter. Marvin and I started dating during my senior year. He was a dark chocolate brother with a beautiful smile and wonderful personality. He knew how to treat a lady. Hailing from uptown Harlem, we met him at the Doc Turner Christmas Basketball Tournament. After our loss to Paul Roberson for the championship game, some of my teammates and I stayed to watch the boys' game. Coincidentally, we ended up sitting in front of Marvin and his friends, and that's how our conversation began. Him and his friends admired the game, and he in particular expressed how much he enjoyed watching me play and how I had skills. He called me a "superstar" a name to this day he still calls me. We vibed and exchanged numbers. He started coming to more of my games, and from that point on, we started spending a lot of time together. My mother adored him. We had a special relationship, and we really loved each other. As we approached the airport the anticipation of the trip combined with Marvin's embrace, filled me with emotions. They walked me through the airport and as far as not having a ticket at the time would take them. I gave them hugs and kisses before tearing up and heading toward my gate. My mother had already started tearing up in the car, and Marvin was fighting back his tears, but I could see his eyes turning red. It was getting close to my time for me to board, so I began walking away, stealing glances back at them watching me leave. I kept looking back until I couldn't see them anymore, and I lost it. Tears fell down my face as I began to miss them already. I started focusing on the flight hoping it would stop me from crying, as my thoughts became fixated on my new journey. As I boarded the plan and the stewardess greeted me, she recognized my nervousness and checked on me throughout the flight.

All I could think about was that in a few hours, my life would forever be changed.

Neither Marvin nor I were prepared for the distance that was coming with me leaving for KY, but we made a heartfelt promise to call and write as often as we could, and we did so for several months. Little did I know how busy college life would get with basketball, classes, and bonding with my new teammates and classmates. With the decision to take classes through the Summer, my trip home was a week long, and I was right back at school. But before I delve too far into this journey. Let me start by recounting ...

When I landed at Blue Grass Airport in Lexington, KY, my heart pounded with gratitude for a safe flight. This was the first time I would be meeting the coaches face-to-face, having previously spoken to them only over the phone. I was not sure what to expect, and I was sure they were too. All I knew was they had really country accents and were pleasant people. As I deboarded the plane and cleared the tunnel, at the gate waiting for me was Coach Laura Litter, a petite white lady with blondish hair. Standing at about 5'5", While Corbett Grisgby, an older white slender man, was around 5'8" with mixed grayish-white hair. While she dressed in sweats with shoes, while he was dressed in a button-down business shirt , Khaki pants, and holding his jacket in hand.

I spotted them waiting with warm smiles at the gate. They greeted me with big smiles and handshakes. They asked how my flight was, complimented my looks, and asked if I wanted a bite to eat? Being an 18-year-old athlete; I was always hungry, so I gladly accepted. I felt a burst of excitement about the new venture ahead and couldn't help but be in awe of their southern accents. Coming from the city, their accents sounded quite country but intriguing. During our meal together, I enjoyed getting to know more about them and the program, eager to meet my new teammates and to see where I would be living for the next two years. As we drove from the restaurant to the apartments I couldn't help but look for bluegrass, which was often associated with the state. As funny as that sounds, in my research about Lexington, what kept coming up was the University of Kentucky and Kentucky being the "bluegrass" state. Needless to say, there wasn't any. I found out later it was named the bluegrass because of the huge meadows of blue-flowered grass that grew in the area.

As we rode down a winding two-way road, we approached the apartment complex, and I was very impressed. It was neat, clean, and had a pool right outside my apartment. It was a three-level complex right off the busy street with units on both the right and left sides of the road. My apartment was on the lower level, and what I didn't know was I would have not one, but two roommates. The apartment was a cute furnished two-bedroom, two-bath space with a large living space, an open kitchen, and a balcony that faced the street. One of my roommates turned out to be the point guard for our team, and the person whom I would be sharing a room with was the team's manager. I had never shared a room with anyone before, so I knew it would be a bit of a challenge for me. Not that I couldn't do it, but as a New Yorker I wasn't accustomed to having strangers in my personal space for long, so that was an adjustment for me. However, they were cool and greeted me with a friendly welcome along with the other teammates who came to the apartment once they heard I arrived. My first observation of them was that they were hilarious. Outgoing personalities and real jokesters. My first day in Lexington was a good day. I was ready for this new chapter with my new basketball family.

After the introductions, I started unpacking. I was anxious to see what the campus looked like tomorrow. I had an 8:30 a.m. pick up time. I would ride over with the players and coaches. As we approached the campus, I was expecting a big building, but Sullivan was a small college campus located amid a commercial strip on Harrodsburg Road. From the outside the building looked like a small business office, but on this small campus lived big opportunities for students and its student-athletes. This campus was the home of the women's basketball program. The men's basketball program was located in Louisville, KY. The inside of the building was a Z like shape that zig zagged from front to back with classrooms and offices. I liked that the campus was small, it was easy to get around and intimate enough to get to know people. The professors and administrators were attentive and went above and beyond to make sure students excelled. Literally every professor introduced themselves to me and extended themselves to help with whatever I needed. It was easy to see that if you failed a class it was because you didn't try. I adjusted quickly and excelled right away in my classes. The professors worked around our basketball schedule and set time aside whenever we needed extra help. I was the first New Yorker to join the team and that meant something to me. I knew if I did well here, it would open the door for other Martin Angels to attend in the years to come. The campus was less than a ten minute ride from the apartment complex and on a good day the walk wasn't bad. Most of the time Coach Litter or Corbett would pick us up and drop us off if we needed to. Other students that stayed at the apartments or were friends with the girls on the team would offer us rides. The team had a school van which was used to transport us to and from practices and games. I was really impressed with the culture of the college, the team, and Lexington as a whole. I still had much of the city to see, but what I've seen so far made me very comfortable. My first take on the team was, "WOW, these women could ball." I got to see firsthand why they were undefeated and blowing teams out. Upon my arrival, they were already well into the season, which allowed me the opportunity to observe the team's style of play. They were just like the Martin team.. Competitive, athletic, strong, and fast paced. Sullivan didn't have their own gym, so practices were held at the Lexington Athletic Club and home games were played at Midway College. The team had an excellent graduation rate, and their impressive record was a draw for Division I coaches. Coach Litter and Coach Corbett both stressed academics. Before my arrival, Sullivan grads went on to NCAA Division I programs including schools such as The University of Maryland, Western Kentucky University, Tennessee State, Edinboro University and University of Cincinnati. The Executives led the nation in scoring with 99.8 points a game. We were a fast break team. Coach Litter's style was "get the ball off the boards and run the break." She stressed early offense, which explains the high scoring averages per game. Our primary offense was a motion offense that resulted in quick scoring. Get the ball and go. Watching the girls play and finish out the season left me excited to play. They finished the year with a winning season and every senior graduated and continued their careers at other major college programs. By watching, I got to plan my strategy for the upcoming season, and I knew from the gate I would be in the best conditioning shape of my life.

As the school year commenced, I did really well academically. I made an honor roll and decided on studying Business Management. In high school, I enjoyed math, but that changed quickly when I got a taste of college-level math. The love I once had for the subject turned into a mere liking. Despite this, I chose Business Management because I had a clear vision of becoming a business owner. While I wasn't certain about the exact nature of the business at the time, I was confident that the right opportunity would present itself in due time. As I got familiar with living in Kentucky and learning my way around the city I ran into my first snag. The roommate situation had taken a turn for the worse. The manager I was sharing a room with had pushed me past my limit of tolerance. My first class didn't start until 9:45 a.m., and since I'm a light sleeper, every little noise around me I heard. This wasn't her problem, but with her knowing that she exercised no courtesy.

Unfortunately, her first class started at 8 a.m., so she would get up around 6 or 6:30 every morning. Her habit of slamming drawers and doors, along with making a lot of noise while getting ready, made it difficult for me to stay asleep. No matter how many times I politely asked her to keep it down, she seemed to only get louder and more inconsiderate. At first, I thought she was upset about having a roommate after having the room to herself. However, I soon realized that she was simply rude and had an attitude about herself, so whenever we interacted she was so extra. After dealing with this for a while, one morning, I finally lost my temper and threatened to put paws on her if she didn't keep it down. In truth, I had no intention of fighting her, but I wanted her to think I might. I had been through so much to earn my scholarship, and I wasn't going to risk losing it over a pointless interaction. All I wanted was my roommate to stop making so much noise. Even when she went into the kitchen, you heard her all the way into the other rooms. I spoke to my teammate and roommate, Tee, about the issue so many times, but she grew so used to it that she closed her door, and it didn't bother her anymore, plus she often stayed at her boyfriend's house. On this one particular day, I scared this poor girl so badly that she asked to be moved. Within a few weeks, she left, and I had the room to myself. I felt so bad about what happened, I couldn't undo what I said to her. I, too, would have been scared too by a New York girl who was so assertive. I would have left, too. Although I apologized to her, I couldn't help but feel relieved that I now had my own space.

I had my own room until after the season was over, and Nee joined the team and became my new roomie. We hit it off instantly, sharing a great sense of humor and becoming fast friends. It was her, Tee, and I until Tee got engaged and moved in with her boyfriend. That is when I moved into Tee's room, and Nee had the large room all to herself.

Since I wasn't playing this season, I decided to enroll in a heavy load of classes. The advantage of being on a quarter system allowed me to take more courses. Due to the attentiveness of my professors, it was easy to get one-on-one tutoring if I didn't understand something, which made learning beneficial for me. Their support and guidance ensured I stayed on track with my studies and made the most of my academic opportunities.

Thank you Coach Litter, Coach Corbett, my Sullivan basketball sisters, and the Sullivan campus for all you've done for me. I wouldn't trade my experience with you for nothing. For me, life was just beginning.

Summer of 1992

As the basketball season came to the end, I eagerly looked forward to the start of summer. I finally had the opportunity to play with some of my teammates for the upcoming season. Coach Litter told us about the Bluegrass State Games 3-on-3 competition at the Seaton Center outdoor courts; a few of us were immediately interested in playing. Myself, and four of my teammates joined forces and registered as "Fast Break." The competition was good but no match for us. We rose to the occasion, winning four games in a row, including the title game with a close score of 16-15. It was an opportunity for us to highlight our talent and build a strong connection with each other. We complimented each other's games so well and we couldn't wait for the season to kick off.

The momentum carried over into another local tournament, garnering the attention from local media outlets like the Lexington-Herald. Talks started quickly creating a buzz about the new class of Sullivan Executives coming onboard. We started the summer winning tournaments, and we made it clear that we were determined to maintain that energy going into the season.

1992-93 Season

Our season began with intense conditioning, and Coach Litter did not play when it came to being in shape. Our regimen was intense. Her run-and-gun style of play just intensified with us. I was familiar with what to expect from her training and how it was going to take my game to the next level. We started pre-season with two practices a day lasting anywhere from two to three hours each. The first half of all of our practices was strictly conditioning without the basketball, suicides and timed sprints. Ball drills followed, which were just as intense and demanding. We went over plays, although we rarely ran because we scored so fast. Under Coach Litter's rigorous conditioning and coaching style, we transformed into an unstoppable force. I never ran so much in one season in my life. I lost so much weight I had 4% body fat. I loved this new look, but geez, it came with a price. Our conditioning and her coaching style caused us to blow teams out by 50 to 60 points by halftime. Once we established this type of lead, in the second half we had to make three passes before taking a shot; otherwise, we would have run the scores up well over 120, 130 points. Our dominance was evident in our astonishing 34-0 regular season run, losing our very last game, which was for the JUCO title/championship game, and we were cheated out of that game. Despite our grand lead, the referees started calling a very lopsided game and barely made any calls in our favor. It was obvious it was 7 against 5, and with the refs controlling the pace of the game, they were able to come back and give us our first loss of the season. It crushed us because we should have finished the season with a perfect 35-0 record, but they stole that title from us and that is without exaggeration. It was very difficult for us to hold our heads down because we knew they had to cheat us to beat us, but we deserved that win and that winning season. We earned it. We worked hard for it, only for it to be snatched from us. However, we had fun. We bonded and we created experiences that would never be taken away.

With all my basketball experience, my time here represented the best basketball experience I have ever had. The girls were fun to be around, and we laughed so much and truly got along with each other. Like any team, there were cliques, but even with that, we got along. The memories of traveling in the team's van driven by Coach Corbett or Coach Litter. We would often tease Corbett because he drove so slow. We used to crack jokes about old ladies in walkers passing us on highways. Corb did most of the driving. We always took turns falling asleep on long road trips because when Corb got tired, he would doze off behind the wheel, so some of us would always stay up to keep watch and make sure he stayed awake. There was always a loud voice from the rear of the van shouting "Corb you ok" and when we saw he was getting tired everyone would stay up the rest of the ride. It was so funny. These were my prized days with this team.

I was able to bring a few of my teammates to NY for a visit. My mother had just purchased my first car, a four-door white Pontiac LeMans, and in it, I drove us from Kentucky to NY. We bunked up in my mother's apartment, on floors, couches, and beds. While in NY, we went to the basketball courts in my neighborhood with my brother Jeff, and scrimmaged against some guys I grew up with. It was my three teammates, me, and my brother against anyone who dared step on the court. On a whim, we ended up playing and beating every one of those guys so badly. We ran them like we did our opponents during the season. They could not keep up with us. One of my childhood friends got so mad at my brother for rubbing the wins in his face, he was about to fight brother. We calmed him down, but he was definitely salty about getting beat. He disliked my brother for rubbing the loss in his face and embarrassing him. My brother had his way of getting under players' skin when he had the competitive edge. Word spread so fast about how we were out there beating up on everybody. People kept coming one by one, thinking they could beat us. They all got very disappointed, but it was good fun. The courts had never seen a crowd like that in years. We ran those guys into the ground. Our conditioning had those guys out there sucking air. We played, I think, three or four games against a different five while we kept our same five. While they were exhausted from us running them, it was routine for us. After that visit, people would come up to me when I visited and ask about my teammates and when they were coming back to clean the courts up again. It was the best.

The business degree I registered for would have normally taken two years to complete, but I earned my associate in science in Business Administration in a year and a half instead of two years, which allowed me to graduate in May of 1993 and attend Western Kentucky, having three years of basketball eligibility. I ended my career at Sullivan, earning the team's Most Valuable Player Award, Award for Highest Free Throw Average, Academic Honor Roll, 1993 JC/CC Kodak Women's First Team All-American, the Bluegrass State 3-on-3 Title and winning a Gold Medal on the South team at the U.S.A Olympic Festival in San Antonio, Texas, hitting the winning shot that beat my new head coach Paul Sanderford who had just signed me to play Division I basketball for him at Western Kentucky University. The Olympic festival was a great experience. There were players from colleges all over the world in every sport competing for Gold, Silver, and Bronze medals. I got to play against the likes of Veronica Cook and with Missy Jackson who were my two of my soon to be teammates at Western. In addition, greats like Charlotte Smith of North Carolina University,

Crystal Robinson of Southeastern Oklahoma, and Nykesha Sales of University of Connecticut. Were also amongst the talent.

What a year and a half, what awesome experiences. I passed over attending my college graduation from Sullivan in June 1993 because I left for Western Kentucky University in May after my last quarter at Sullivan. WKU offered me a full basketball scholarship right out of Sullivan. I could have returned for my graduation, but I opted out and chose to do some traveling that summer before returning to Bowling Green, KY in August for the start of the school year.

With this being my first time away from home, I learned so much about myself. I gained maturity and a little independence, and I developed greatly as a basketball player. Thank you, Sullivan College Family, for blessing my life the way you did. I wouldn't trade my experience with you for anything. For me, life was just beginning.

Division I Basketball @ Western Kentucky University 1993-1996

As I progressed beyond my career at Sullivan College, I am thrilled to welcome this new journey as a member of the Western Kentucky Lady Toppers, playing. Division I basketball. I gratefully accepted a full basketball scholarship from the program, which covered 100% of my college academic and athletic expenses. This opportunity represents yet another milestone in my life, and I am eager to make the most of it and continue to grow as an athlete, student-athlete, and individual.

WKU stood among the top 10 NCAA teams in the country, having recently achieved a remarkable run for the Final Four. I chose to join the Lady Toppers after taking an official visit to the campus after my Sullivan basketball season ended. Western Kentucky was one of the colleges interested in me when I was in high school, so I was already familiar with them, thanks to Trina, a former Martin Angel who had high praises for her time as a player there. Her impressive skills as a 6'6" post player left a lasting impression at Western.

Having adjusted to the southern style, I gladly accepted Western's offer to join their program. Right from the start, the coach Sanderford took excellent care of me, ensuring a smooth transition from Lexington to Bowling Green. I had been fortunate to come across coaches who genuinely care for their players, and this continued with one of the top 10 coaches in the nation at WKU. He did not make my visit very comfortable but helped me move to the campus, and his act of kindness I will forever be grateful for. Even if I missed how big those moments were then, I am humble about them now because I've truly been blessed with incredible coaches.

When I came from New York from a one week break I finally got settled into Gilbert Hall. Gilbert Hall would be my home away from home on campus. Its location was perfect, granting me convenient access to the dining hall and a direct route to E.A. Diddle Arena where we practiced and played our home games. Western was a nice size campus sitting on the hill of Bowling Green, hence the name "Hilltoppers' '. Campus struck a great balance-it was large enough to embody the quintessential college experience, yet small enough to avoid feeling overwhelmed commuting to and from each building.

The town of Bowling Green had a strong sports-oriented community. Positioned a little over two hours away from Tennessee, where we caught our flights from, and about an hour and forty-five minutes away from Louisville, KY. Despite being new to campus, it seemed like everyone already knew me; such was the close-knit community. And when it came to events or incidents on or off campus, I found out quickly how incredibly small it was. Coaches often knew what we did, where we did it and who we did it with, no matter the day or time. Missing a class was no secret either; our coaches quickly got wind of it once class concluded. Their vigilance was impressive! My excitement about being at Western was met with my diligent work from each level of my career. This is what I worked for; this moment served as yet more building blocks forming the foundation of my career. Academically, it was a fresh challenge, while athletically, I knew I'd reach new heights. I looked forward to competing against some of the best collegiate programs in the nation and playing alongside some of the best in the game. I felt good about the growth of my status and my game.

Considering I had only played one season with Sullivan, the three years I was eligible allowed me to come in as a sophomore even with a two year degree under my belt. Fortunately, most of my credit transferred smoothly, placing me on track to graduate in 1996.

Dorm Life

My first experience with dorm life was a lot different from the apartment I had just left. It was a plain room with two beds, two desks, two hairs, two closets, and a big window. The down side was the shared bathroom and showers with all the other girls on the floor, which I wasn't crazy about at all, but I got used to it. I hated the fact that the bathrooms consisted of four stales, so when I had to poop, I usually held it until the floor got quiet and no one else was in that bathroom. If there was one aspect of college life that I disliked the most, it was undoubtedly the shared bathrooms and showers. But hey, when you have to go, you go.

My roommate Vee, was a junior on the team and an absolute riot. She always had something funny or sarcastic to say. She would often joke about how her "poots" smelled like roses. It was all good fun, and her sense of humor lightened the mood. We stayed across the hall from two other teammates Tara and Gwen. Whenever she walked into the bathrooms, she was always the first one talking about how something stinks, duh it was the bathroom. It was funny, though. We were roommates during my sophomore and part of my junior years. The second half of my junior year I lucked up and had my own room, so I pushed the beds together and made a Queen size bed. I set my dorm room up like an apartment and made a mini kitchen with a microwave and a deep fryer, and a mood light. In my senior year, I moved off campus into an apartment with my teammate, Stacey. Our coach only allowed junior and senior players to live off campus if their grades were good. Other than that, home was the dorms.

Pre-Season

I spent about a week on campus in the summer of '93, getting my feet wet and learning where stuff was. After that, I drove home for a couple weeks before heading back to campus to start pre-season conditioning. You would think after the rigorous conditioning regime we had at Sullivan, WKU training would be a piece of cake. Um, not so much. Although we didn't run sprints for an hour and a half straight, our training included a variety of other activities, including track work, pool exercises, floor workouts, running the stairs of our arena, running around the campus, aerobics, and weight lifting. My body went through a whole new level of shock; the intensity sank. Our team trainer John, who had a military background, showed no mercy. I was doing all kinds of complaining, and he just added more to the workout. I complained about this body part hurting, that body part hurting, how tired I was, getting on his nerves and driving him crazy. He was serious about his work, and like us, he was there to get the job done. He was a great guy, though. I had a lot of respect for him. We knew he had to get us ready to compete against the best, and his job was to make sure we were prepared for everything.

What Happens After The Game

The pre-season workouts started off with two a days- 5:30 a.m. workouts followed by afternoon sessions. It was a clear sign I had entered into another level of the game. Now, I was someone who could run wind sprints all day, but running long-distance on the track was torture for me. One, it was early; two, it was morning chilly air; and three, I hated it. My junior year I had developed tendonitis in my left knee, which forced me to run on the grass, which further slowed me down. Our condition required us to make specific time targets, and each time we didn't make time as a team, we had to do it again. Picture running from sideline to sideline hitting the lines a total of 17 times in just over a minute. Then you have 30 seconds to rest before you now have to hit the lines 16 times, then 15 times, and so on and so on until you finish at 1. Then we would switch and do the same thing sprinting baseline to baseline starting as high as 21. Again, any set we didn't make as a team, we had to do that set again until we did. And that was just A.M. practice. It hurt like hell, but if we wanted to compete at this level, we had to fight through it. As a team, we did.

Adapting to the Game, Sophomore Year

To compete at Division I college level, I recognized the need to enhance my mental capacity for the game. While I possess the intensity and desire to be here, I knew adapting to this different style of play was going to challenge me by the first few practices. Instead of being fixated on how different the Lady Topper system was, I had to learn to focus on effectively developing the areas I struggled in, starting with the tempo. Every team I played for was an up tempo run-and-gun team. Western was more half court and played runners. A style of play I haven't done since junior high. When I came in my goal was to become a starter, now my goal was to earn a spot as one of the sixth or seventh players to come off the bench. Honestly, I knew it would take time for me to adjust. Despite my accomplishments in JUCO, I whipped my slate clean, set new goals, and set my sights on figuring out how to fit into this slower style of play. What I achieved helped me confidently remind myself I deserved to be her, but it was going to take a lot of hard work to mentally shift to the coaches system. It was one thing to have set out of bounds and defensive play, but it was another thing for the game to be dedicated to various options of offensive plays. Don't get me wrong, there were plenty of opportunities to run the ball, but we focused a lot of plays out of multiple scenarios. This frustrated me big time. My timing was off, and I felt out of place on the floor.

The coaches recognized my frustration but stayed on me to keep going. Those words hurt more because they were true and because he said them in a newspaper article. However, in the same article, it was replaced with "dedicated," "respected," and "a leader." It got to a point when I wasn't looking forward to practices because I just didn't care for this slow tempo. However, this is where I needed to put my big girl draws on remember it wasn't about me, it was about the team. This wasn't a game that would be customized just for me, it was designed for us to win within a system that works. Being that this was a winning program, it clearly works, I just had to figure out how to play within it. This is when I wish I had my big brothers in my ear reminding me that I got this and that everything would work out. I had to battle through this, toughen up, and be patient with myself. This was yet another obstacle of my life that I can work through, and my coach often reminded me that anything worth having is worth working hard for, and this game is no different. The coaches would often tell me to use my athleticism and my talent to stay inspired. The question was never whether I can adapt, it was how long will it take me to adapt. Although I played between 8 to 10 minutes a game and averaged almost 9 points, I had some growing to do. Needless to say, my sophomore year was a learning year, and I was so happy that I had two additional years to get this right.

I needed to get out of my head and work on my weaknesses. Two weaknesses for me were the tempo and playing better defense. Coach was big on playing defense. If you didn't play defense, you weren't going to see much playing time. His saying was "defense wins games," my smart mouth ass always mumbled, "Scoring wins games," but I learned quickly what he meant by that saying. Simply, if I wanted to play on his team, I better play team defense. I grew into the system one practice at a time. Playing against the starters and watching how successful they were at playing his style of play, I used watching them as a way to learn what to do and what not to do. I learned to feed off of their energy, their skills, and their leadership. Although when called upon I contributed to the team with quick baskets in small amounts of time, I still had a lot of growing to do. The crazy thing is it wasn't hard; it was just an adjustment and required me to be patient with the process. Plus, I was getting tired of being singled out for missing my marks while learning the plays. I hated when the coach yelled at me and often would take it personal, and I didn't know how to let those moments go. I used to think he hated me, but he didn't, he yelled at everyone. I just took it personally because that was my way of dealing with being frustrated with myself.

We finished the regular season 24-8. We lost the conference championship to La Tech 68-43 but was still guaranteed a selection pick in the NCAA Tournament. As we gathered to watch the NCAA selections, I was excited that we would finally play an East Coast game against C. Vivian Stringer's Rutgers University. I couldn't wait to get back to my dorm to call home to tell my family. I can't tell you how excited I was to see my mother, brothers Jeff and Dee, and our childhood friend Ninja walk in the gym. I ran off the layup line and gave each of them a big hug. My coaches wondered where I was going.

Needless to say, that was the best game I played all season. After the game, I introduced the players and coaches to my family. To hear my coach jokingly tell my family how he needed them to show up at the rest of our playoff games if I was going to play like this felt good. Time was short after the game before we had to board the team bus and catch our flight. As we boarded the bus, my family stood outside waving until we disappeared, and once they were out of my view, I lost it. Tears wouldn't stop falling. This was a big moment for me; this was the first time my family attended one of my college games. I felt on top of the world. Their presence meant everything to me, and I needed that so much.

We went on to lose the next round to Southern Mississippi 72-69. After the season ended, the coaches sat us down as a team and individually to discuss our performances and gave thanks for our commitment to the season. We discussed the highs and lows, and they gave me some encouraging words to prepare me for my junior year. I respected these moments, as they showed their sincere care for my development as a student-athlete. Their guidance gave me insights on what to work on during the off-season. Both the coaches and I had high expectations for my growth and potential. I was committed to what I needed to do mentally and physically to have an impactful next season, and it started with me building up my confidence and patience. I told them, "Trust me, next season, I will be ready."

Junior Year

To me, running half-court sets seemed robotic as opposed to run-and-gun style, where there's always movement and no time to really think. Half-court sets required a lot of thinking for me, and until I learned to simplify this process, I was going to struggle. So now that my sophomore year was over, I was determined to figure out how to adjust my game. I took my playbook home with me over the summer and studied it page by page. Whether these same plays were going to be used next season or not, my goal was to view the game the way the coach saw it and practice being in that mind frame. By the time pre-season practice started, I wanted to be better prepared. Although I went home for a short two weeks, I came back to campus, took a couple of classes, and worked a part time job at the local radio station. I needed to make some money to cover these new credit cards that were just showing up in the mail with my name on them. All I had to do was call and activate them. For the first few months, I thought these cards were a part of my scholarship, until those bills started coming in I learned quickly these were my responsibility. Thankfully, the limits were low, and I made enough over the summer to pay off the balances. I spent the summer enjoying my time off and playing pick-up ball with the students on campus at the campus sports facility. I don't know what it is about playing against guys, but it just brought out the best in me. I had more fun, and my game just elevated. If I had the option to play on the men's team, nothing against the women, but I would. I just loved it. Playing with them helped me develop my confidence, which is what I needed going into the new season. I wanted to erase the negative thinking I had last season and walk into practice with new goals that will move me into the rotation.

Pre-season conditioning went the same as my sophomore year. I knew what to expect and called myself coming into the work in better shape, but John still kicked my butt. If he thought he could push me more, he did. Man, he knew how to get under my skin. He was good though. My eagerness to improve from last season had me running with the point guards and beating my times. I was still complaining a lot, but I got through it. For some reason I kept turning my ankle. Early during conditioning, I turned my ankle, and it swelled up like a tennis ball. I was out for about a week before working my way back.

Throughout the season I had a series of ankle sprains. The trainer would tape my ankle before every game, but somehow I would still turn it. This bothered me so much because it would mess with my conditioning. At the same time, I had developed tendonitis in my left knee which I refused surgery because I wanted to play through the season. I was now getting comfortable with the system. I knew I was developing when I read an interview Coach Sanderford did with Bowling Green Daily News when he described me as "moody," "inconsistent," and "unpredictable": however, in the same article, it was written that "he wondered when he would replace those words with 'dedicated,' 'respected,' and 'a leader.'" And that day came the second week of practice. He said, "Michelle has finally decided that she wants to work hard," and "Now the sky's the limit for her. She has matured and improved physically and has the look of an outstanding player." The best part of that article was not just his words that encouraged me even more, but the fact that he was adjusting our style of play to an up-tempo style of play. Music to my ears. LI mentioned in that article how I cheated myself last year by letting a lot of things bother me. This year I was going to let the game come to me. In practice I was aggressive and gained the respect of my teammates. Last year when Coach used to yell and correct me, I took it personally. This year, I listened, corrected myself, and played through it. He noticed the change, I noticed the change, and my teammates noticed the change. I was still moody, but I was getting the job done.

I was a starter in the first half of the season before becoming a consistent six coming off the bench. Averaging between 10 to 14 points, and about 5 rebounds per game. When called on I was an immediate impact for the team offensively and defensively. I was even growing into taking pride in playing defense. I was able to put up good numbers in a short amount of playing time. For example, in 21 minutes of play in a game against South Alabama, I scored 16 points. This was where my strengths added impact to the team. Coming off the bench I was able to instantly contribute, and I enjoyed that role. We had enough talent on our team to adjust the line up and still win games.

I was leaning into my junior year with way more confidence and began finding my place on the team. Whether I started or came off the bench as the sixth player (something I actually enjoyed), I was ready. Being the sixth player off the bench allowed me to bring that extra spark when I got in the game, adding to the stat lines in every category. As the sixth player, I got to see the game in motion and see what I needed to do when I took the court. I got to see where the open spots were, who the weakest and strongest players were, and what areas my team needed me the most. I could take advantage of both ends of the floor just by observing the start of the game from the bench, and this was how I used my skills, and athleticism to gain a competitive edge over the competition. It allowed me to assess and attack, and I was able to effectively contribute every time. I started having more fun with how I was learning, and game by game, Coach started having more and more confidence in calling on me. By January of 1995 we were undefeated 10-0, looking for 11-0 going up against Iowa in a home game. This was the first time I would see Coach C. Vivian Stringer again since she sat in my living offering me the opportunity to play for her team in high school. We were on a winning streak, but off the court, as a team our energy was off. Off the court we were bickering a lot. We would have several team meetings, we had team building sessions, and team interventions. I don't know what it was, but as strange as it was, we played better. By the end of January, we were 14-0, 3-0 in the Sun Belt conference. During our winning streak we were ranked No. 9, undefeated, and went up against No. 4 ranked Louisiana Tech who was always our toughest competitor in our division. In front of a crowd of 8,214 fans at Diddle Arena, the second largest crowd in Lady Topper history, we beat La. Tech 79-71 giving a 14-0 undefeated mid-season.

As great of a basketball season we were having we met a scare that no one is ever prepared for.

The Flight That Could Have Changed Everything

In January 1995, following a tough loss playing at Auburn University, we headed to Louisiana to face off against La Tech, we boarded what appeared to be a 30-passenger plan for our next destination. The initial part of the flight was smooth, but as we entered a stormy area, turbulence got really bad. The plan began to drop erratically, spreading fear throughout the pan especially after being lifted from our seats despite wearing seat belts. We would scream in panic each time the play swayed and dropped. In response to the conditions, we heard the announcement from the pilots deciding to make an emergency landing at a small airport. When we landed, some of us experienced motion sickness, and collectively many of us were shaken so badly that we begged the coaches to arrange a charter bus as an alternative to getting back on that plane. We overheard the pilot tell the coaches that the wing of the plane was struck by lightning, which only intensified our apprehension about continuing the flight.

After waiting for the weather to improve, he mustered the courage to reboard the plane. Thankfully, the rest of the flight was better, and we made it safely to our destination. To be honest, during that ordeal, I genuinely feared for our lives. From that flight forward, flights in bad weather made me fearful about the flight. I would always say extra prayers before, during, and after each flight. I couldn't help but to be grateful for every safe life thereafter even to this day.

Sun Belt Conference Championship, 1995

Once again we meet up to play La. Tech this time on their home court for the March Madness Sun Belt Conference Championship game. We finished the regular season (26-3), and La. Tech was (26-4). In Ruston La. We would beat them for the Sun Belt Conference Championship 7-68, by a three-point shot made by our point guard Dawn Warner with two seconds left on the clock. The plan was run for Veronica, but with the clock running down Dawn sank the three. The final buzzer sounded, the game was over, and we had just won the 1995 Sun Belt Conference Championship in Ruston, Louisiana, against Louisiana Tech, a team full of talent who always gave 100% from start to finish. They wore their confidence and pride on their faces and backed it up with their play. On March 11, we cut down the nets in celebration on their home court, walking away with a buzzer-beater victory, 71-68.

We often had a hard time hearing each other on the court in this arena. To win a conference championship with all that, sealed the deal. Players like Vickie Johnson made going up against them really tough. This team's roster was just as competitive as ours. This win put us in a great situation going into the NCAA seeding and gained us home court advantage in the first round of the NCAA tournament. Coming off of a win like this, our adrenaline was racing. We had accomplished what we set out to do. Filled with exciting emotions, we managed to settle down and do post-game interviews with the media. These moments gave us the opportunity to celebrate the victory with the hundreds of fans that filled the stands of this game, and those who were at home watching it live.

NCAA Tournament

Winning our conference gave us a great seed in the NCAA Tournament selection. Upon gathering as a team, along with some alumni, we learned we would play against Toledo in the first round of the tournament on our home court. Our coaching staff went to work on scouting this team and putting together film on them for us to watch before practice. Our coaches were amazing at putting films together. Sometimes, watching films was exhausting, but it was necessary. It trained us on how to prepare for battle and be ready for whatever was to come our way. It was better to be prepared than to be surprised and unaware of what our opponents were capable of, especially the teams we had never played against. Because of our filming sessions, our preparation practices were intense. Not only did they allow us to walk through their offense and defensive sets, but they also allowed us to adjust our own. Pre-game is equally as important as post-game.

We all took pre-game preparation seriously because, unlike regular season play, the NCAA Tournament was single elimination. We were one of 64 teams battling for the same goal, and that was to win the NCAA Championship trophy. So, every film session, practice, and pre-game was met with an urgency that left very little room for errors.

The hard work paid off, as we went on to defeat both Toledo first and then Oregon State at the Diddle Arena. These wins advanced us to the Sweet 16, where we would face Tennessee (34-3) on their home court. This was my second time coming face to face with the legendary Pat Summit, but my first time playing against her and her team. The first time I met her was at a basketball camp in PA in high school, and she was one of many coaches who was recruiting me out of August Martin.

What Happens After The Game

At Diddle Arena, we had an amazing fan base, averaging over 5,000 or so fans per game. On road trips, our fans filled entire sections right behind our bench. For major matchups, our arena was standing room only. It would be so loud in there we had a hard time hearing each other and then we would stand right on top of each other. Tennessee had the same reputation at their home games. The first impression I got of their arena was, it was huge. The court seemed longer than usual, and the seating seemed endless. As their fans began to fill the arena, it was maxed out and loud. From the floor seats the nosebleeds all you saw was orange.

Reaching this level came with perks. They gave us NCAA Sweet 16 gear and the media was at a level I never seen before. They even drug-tested us before the game. Now in all my years of playing basketball at the college level, we were never drug tested. This gave a different spin on the level we had reached. The funniest part was some of us peeing in the cup NCAA staff was literally standing right outside the staples of the bathrooms to keep an eye on us. While others were finished and, on the court, warming up, the rest of us had to listen to running water to help us use the bathroom.

The game was broadcasted live on ESPN and several other networks. The good thing about being nationally ranked was quite a few of our games, especially the big ones, had ESPN coverage. This was great because this allowed family and friends from around the world to see the games live, as well as catch the replays.

We were warned well in advance that this was a difficult gym to play in, not necessarily because of the roar of the loud crowd but the favoritism the refs displayed toward Tennessee. We were used to that because we often faced one-sided refs, but this event played out a lot differently.

We had no idea what was truly ahead of us. When I tell you this game was 7 against 5, I am not exaggerating. We gave Tennessee the business in the first half, but that quickly turned. I mean these refs controlled every aspect of the game's outcome in the second half. They started fouling out our players one by one, rarely making calls for us. It got so bad that I could hear some of their fans in the stands screaming, "Let them play." This was a game that could have easily been a battle to the buzzer, with the best team advancing, but the refs made sure the game wasn't close enough to give us a fair chance at the win. Tennessee would claim the win 87-65. Don't get me wrong, this was a talented team with players like Nikki McCray, Michelle Marciniak, and my former USA Olympic Gold Medalist teammate Latina Davis. But we were stacked too with the likes of Gwen Doyle, Tara Cosby, Ida Bowen, and Veronica Cook. The Tennessee team was extremely talented, but they weren't 22 points better than us. Whether you watched the game live or watched the replay, you would agree with that, too.

We were hurt. I mean HURT! The bus ride was silent. Usually, our coach would put the game on for us to watch on the bus, but the tension and raw emotions permeated the bus. At some point, we did eventually watch the game and witnessed the disgrace. We could hear the commentators speaking about the one-sided calls, that's how blatant it was. It's amazing how nothing was done about that game, but that's the way our season ended.

We finished the season 28-4, ranked No. 12 in the NCAA Top 25 Coaches Poll. We felt good about what we accomplished that year, but we wanted the championship for our seniors. They had such a deserving season it would have been nice to send them off on top. We had a strong squad consisting of All-Americans and all-around great women. It was a fun season. We spent New Year's in Las Vegas and were 12-2 in our conference and 14-0 at home. That loss at Tennessee was a real dagger, but it took nothing away from what we accomplished as a whole.

With games like this, the hardest part was having to replay the experiences during post-game interviews and press conferences. Regardless of wins and losses, big games, and rivalries, it was a routine that came with the game. As players and coaches, we always hold an appreciation for the media because it's another way for us to interact with the public, and we get to share our perspective of the game. As harsh as they can be at times, they were also a voice for us too.

The Media and the Press

Post-game interviews and press conferences play a pivotal role in sports. My personal experiences began from high school, where local papers and commentators frequently interviewed and wrote about me. These interviews cover a wide range of topics, including their personal opinions about the game, our performance, our opponents performance, and the strategies employed. Journalists never held back tough questions. If you had a bad game, they wanted highlights with details of what went wrong. If a teammate underperformed, they wanted statements about that too. Injuries were not off-limits; they wanted the inside scoop and if they could get it from you they would. While some of these interviews often felt repetitive, they served a crucial purpose. Throughout my athletic career, I've strived to be open and honest in my responses, but I did so without sacrificing the integrity of my teammates and coaches. It wasn't always easy, especially after a disappointing loss, but with time I learned to maneuver through it.

It is important to always be mindful of what you say and how you say it. Public perception can potentially impact the program and careers. Talking to the media also allowed me to show my appreciation to them for taking an interest in what we do as athletes. I always felt how I approached the game, and the media was one and the same; both had a vital role in how we represent ourselves and the programs/franchises I played for.

The Season's Takeaways

My biggest take away from this season was learning the power of getting out of my own way to allow great things to happen. I am confident that my performance today helped prepare me for what's to come. I stepped out of my comfort zone, embraced the challenges presented to me, took the shackles off, and leveled up my game. What felt uncomfortable manifested into confidence and earning the respect of the coaches and my teammates. The obstacles that were once burdens on me were now transformed into stepping stones for growth, no longer blocking the opportunities in front of me. On the other side of stress, I discovered clarity and resilience, shedding the weight of unnecessary doubt and welcoming positive changes. This involved me being patient with the process and a newfound confident in my abilities to figure it out. As I matured into a young adult, I began to see the opportunities for me to excel, both on and off the court. I acknowledged my mental and physical weaknesses and began to learn more about my personality. I knew for me to continue to offer the world my unique gifts and talents I had to get out of my own head. This would be vital going into my senior year, which was already filled with promise and anticipation. Now, I had to get past the biggest missing and needed pieces in my life, and that was getting my family to some of my games. This was the last year of my college basketball career, and I didn't want them to miss yet another year of me playing. I struggled with letting go of this need, it meant a lot to me, and I hoped that summer when I was able to go home, I could have this conversation with them again. What

I didn't know is how much it would affect me when the conversation didn't go as I hoped.

As the season came to an end I found myself preparing for arthroscopic knee surgery. I played the whole season with tendonitis in my left knee, even with the help of pain-relieving medication I endured constant pain throughout the season. I knew I couldn't play another season with this pain. The discomfort not only affected my performance on the court but also made everyday activities challenging. As apprehensive as I was about my first-ever surgery, the surgeon explained the procedure and the healing process, offering some comfort. Despite not feeling particularly excited about the surgery, the relief of ending the pain outweighed my nervousness. Thankfully, the surgery was a success, but it meant I had to spend six to eight weeks on crutches and wearing a full leg, unable to bend my knee.

After the sixth week, the rehab process began in Bowling Green, and once the brace was removed and my knee regained flexibility, the doctor arranged for me to complete rehab in New York during the summer break. I was so happy about that because the campus was a desert, and I was in the dorm pretty much by myself. I was excited to go home and be with family and friends, but unfortunate conversations with some family members reminded me of the feeling of invisibleness I experienced in their presence. Being that I was going into my senior year, I hoped my family would come to KY to watch me play, but once again, I felt unimportant and overlooked. The pain of this recurring situation brought back memories of why being away from home had often felt better than being there. Watching others in the community being celebrated for various reasons by them while my achievements were ignored and intensified this feeling. I then talk about upcoming parties and events being held for movers and shakers from the neighborhood and I just kept asking myself what I was doing wrong that my own peeps aren't acknowledging and celebrating me. It just didn't make sense to me. Despite the games on ESPN, winning a Sun Belt Conference Championship, and making it to the Sweet 16, it was made to seem so small.

My mother always made sure she bragged about me and told her co-workers and peers about my success. She gloated every chance she got, and I loved her for it. She made sure her job and community organizations knew about my achievements and acknowledged me in their quarterly or annual bulletins. People I grew up with from the neighborhood showed me love by taking pictures, giving me hugs, wishing me well, and excited for seeing me play on TV. This felt GREAT! The best greeting I got the entire trip. After completing my visit and fulfilling my rehabilitation for my knee, I was ready to return to campus. On the trip back, I couldn't shake the negative energy that was invading me. After working through so many insecurities during the year, this was a big trigger that manifested into anger.

Senior Year of College

When I stopped moving in my purpose, I crossed into the lane of overthinking and pain. In my junior year, I was coming into myself and figuring out exactly what the team needed from me. I was doing good in my classes but could have done better. I was averaging a C as I finished up my junior year and had pretty much taken all of my core classes. My senior schedule was filled with electives. Coming in with the classes that transferred from Sullivan left me to focus on taking the classes specifically for my major in both my sophomore and junior years. By my senior year I had only had to take one class to complete my major and the electives with easy classes to remain registered as a full-time student. I was happy about this because I could commit more time to figuring out what I was going to do once I graduated. I knew of a few of my prior teammates going overseas to continue their basketball careers as professionals, but I haven't had that talk with anyone as of yet, so my focus was on completing a successful season. I knew I really didn't want to return to NY, and it was important for me to decide what things look like for me after graduation. Having a successful season would create options for me. This was the time I needed my pure athleticism and talent to shine brighter than it ever has. I didn't want my career as a basketball player to end after this season.

What I didn't expect was my trip to NY to have me returning to campus feeling defeated. I thought maybe it was mental fatigue, and I just needed to enjoy campus life and go to some parties. I went to some events with some of my teammates and friends on campus a little more; laugh and have a good time. I started going to campus parties and traveling with a friend of mine back and forth to Cincinnati, Ohio, to hang out with her and her friends. We took these trips on the weekend when we had off time from preseason conditioning. This was the fun I needed to venture into something different and to just stop thinking so much. When we couldn't make these trips anymore, I would spend my off time at my apartment, dating, and inviting friends over to keep from sitting alone feeling miserable. I was tired of feeling disappointed, yet I could hide from the stress brewing in me. Two of my teammates had an apartment on the other side of town, and several days out of the week I was hanging out with them. They gave the best parties. Most of the time, the men's basketball team was at their spot hanging out. If you wanted to have a good time, this was the place to be. What happened there will stay there. I began attending scrimmages at the campus sports facility to start getting in shape. I knew John was going to go hard with our conditioning, and I didn't want to go into the preseason out of shape. I wanted to be better than what I was described as in that article and show up with a positive attitude toward the season and my teammates. I did everything I could to shake off my NY experience but like a song on repeat, it kept playing. It was obvious something was bothering me, and people would ask me often if I was ok? I would brush it off as being tired. At this point I was carrying a full class schedule, we were having two a day practices, so using the excuse that I was tired worked. I wore my emotions on my sleeve and wasn't very good at masking my moods. In the locker room, one day, we gathered to review the new program for the upcoming season. I was excited to see me on the front cover with Dawn, our senior point guard, and Coach Sanderford. We were excited about the upcoming schedule, especially our trip to Nassau Bahamas for our Winter break tournament. Bahamas would top our trip the year before to Las Vegas. There, we won the tournament and got to spend New Years on the Las Vegas strip. Don't get me wrong, I had a blast in Vegas, but learning we were going to the Bahamas with its beautiful beaches and blue waters was music to my ears, especially after our trip to Puerto Rico during my senior year. All the beaches were eroded from a big oil spill in the ocean.

We were also excited for our teammate Jaana who was from Finland, and on the schedule was an exhibition game against the Finnish National Team. With her being so far from home, the coaches put this game on the schedule just for her to feel home away from home. As we read further down the schedule, Dawn pointed out that the last home and senior night game would be played against New Orleans on February 22nd, and she asked me if my family was coming. This game was of importance for me and her because we were seniors, and this night would be a celebration of us. Immediately, sadness consumed me. I went into the bathroom to avoid them seeing tears forming in my eyes. For the last two years, I watched the seniors be celebrated by the program at half-time of our last home game. They were escorted by family members to center court, acknowledged by the coaching staff and members of the university, presented with flowers and their basketball jerseys in a beautiful frame. Those moments filled with so much happiness and tears as we honored their achievements and wished them well beyond college. I knew my day was soon coming and hoped that if there was no other game, my family would show up for this one.

At this point, I had to be honest with myself as to why this situation with my family was bothering me so much. It all balled down to "senior night," which was my final moment to celebrate my final year of playing college basketball. It meant the world to me when my family came to see me play at Rutgers in my sophomore year. I hadn't had another moment with them at a game, and I hoped this could be it. We kicked off the season with an exhibition game against Athletes In Action and the Finnish National Team. We got to see what our team would look and feel like. With some key players having graduated and eight new players on our roster, we had to learn to play together under the coach's system. Although six of us were returning, we had a lot of developing to do. The great part is we all got along well and pushed each other through preseason conditioning. We had some real talent on this team, and I was confident that we were going to achieve some great things that season. With Dawn and I looked at leaders as the seniors of the bunch, we assumed our role and knew it would take a lot of mental toughness on all of our parts to have a successful season.

Just What I Needed-Another Ball To Drop

Late one night, the phone rang, and on the other end was my Aunt Alice. Instantly, something felt wrong because I usually got calls from her wishing me happy birthday. We often spoke in person. However, this time, she had somber news to share. My mother had been diagnosed with colon cancer and was in the hospital. My mother requested that no one tell me to prevent adding stress on me. My mother didn't want her diagnosis to become a distraction from my studies and ongoing season. However, my aunt felt I should know.

I was grateful my aunt told me because it allowed me to fly home for a few days to be with my mother, all thanks to the understanding and support of my coach. Although it was a challenging time, I did my best to stay focused, being able to spend time with my mother and see for myself that she was healing, and that brought me a sense of relief. Fortunately, they caught her cancer early, sparing her from the need for chemotherapy. Despite the difficulty of the situation, I found comfort in knowing that she was recovering.

After speaking to my mother's doctors, I realized it was impossible for my mother to travel for a while, which meant her being at Senior Night was out. She was never much of a traveler, but for this special moment, I would have moved heaven and earth to get her to Bowling Green. Her life had always revolved around taking care of us as a single mother; even as we grew older, she had this need to keep up her nurturing ways and always be available whenever we needed. However, due to my brothers' choices and her concerns for their safety and her home, she often became fearful of traveling, effectively enslaving herself with worrying over their life's choices. It saddened me that her fears kept her from enjoying traveling and being a part of my college career. Here it was a moment in time that I yearned for my family's presence, only to have yet another ball drop.

My emotions spiraled as I sank into a dark place, with my mind constantly filled with the conversations from the summer and now my mother's cancer. I just wanted the noise to stop, for a moment of peace without responsibilities or reminders of the pain. I was showing up for practice but wasn't fully present. I went through the motions. The leadership role I once embraced was honestly deserving of someone else to have. The excitement about being a senior and all it represented lost its meaning, and I found myself trapped in a web of self-made excuses and yearned for an escape to somewhere free from burdens that now controlled me.

I found relief as I was getting to know a woman I met in Cincinnati. Our evening phone calls became a lifeline, helping me get through each day. I felt a connection with her, and when she came to visit me, it felt good to have her at our season opener against Athletes In Action. Despite the loss of the game, I managed to score a team high of 16 points and grabbed 8 rebounds. Though my individual performance was decent, the loss dampened my pride, but I admired how as a team we rallied together during and after the game, committed to learning from our mistakes. I loved these ladies; I cherished being in their presence. Their passion for the game ignited a fire within me, allowing me to feed off of their energy. However, my mind couldn't escape overthinking. Thoughts of things that hadn't even happened yet consumed me, clouding my focus in my classes and preoccupying my mind with worries about the upcoming season, my social life, and the absence of my family for yet another season. I had no idea why my family's absence invaded my thoughts, but their presence was very important to me, and it affected me big time. My actions had become unpredictable even for me. The game that once brought me so much joy was losing its luster, and haunting thoughts lingered, affecting my state of mind. I yearned for a way to break free from the mental burden and rediscover the passion I once had for the sport.

My teammates noticed the change in me. I noticed the changes within myself. At times, they were unsure whether to engage with or give me space. I developed the habit of keeping my struggles to myself, stemming from a lack of feeling safe to express myself and feeling acknowledged at home. Holding things in persisted throughout my life, to avoid conflict at home due to my family's unhealthy ways of communicating, it felt safer to practice avoidance. Never did I know then that keeping silent would break me down at this stage of my college career. I unknowingly burdened my team with traumas I didn't know I had, and it hurt me to know my frustrations were now theirs. *To my teammates and coaches reading this, I want to apologize wholeheartedly for that. I genuinely mean it.* A pivotal moment came when Dawn brought up my moodiness during an interview with a local paper. There was a time when my coach did, too, but at that time, I was able to brush it off. This time, I got defensive, feeling hurt she had publicly embarrassed me like that. Those words cut like a knife. I believe that airing personal matters like that was inappropriate, as we should have handled such conversations privately. I grasped the lesson in that statement much later, but at that time, it caused more harm than good for me. As much as I appreciated her honesty, I believe I would have received it better if she spoke directly to me. I needed help at that time, and that article actually made me feel worse. The article made me confront my inner struggles, and while I wasn't mature enough to handle how to deal with things, it did resonate within me enough to acknowledge the need to face my them.

I'd been successful in the past with burying my emotions while on the court, but this time was different. The only way I knew to deal with this was to isolate myself in my lowest moments. It was clear I needed someone to confide in, but I struggled with asking for help. The fear of judgment and the lack of discussions around mental health kept me from seeking the support I needed. Deep down I knew I needed someone to help me through this, but I just didn't know how to ask. And being called names publicly made it harder to feel comfortable asking for help, which only led me to isolate myself even more.

I hate the fact that I was depriving my teammates of having the best version of me during such a great time in our careers. The team wasn't about me; it was about all of us. However, I couldn't prioritize them because I felt lost in my own life and achievements. As the weeks passed, my interest in the game waned slowly. The turning point came after taking all of my class finals, I woke up one morning with absolutely no desire to go to practice. It was Winter break, and the excitement of Christmas had just passed. The team was preparing for our upcoming trip to the Bahamas, which was a short time away. I had been going through the motions. I was physically present in my body, yet mentally disengaged. During practice, I did what was required of me, but internally, I was no longer enjoying the game. One afternoon, after crying all night in my dorm room, I mustered the courage to walk into my coach's office in Diddle Arena and shared my decision to leave the team. His expression turned to shock, and his face reddened as he waited for me to explain why. As a natural reaction, he said, "What?" and just stared at me for what felt like forever.

I opened my mouth to respond, and *everything* but the real truth poured out of me: I explained my unhappiness, how I wasn't having any fun playing anymore. I didn't go into my family situation, all I could say was, "I didn't want to hold the team back and I wasn't happy playing anymore." While some elements of the truth were obvious, it wasn't the whole truth. This was my chance to be honest and seek help, but I found myself unable to open up. Mentally, I had shut down, and the idea of expressing my fears only intensified my emotional distress. Inside, I could see the younger versions of me, longing to speak up and be heard, yet the young adult sitting before him was afraid of being ignored again. Running away was easier than facing any further pain. I honestly believe he would have exhausted every possibility to help me, but in that moment, my thinking was clouded by fear and irrationality. I saw asking for support as a set up for failure, and I just couldn't handle that thought. I had tunnel vision, fixated on everything that was lacking in my life, rather than appreciating what I already had.

Coach suggested I take a few days to carefully consider my decision before making it. He suggested I continue attending practices to support the team, to not totally remove myself. I think he hoped I would change my mind if I watched from the sidelines. I agreed with his suggestion, although I had already spent the last few weeks doing so. Sitting meant I now had to explain my decision not only to the rest of coaching staff but to my teammates as well. It wasn't an easy thing to do, and it brought up emotions for all of us. Although they offered support, I was in such a dark head space, I couldn't see that everything I needed was right in front of me. As I sat observing the practices, tears would form in my eyes, and I would catch them before anyone could see. I felt so out of place in my own body, in my own thoughts. I just sat there quietly as my teammates came over at random moments to hug me, give me encouragement, wave at me, and try to make me smile whenever the coach would turn his back. I would try to muster a smile, but my heart was hurting so much. I wanted to be out there. I wanted to be honest. I wanted that call from my family saying, "We are coming. We will be there for you." Yet, my reality was I was letting my team down and I had finally reached my low. Here I was, the leading scorer from previous games, averaging 12.8 points per game, coming off a career-high 22 points against North Carolina State, and I was walking away from it all, just when the ball was literally in my court. I was leaning on the excuse that I was leaving the team for personal reasons when in reality, I was leaving the team to keep from being embarrassed walking out on Senior Night alone or with a family that was not my own. I just could not face that pain. That wasn't just that moment, but every moment before that I'd gone my entire career alone. Yes, I was walking away from the game, and running directly into misery. Blinded by what making this decision really meant for my life and how much this was leading me into a web of poor decisions and more heartache.

What Happens After The Game

The situation took a turn for the worse when the news got out to the public. A reporter from the local paper showed up during one of our practices to interview me and took a photo of me watching the team while I sat in the bleachers. He then wrote a full article speculating whether I would stay on the team or not. This was a critical moment that required thoughtful consideration, yet it had turned into a public conversation that should have remained private. Reading that article, I felt overwhelmed, and a couple of days later, I made the decision to leave the team. For me, this was never meant to be a public spectacle. I had hoped for private, closed-door conversations to aid in my healing process, but it turned into an embarrassing and overwhelming experience instead. At that point, I simply wanted to step away from the team. Even though it meant leaving when I was only nine hours away from earning my degree, forfeiting my scholarship, ending my athletic career, and letting go of any potential benefits the season could have brought post-college, I felt it was the right choice for my well-being. Despite the challenges, I made the decision to complete my last semester, refusing to give up on what I worked so hard for academically. However, to do so, I had to take out a student loan to cover all of my expenses. As much as I tried to push through, the discomfort and judgment on campus became too overwhelming, and I ultimately decided to pack up and leave Bowling Green. What I truly needed during that time was support, not further criticism, which was why I had chosen to stay silent initially. From my perspective, it seemed like the best course of action at the time. However, I didn't let these setbacks define my future entirely. A few years later, I mustered the determination to complete online classes and earn my bachelor's degree. I refused to give up on that part of my journey and ended on a high note, proud of the achievement despite the challenges faced earlier.

I take full responsibility for not speaking up, acknowledging that things may have played out differently. I share this experience hoping that readers take heed to the significance of addressing challenges as they happen and how neglecting them can lead to unhealthy habits later in life. Unfortunately, mental health is often not given enough attention, especially in the context of athletes. The primary focus tends to revolve around the game and our contributions to it, while the issues outside of sports are disregarded as they go unnoticed by those around us who lack the training to recognize them.

It is crucial for every player, coach, and parent to prioritize mental health by engaging in open conversations about its impact on our lives. Mental health challenges transcend age boundaries; they are universal experiences we all face at one time or another in our lives. Being equipped with the necessary tools and resources to first recognize the signs, second, knowing who to ask for help, and three, learning how to navigate through those times in a healthy manner is sometimes the difference between life or death. As much as we embrace our roles as athletes, we are individuals first, and our well-being takes priority over any sport we play. Staying silent is not an option, nor is it the best option. Instead, we must encourage open dialogues and create an environment of understanding and support for one another.

Looking back, I now recognize the importance of reaching out when faced with challenges. Even if home is not the first safe space, there are so many other resources available, and public services should do a better job making these places known. I regret not speaking up and asking for help sooner, and I understand the impact it had on me and everyone around me. It is my hope that by sharing my experiences, more supportive and safe environments are created for the mental well-being of us all. By opening up about my journey, I hope to encourage empathy and compassion, paving the way for our communities to see the benefits of mental health awareness in our communities, our educational systems, and within our households. Together, we can create a world where everyone feels seen, heard, and supported in their mental health journey, importantly without ridicule and judgment.

If I could take anything back from my decision making in college, I would have asked for help rather than living in pain. The pain attracted more chaos and destructive behavior than I was prepared to handle. The second takeback would have been the day I walked into my coach's office and made the decision to quit on my team and myself. Instead, I would have walked in his office and said, "Coach, I need your help!"

Renewing of the Mind
The Art of Failing Forward

This is a subject I hold near and dear to me because the fear of failing at anything was crippling for me. The only thing I've never feared failing at was playing basketball. When I competed, I showed up with the level of confidence that I was ready for any and everyone, even those who challenged me the most. The confidence I developed early from playing with and against boys and men always made me feel a step above playing against girls/women. It was something about playing against guys that always took my game to another level. The Michelle you saw play against guys and then play against women was so different. I always felt the challenge to be greater playing the guys. It was the grit, the trash-talking, the need for me to level up every time I played because I knew I wanted to be better than them. Not to say I didn't have that playing against other females, but it was just different against the guys. I was sometimes intimidated, but that intimidation forced me to step my game up, and I loved that. When I played against other females, I jumped higher, I felt stronger, and I was much more creative in my play, so much of the time, I felt I wasn't always challenged enough. Failure was an afterthought.

I felt prepared and ready for battle. I was more afraid of failing at WKU because that was the first time in my entire career as a ball player that I was on a team that didn't have a run-and-gun style of play. From JHS to JUCO, we ran very few plays, and if we did, they were quick sets that went off quick baskets, so the transition from JUCO to WKU was rough for me. That's all we did was play a fast-paced style of play at Sullivan. I loved it. Get the ball out, and we were off. No exaggeration. By the halftime of our games, we would have at least 50 points more than any other team on the scoreboard

We had a powerhouse. Everyone knew their role, and our practices were mostly conditioning drills every day. Playing at Sullivan put me in the best shape of my playing career, and I had the most fun I ever had playing the game of basketball. I truly enjoyed playing with my teammates. We challenged each other every single day to be better. Even during conditioning drills, we were exhausted, but we pushed each other non-stop. I guess that was our way of getting through the journey together.

As excited as I was to play at WKU, on one of the top NCAA women's basketball teams, for the first year there, I didn't know if I would make it off the bench. It was an exceptional group of talented women, but I felt like I was learning the game all over again because, for the first time, I was learning a half-court style of play. Compared to the run-and-gunning I was used to, here, there were more half-court plays, which required lots of ball movement, pick and rolls, double screens, etc. It was like the game was in slow motion. I was so frustrated. This experience was hard to adapt to. I went from being a starter at Sullivan to coming deep off the bench, which was fine, but coming off the bench took some time because I had to adjust. I struggled badly. The coaches didn't give up on me, though. They recognized the frustration and kept me in the rotation, but it wasn't until my junior year that it began to make sense to me. I literally became a student of the game, which I felt was a good thing because it gave me a challenge, like when I played against the guys, but this time, it was more mental than physical.

I wasn't scared of the players; I was scared of failing at learning this new system. Of course, the more I practiced and sat on that bench my first year, the more committed I was to learning whatever I needed to adjust. I knew I could help the team, but I couldn't do it the way I used to. This new challenge introduced new opportunities to learn a new approach to the game. I was determined to move from 3rd or 4th person being called on to the first person, then ultimately starting. When I earned that 6th player role, frankly, I enjoyed it because whenever I would come into the game, I brought quick buckets, which gave the team the spark they needed to the floor, which blended well with the starters that remained on the floor. That transition worked very well for the team.

Being the 6th player on the floor championed my role in the system I initially struggled with. One key aspect of experiencing that struggle in my sophomore year was being able to gradually and accurately identify what and how I needed to adjust to get into the lineup consistently. This required me to be honest with myself and evaluate my performance when we watched the films. Watching films helped me so much. I got to see not only how our opponents performed, along with my teammates, but also how important I was in the right places and positioning to be effective. It also required having the humility to admit my mistakes and the courage to keep working at it until I got it.

Each practice and game was crucial and provided lessons that helped me improve my performance. This required me to retrain how I thought about and played the game, evaluate my ability to grasp the WKU system that had made me so successful, and adjust my game to fit into this system. I knew I could play the game; I just had to approach it from another level, and that required me to be patient with the process, and patience wasn't one of my strong suits. I got discouraged, but I stayed with it. I believed in the coaches, my teammates, and myself. I held myself accountable for learning, and I ultimately became an important piece to a grand puzzle.

In a nutshell, I didn't accept failing; I learned from my mistakes, I gained the knowledge I needed to become a vital part of the team, and that encouraged my growth.

Your Decisions Shape Your Destiny

I will admit that I have often thought, *Would my life have been less difficult had I never left college and graduated?*

To this day, I feel like after making that one decision, the course of my life that followed were constant roads of test after test. There were my financial struggles. I wasn't happy with a series of jobs I had because I'd rather be playing professional ball instead of punching a clock. I had a failed relationship that, in my head, would bring me peace but didn't.

That one decision caused me to stray off course, changing the trajectory of every sequence that followed. I was looking for an explanation for the pain I was feeling, the absence of desire, and the self-ridicule of my thoughts. It always seems easier to make negative decisions rather than the right ones and then adjust accordingly. I left school unhappy, and that unhappiness stayed with me wherever I went. I thought by leaving school, absconding from my issues, and, instead, embarking on new experiences, I would eventually put my life back on track. It didn't.

I knew I had to do the work. The same way I got myself into this reckless lifestyle was the same way I had to make the consequential decisions to set me back on course. I tried to mask my pain by making impulsive decisions, hoping they would provide me with answers. All it did was bring me right back full circle, right back to the place my pain started, right back home. I tricked myself into believing that I could add more value to my life by running from my reality. My awakening came when I faced the reality that I couldn't run from myself or the demons that had taken over my passions and interfered with my purpose. I was expecting time to relieve my hurt and confusion by replacing the people and the value I hoped they'd bring into my life. That was my first road to destruction, thinking that people would fill a void that only I could.

When I moved to Cincinnati, Ohio, I entered into my first-ever female relationship. This was a decision I made trying to run from my problems and thinking surrounding myself with things and people would provide me answers and healing. For me, this was about the escape more than it was about finding solutions. There was no one to push back against my decisions, and there were hardly any questions asked about it beyond my WKU coaches—until my mother found out. However, even then, when I shared with her how invisible and unsupported I felt within our family, she made the conversation about her and didn't listen to what I was saying.

I stayed a few months with my girlfriend and her mother, and I enjoyed her company. Being with her felt better than feeling empty at school. However, my decision making didn't get any better. I worked at a credit union by day and UPS at night, earning enough to get my own apartment. What seemed like answers, turned into more problems. My vulnerability led to me getting cheated on, and after that, the relationship became challenging. Her choices sent me deeper into darkness, and I really felt on an island all alone. I withdrew from the circle we hung around, quit both jobs, and began working at a car rental company at the Cincinnati/Northern Kentucky airport and a 311 call center to separate myself from her. I really felt alone, and I had no one to blame but myself. Not long after, on my way to a party with some friends, as a passenger, we were hit head-on by a drunk driver. The only people I knew to call for help were my girlfriend and her family, and she arrived at the hospital, making me feel bad for choosing to go out. With the injuries I sustained, I was out of work for a couple of months, doing physical therapy. I lost both jobs, Mom was sending me money for food and rent, while at the same time trying to convince me to come home. I got behind in my car note, and despite my attorney sending them information about my accident, they came and repossessed my car. Once again, my life headed further downhill. My bills were mounting up, and bill collectors were blowing up my phone, threatening me to make payments. The furniture store I rented my stereo from finally caught up with me and came to take back their system. All the while my mother was still in my ear begging me to move back to NY, but I vehemently would say no.

As pain and pitfall after pitfall fell upon me, I woke up in my apartment in Ohio and realized I couldn't run from myself anymore, and I was tired of making the same mistakes. "Michelle," I muttered, "if you don't fix your life now, you will lose out on everything you worked so hard for." In my darkness, I realized that I had lost sight of who I was, what I wanted out of life, and where I was going. I also realized that my mom was right: I had to return to NY. As much as I didn't want to, I had to. I had to go back and face where my pain came from and understand why it was holding me back from being my best self. I successfully sabotaged my course of life when I walked away from my scholarship. Now, I would have to face the trail of unknowns I created and trust myself to battle through without making all the wrong decisions. My first task was to stop running

and deal with what was plaguing me. I had to start with identifying the hurt and addressing it. Whatever I couldn't address, I had to learn how to heal from before it destroyed me.

On my first day back to NY in 1997, the band-aid I loosely covered past hurt with was ripped off by my brothers, whose actions reminded me why moving to Ohio was a better option than returning to NY. I needed help unpacking my U-Haul truck, and two of my brothers never came to help after a family friend told them I was about to unload the truck. One never came from around the corner, and the other never got out of the bed. The same hurt I left with and endured while being away at college started immediately upon my return. I walked right back into the BS.

Thank God for my mother, Tim, and Greg because we just did what we had to do. I did nothing but go away to school and make something of my life, so why was I being treated like this? Why did brothers' friends, who came home from jail or passed away, get parties of celebration, and all I got was the cold shoulder? I began to resent them even more. I even held a little resentment for my mother for every second this treatment went on and she said nothing. I always wondered why she didn't correct this behavior and speak up for me. I hated everything about them. I hated everything about moving back to NY. I hated everything about my life at this point. I wanted to be anywhere but in NY and around this madness. That is why I invested all of my time into getting back into the game so I could get my life back on track, leave, and never look back.

Road to the WNBA
1995-2000

American Basketball League (ABL)

The American Basketball League (ABL) was a professional women's basketball league established in the United States in 1996. It attracted some of the best talents coming out of college and current pro players overseas who expressed interest in joining the league, and it heavily scouted players. That gained my interest when I saw women from college I played with and against on the rosters. The ABL had great players, such as Nikki McCray, Teresa Edwards, Natalie Williams, Taj McWilliams, Katie Smith, Jennifer Azzie, and Dawn Staley. The season went from October to March, which I thought was great. Plus, they offered attractive salaries, ranging from $50,000 to $150,000. With a salary like that, a player could choose to go overseas or stay home, and I wanted in.

Now that I was settled in New York, my immediate goal was to find out where the best of the best basketball was happening and with whom. I was told some of the best games were happening at West 4th Street, Tillary Park, and River Bank tournaments. If I wanted to find the elite players, these were the places I needed to start with, and that's exactly what I did. I got with a competitive semi-professional women's basketball travel team that was full of women who were chasing the same dream as I was. I connected with them to start my mission off right. Before long, my name was ringing bells, and my game spoke for itself in those NYC streets. My journey was playing out just as I had prayed. The right people were coming into my life, and doors were opening both on and off the court. I hired an agent to help me jumpstart my pro career by going overseas and, ultimately, into the ABL.

My agent had developed a business contact with quite a few of the ABL coaches, one being the New England Blizzard coach in Connecticut. I had a scheduled visit that allowed me to meet with the team's head coach to discuss the opportunity. My agent and I felt good about the trip and were confident I would be joining the Blizzard's roster.

And then the news hit the airwaves: The league was folding.

My heart sank! This was shocking because their rosters were filled with talent, the interest from the fans was there, and their compensation package was pretty good for a new league, but it was done, finito. Then the news dropped that the WNBA was gaining traction, and many of the ABL players began signing with the WNBA. Now, it's not for me to discuss the reason for the demise of the ABL. I wasn't in the room to hear the exact facts, but 1997-98 was the final season, and the WNBA's first tip-off was in 1997. The WNBA season was a shorter season, operating on a non-traditional summer schedule. This was a big blow. This meant starting my hustle all over again to tap into a brand-new audience of owners, coaches, and managers in the WNBA. The bright side of things was the opportunity for players who still remained in the States. The downside for me was that to build up my resume, I had to consider international play. I played away from my friends and family my entire college career, and I was looking forward to creating an opportunity to play close to home. In order to achieve that, joining an overseas ball club needed to happen. While my agent sought overseas teams, I continued playing with Prime Time. Not too long after, an opportunity arose for me to play in Croatia, Europe, under a three-month contract.

Getting to this point took a lot of hard work. From the time I moved back to New York in the summer of 1997 to the time I joined the Sparks in July 1998, my hustle was real. I played in every elite tournament throughout NYC, whether on hardwood or outdoors. If they were competitive, I played. The city's renowned summer leagues like Tillary Park, West 4th Street, and River Bank saw me on their courts. Playing with Prime Time, which was one of New York City's best semi-pro women's teams. Prime Time was a travel team and we played in New Jersey, DC, LA, PA, CT, and other states to compete. These events drew players from all over and included overseas and WNBA pro players. Our opponents ranged from college teams, military squads , and various semi-pro teams, at different levels. Our team was stacked with women whose goal was to play professionally and to continue to play professionally. The women on our team were driven to play professionally and to continue their careers at that level. To add to the team's strength, our head coach also acted on our behalf as our basketball agent. With her extensive network in the sports industry, she made sure our presence was known. She took me under her wing and helped me further my basketball career. Through her support and my unwavering dedication, I gradually made strides toward my goal of playing at the professional level first internationally in Croatia, Europe and upon my return, and joining the WNBA LA Sparks.

Croatia, Europe

The transition from playing away at college to playing in a foreign country required a total mental reset. Zagreb, a place I had never heard of before, was now the next phase in my professional career. My agent and I spoke about getting international experience on my athletic resume. She explained how this would increase my odds the WNBA taking me. I agreed to her plan, she worked out the details with the team, and the next thing I was looking at was my flight itinerary, which consisted of just over 13 hours of travel. I immediately thought, *What the hell can I do on a plane for the first 11 hours?* and *How do I pack for three months in Croatia?* I was the person who always had to have a pair of sneakers for every outfit, but for this type of travel, I had to pack light. I went with a simple sweatsuit and four pairs of sneakers. For me, that was the lightest I had ever packed going anywhere. Either way, the venture began. I had some magazines, my CD player with my case of CDs, some books, my pillow, and I was ready. As I walked down the tarmac to board the plane, I noticed the different nationalities boarding and just how huge the plane was. My nerves elevated as I stepped on the plane into unknown territory. I had no idea what to expect on such a long flight, I just wanted to be comfortable. I thought about the stipulations that came with this trip. The agreement was pretty much a trial situation based on how I played in the first game. If they wanted me, they would offer me a three-month guaranteed contract. I wasn't concerned about that because I knew I could play this game. Plus, I didn't take a 13-hour trip with a layover to turn around and go back home. My concern was the culture and language barrier. I had no idea how or if they would receive me. After all, I had to adapt to them more than they did me. Despite my anxiety, I was impressed with the flight attendants on this huge double-decker plane; they were exceptionally kind and helpful. The plane itself was also impressive, with three different large sections separated by curtains, including an upstairs area, something I had never experienced before. My first international flight was a mix of nervous anticipation and excitement, and I was eager to see what this new chapter in my life would hold.

I was so relieved to finally land in Zagreb, the capital of Croatia. As I exited the plane, I was greeted by the coaches who held up signs with my name on them. One coach spoke English, and the other partially. They were excited and very touchy but friendly. The pair took me to a town called Osijek which was almost three hours from the capital. Osijek will be my new residence for the next three months. Here, I would play for the Drava Visual. The ride consisted of mainly a single road with two lanes one going in each direction. That made me nervous because they drove fast along these winding roads. As they told me about their history and culture, I immediately noticed the difference in the look of the town compared to Zagreb. Zagreb had more of a city vibe, while Osijek was more of a small town feel. They gave some history of how Croatia declared their independence from Yugoslavia in 1991. How they were still at odds with some countries and could face a war at any given time. He spoke about the town having one entrance and exit. That immediately made me nervous because I was three hours away from the airport and had no car of my own to leave if something did happen. I have to admit, that left me unsettled, but I tried not to think too much about that because I would have wanted a ride to the airport and back home. I needed this experience to work for me. As we approached this big beige building with multiple floors, the first thing I noticed was holes in the building with shrapnel sticking out. I also noticed missile debris left on the sidewalk from the last war they had. This bit of history was being shared with me as they noticed the puzzled look on my face.

"Are y'all still at war?" I asked.

"We haven't been at war for some years," one coach responded, "but war can break out at any time."

I instantly wanted to get on a call with my agent to ask her what she had gotten me into, but I paused on that and continued the tour around my new living quarters and the restaurant I would be eating at for my meals every day. My apartment was on the second floor in a modest space with a small living room and a nice size bedroom with a king bed, TV, and a nice kitchen area. The TV had plenty of stations, but the only two networks that played in English were a news station and Cartoon Network. After dropping my bags off, they took me to where I could get my daily meals covered by the team. I noticed the nice ice cream shops, boutiques, and other quaint stores. Of course, they had a McDonald's, which ironically tasted much different than it did in the States. It tasted better; even the Sprite tasted better, and I wasn't much of a soda drinker, but while there, I grew to enjoy a nice glass of Sprite with lemon. This was the first time I got to experience not just the difference in culture but how much healthier and rich international food was compared to the United States, how their products were grown and processed much differently than ours, and that explained our obesity and illness rates being so high.

After the tour and meeting people on the street who were excited to see the American Basketball player there to represent their team, I was ready to relax and get ready to meet the rest of the coaching staff and team the next day. I wasn't provided with my own car, but they did give me a pass that allowed me to use their transit system to get around, which were buses that ran from one part of town to the other. Most places were close, so it wasn't an inconvenience to use public transportation. For the first few days, either the coaches or the players transported me around until I got familiar with my surroundings. My first day with the team was a two-hour practice, and it was cool. Only one girl on the team spoke English. She took it as a second language because she had plans to come to the States for college. She was my lifeline because, without her, I wouldn't have been able to talk to anyone when the assistant coach wasn't around. Those two helped me with translation. The head coach spoke Croatian, so everything he said besides my name I had no clue about. I just knew to look up at him when I heard my name to reference me. I adapted pretty quickly.

The next day, we had a game. They made it clear I was there to get them a lot of rebounds. That was their whole goal. Once again, in my career, I was challenged in my game. I played guard and power forward in the States, and now I was being asked to play the five position. I wasn't afraid of the center position because at WKU, the guards and forwards worked on post moves, and I had played against people bigger and stronger than me all of my career. I always practiced post moves, and WKU helped me perfect it by having those isolation options when we played. The Croatian star player on the team was a 6-foot-thin-built player. She was good. She could definitely hold her own, and I didn't mind playing number two to her. She was a great scorer, had a good jump shot, and as much as they wanted me to rebound, my goal was to show them that I was a well-rounded player, and I wasn't going to just grab boards. In game one, I grabbed 13 rebounds and scored 15 points. They instantly expressed interest in me staying for the whole season, and we completed the remaining contract extension.

The season was going well. My adjustment was getting used to wearing tight-fitted shorts. This was the era of oversized uniforms in the States, but these uniforms, to me, were like biker shorts. We played at the Drava Visual Arena, which held a few thousand people. The men's games were also held here. They usually played on the same nights as we did. Both of our teams pulled in nice crowds. The town was very supportive of their home teams, and they were aggressive fans. They gave the guest teams no mercy. The fans were excited to get to know me, but with the language barrier majority of the time, I didn't know what they were saying. I just smiled as they spoke. They kept talking about how white my teeth were and how tall I was, and how much they loved American players. Everyone wanted to know one thing: Did I know Toni Kukoč and Dražon Petrovic? Kukoč and Petrović were famous Croatian pro players that represented their country in the NBA. Petrović died in a car accident in 1993 at the age of 28. The funny thing is whenever I would say no, they always seemed so sad and disappointed I didn't meet that need for them. They think all pro players know each other.

What Happens After The Game

Our team had a nice run. I would average over 15 rebounds a game and 15 points. For the two months or so I was on the team we lost only one game. It made me feel good to be a part of a winning team in my first pro experience. My first few weeks were hard to get used to. Being there with no one to talk to most days, meant I either ran up a phone bill calling home, or bought plenty of books to read until something good came on to watch on the English tv channels. Most days I sat looking out the window, walked around the town until the sun started to settle, and went to practice and games. I was bored out of my mind. That overseas basketball scene out of *Love and Basketball* was me 100%. Ironically, I auditioned for that movie, not knowing how relatable I was to different parts of the movie's scenes. I was relieved one night when a couple of my teammates invited me to go to a local hangout with them. Many of my teammates were either full-time college students and/or employees, they didn't have as much free time as I did, so this invite was just what I needed to keep from thinking about going home. I admired their commitment to the team and their jobs and studies too. All of our games were on the weekend and our practices were a couple of times during the week. In between that time, I was in my apartment or walking around the town. It would have helped if people spoke English, but I made the best of it. I wrote letters to friends and family every day. This was my only real pass time outside of playing.

I had quite a few memorable moments while with the team. One being a trip we took to Split for an important game that determined our spot in the playoffs. Split is a beautiful location that is about six hours away. The weather in Osijek was cold, but when we went to Split, the temperature was warm, and the water was so clear and turquoise blue. It was amazing. We were there for an overnight trip. This is when my second memorable moment about being in Croatia happened. I went to use the bathroom in the locker room and the toilets were built in the ground. These were called "squat toilets." Now, my first question was how do they do this? The second, was how do I not get my sneakers wet? Third, where was the real toilet? It was the most awkward experience ever. I was trying to focus both on my aim and not splashing anything on my clothes and shoes. I actually took a picture because I knew no one I shared this experience with would believe me.

My two-month stay in Croatia was a unique experience; however, I ended up leaving the team one game before the championship game because my goal was to get on a WNBA team, and I wanted to get back to the States to get in front of the powers-that-be to make that happen. My team in Croatia went on to lose the second round of the playoffs without me. Whether the results would have been different if I had stayed, I don't know. I would like to believe it would, but I made a selfish decision and put my goals before the teams. Was it the right decision? Yes, because one of the tournaments I played in landed me an invitation from to attend the WNBA Draft Camp in Chicago, Illinois.

WNBA Draft Invitation

Upon my return from Croatia, my primary focus was to attend all the basketball events being scouted by the WNBA. One big tournament was the Martin Luther King Classic, held in Washington, DC, in January of 1998. The key purpose for me being there was to capture the attention of coaches observing players during the weekend tournament. My agent personally invited me, and WNBA Chief of Basketball and Players Relations Renee Brown, along with several other WNBA coaches, would be in attendance. This tournament was a big deal for women's basketball. At this time, it had grown its reputation of drawing in great talent. That year in particular, with the buzz of the WNBA, it attracted current WNBA players on teams, which I loved. This allowed scouts to see me and my teammates compete against other pro talent. True to tradition, Prime Time advanced to the championship round where we battled against a standout player from the Charlotte Sting. Our matchup was characterized by relentless exchange of baskets and jump shots; the battle between her and I was intense. My objective was clear: to leave that gym with an offer from one or even all of those pro scouts.

Mission was successfully accomplished immediately after the championship game, as Renee Brown offered me a spot at the invitational only 1998 WNBA Pre-Draft Camp, which was being held in Chicago, IL, April 1998 on the campus of Moody Bible Institute. This camp featured exclusive workouts for players and coaches. They covered all arrangements and expenses from flights, hotel, food, and transportation for the entire weekend. From the moment we landed at Chicago O'Hare Airport to the conclusion of the camp, our schedule was packed with workouts, interviews, photo sessions, meals, and group meetings. Giving us a glimpse of what life in the WNBA would be like. My mother, for the first time, overcame her fear of flying and flew in with my Aunt Alice to provide me with their support. None of us knew what to expect from the weekend, I felt so bad because our schedule was so busy, I would see them for every bit of twenty minutes the entire weekend. It felt amazing having them there. We had hoped the workouts would be open for spectators, but unfortunately, that wasn't the case. Not even my agent had much time with us. I saw her as much time as I did my family. Throughout the weekend, we were surrounded by team staff, current players, coaches, and members of the media. Even our meals were integrated into events that focused on networking and meet and greets.

Our days started as early as 5:30 a.m., between the intense scheduling, workouts, and meals, there was little time for down time. Exhaustion took over by the end of each day, leaving little energy for anything short of ice baths, and rest. Liza D. and I shared a room, and considering how endless her energy is, it was quite telling to see how exhausted she was at the end of the day, showing just how strenuous those workouts truly were. The highlight for me from the weekend was my mother facing her fears, flying to Chicago to be there for me. My family's support meant more to me than words could express.

My performance at the camp was solid. I felt good about my conditioning and my overall play. At the time, both the Assistant Coach Houston Comets and the head coach from Detroit Shock expressed interest in me being a part of their teams. Throughout the final day of workouts, quite a few other team staff shared how much they enjoyed watching my play. As I left Chicago, I carried a sense of optimism that I would secure a spot on a team. The Houston Comets seemed particularly promising, especially since the Assistant Coach had already shown interest during the Martin Luther King Classic in Washington, DC. That boosted my confidence even more.

However, come April 1998, I found myself sitting in my living room, staring at the TV, eagerly awaiting a call from my agent with updates about team interest, only to be met with silence. No phone call came. No draft selection for me was announced. I was deeply disappointed. It was perplexing why these coaches would express interest and build my hopes, only to have no results. I know I had a great camp but, I was passed over in favor of players fresh out of college and with more recent experience than I had. Going overseas was a plus, but many of those players had leverage of recognition over me due to their recent college and overseas performances. I understood that, but knew when it came down to skills, I had it.

With my plans thwarted, it was back to the drawing board. Despite my frustration, I had to stay the course. All was not done. Although the draft selection took place, teams were still looking to fill spots. Teams were hosting individual workouts, my agent set one up for me and Trina with the Detroit Shock, a trip that ultimately proved to be disappointing and a mere waste of time. Trina and I stepped fresh off the plane and went to the gym for the workout, only for the head coach to pop her head in and out twice. By the end of the workout, she told us that she had finalized her roster earlier that day. Though I appreciated the opportunity, the fact that she barely watched us play and then delivered that kind of news made the experience bitter. This was a trip we paid for, not them, so to get that kind of treatment left us feeling some kind of way about how things happened. We called our agent, letting her know how we were treated, caught our flight back, and moved on to plan C. Throughout the summer, I stayed in good shape, hopeful of another opportunity. Eventually, that opportunity came in July 1998, in California, leading me onto the roster of a professional team. This was the turning point I needed to reignite my professional career.

WNBA LA Sparks

Twice, I had the incredible opportunity to showcase my skills at the iconic Madison Square Garden, the Mecca of New York. It was during the P.S.A.L High School City Championships, on two occasions, our team emerged winning City Titles. For a high school player like myself, that was a great achievement.

Stepping onto the same stage where many NBA legends once played was really inspiring. Playing under those intense hot lights, with hollow-sounding wooden floors, was an experience like no other. To me, this was a dream come true. From that little girl watching Knick games on tv to being watched on the same platform was amazing. Each time, I felt on top of the world each experience would be hard to beat. However, fate had more surprises in store for me. Another unforgettable experience awaited at the E.A. Diddle Arena at Western Kentucky University. As I stepped foot on the court, memories of playing at the Garden filled with thousands of seats, and the roar of passionate crowds. Both venues were on a grander scale than any high school gym I ever played in, leaving a lasting impression on my heart.

Playing at the Garden and at Diddle Arena felt like pinnacles of my career, but little did I know that new dreams were waiting to be discovered. Soon, an incredible opportunity knocked at my door-I was offered a chance to represent the WNBA's LA Sparks playing at the Great Western Forum. Out of thousands of hopeful players, I was chosen to be 1 of 120 players to claim a spot on 1 of the 10 teams at this professional table. The moment became real when my agent sent over a contract with a bold letter spelling out "WNBA LA SPARKS" at the top. I eagerly signed on the dotted line, knowing that come July of 1998, I would officially be a LA Spark. It wasn't an easy road to get to this moment, but it was all worth it. The excitement and joy I felt were indescribable. While I had played on many basketball courts, calling the Forum home for the next few months was a different kind of accomplishment - one that I had worked tirelessly to achieve, yet it still seems surreal. The invitation to join the LA Sparks originated from the Queen Latifah Basketball Tournament at Venice Beach in California during the July 4th weekend of 1998. It was during this tournament that I played with a semi pro basketball team, Prime Time, which I've been playing with throughout the year. This was my first time back in Cali to play since college. I wasn't sure what to expect from the tournament, except that it was hosted by Queen Latifah and the games were being played on the beach. With the championship in our sights, we were coming in undefeated. During this tournament we competed against teams from New York, Cali, and a few other locations, all with the intent to claim victory on the sandy courts of Venice Beach. Little did I know that this tournament would be the gateway to realizing my dream of playing in the WNBA. A moment that would forever change the trajectory of my basketball career.

What Happens After The Game

Unlike the scorching sun and heat of New York City, the California sun brought a different kind of blaze. Even though we were playing on the beach, there was no breeze from the water. As we arrived to play our first game of the tournament, it was good to see Latifah again. I first met her at a New Jersey Celebrity Charity Basketball game I played in honor of her brother.

The tournament kicked off on Saturday; depending on the standings of each team, you advanced to the playoffs and championship rounds on Sunday. Our team went undefeated, securing the first-place spot all the way to the championship game, where we were matched up against the second-place team. It was the game to see, with standing-room-only around the bleachers and court. Of all the games we played that summer, this team was our toughest opponent; they actually gave us a run for our money. It was a close game from the very start, with the lead changing many times. Despite our efforts to pull away, they would get on runs to keep it close. Late in the third quarter, we were up by 12 or 13 points, and I was having a great game. My shot was falling, and thanks to our point guard, Estelle, who I loved playing with, our fast-break game was on point. We always found each other in the right spots, and we communicated by eye contact and instincts. However, early in the fourth quarter, I came down on an opponent's foot and turned my ankle. This forced me to sit out elevating and icing my ankle on the sidelines. I tried everything to get back on the court, but the trainer told me it didn't look good, and my ankle began to swell. With our lead shrinking and the pain throbbing in my ankle, I reluctantly sat on the sidelines, hoping for some relief as the time ticked away. Behind by 2 points, our coach kept looking at me hoping I would give her the signal to come back in. At this point my ankle was throbbing. I kept walking on it hoping I could tolerate enough of the pain to play through it. I laced my sneakers up as tight as I could to slow down the swelling and sat next to the coach hoping I could give her a signal any moment to get back in the game. Constantly flexing it, all that was going through my mind was, suck it up and help your team.

In that critical moment, a loud voice from the bleachers behind our bench shouted, "Michelle, get back in the game. Your team needs you." I had no clue who said it until I looked back and made eye contact with Rhonda. At the time, Rhonda was the general manager for the LA Sparks. I knew her face and her history of playing, but I had never met her before. I don't know what it was about her strong and authoritative voice, but it sparked, no pun intended, something in me that caused me to stand up and signal to my coach that I was ready to get back in. Without hesitation, she sent me to the scores table. With less than 4 minutes left on the game clock our team was down by 4 or 5 points, I didn't want to let my squad down, and endured the pain. We didn't come to Cali to lose. Long story short, your girl went off. Estelle, and the rest of our powerhouse elevated their games, and I would like to believe me returning played a big part in that. We went on a run, regained the lead, and together, we walked away with the championship trophy. To my surprise, I was awarded the MVP trophy.

Little did I know that only 48 hours after landing back in New York, Rhonda would call my agent and extend an invitation for me to join the LA Sparks roster. I literally had three days to prepare, I was bound for Los Angeles, embarking on a new chapter in my professional basketball career.

The moment my agent called, going over the details of the contract, I began playing in my mind the amazing opportunity that lay before me. Unlike many players who were drafted straight out of college or recruited from overseas or retired, this invitation didn't feel like anything I ever accomplished within my career. Over the years, my name had faded from the spotlight as I had left college just when I was about to step into my breakthrough role as a player. Consequently, this invitation wasn't handed to me or given as a favor but was the result of my hard work, which made it all the more rewarding. Moving to New York allowed me to rebuild my name and game and doing so paid off. After the decisions I made during my senior year in college, I had convinced myself that my chances of becoming a professional player was over. I had mentally accepted my defeat in 1997. However, my persistence to keep going had me signing a contract with the WNBA Los Angeles Sparks

Welcome to LA

On that unforgettable day, July 10, 1998, the excitement went through every fiber of my being as I started my trip to California. The LA Sparks of the WNBA offered, and I heeded the call with my heart bursting with anticipation. Picture me walking through the airport, an aura of pride enveloping me, as I set my course for the TWA gate at the busy LaGuardia Airport in New York. Oh, the pride that flowed within me was like a symphony of triumph!

It was more than just a flight; it was the unveiling of a chapter destined to be etched in the chronicles of my life and career. With each step onto that plane, the surge of excitement was matched only by the pulse of determination that coursed through my veins. Settling into my seat, my thoughts raced faster than the airplane's engines, fixated on the thrill of donning that jersey for my first game as a Spark. Sure, the Sparks roster was already recognized for its remarkable talents, but there I was, added to the roster midway through the season, ready to unleash my own brand of brilliance. The clock of time urged me on; the challenge was immense, and the time to rise to it was limited. The opportunity was mine for the taken, and the expectations soared. The stage was set, the pressure was on – to fit in, to excel, to display my unique talents into the canvas of Sparks history. As I settled my anticipation and calmed my nerves, I began to imagine that destiny had summoned me to capitalize on this opportunity, to gain the coaches confidence, and to blend seamlessly into the system of the LA Sparks. The journey ahead filled me with intensity, passion, and I was ready to seize it all. July 10, 1998, wasn't just a date – it was a magical date that stamped a new place in my basketball career, and oh, was my adrenaline-fueled and flowing.

As I touched down in LA, the sun was shining bright and so was my outlook on life. At the airport I was met by staff management who extended a warm welcome. Our first destination: the team's practice facility. Ready to meet my new teammates and coaches that formed this franchise. I looked around at the clean gym that reminded me of many that I played in before. It wasn't just a gym; it was one part of the professional stage as the LA Sparks. Gone were the doubts that once plagued my thoughts, replaced with a true sense of purpose. All of those sleepless nights questioning whether I would ever get here, were now signed, sealed, and delivered. This was no longer a distant dream; it was unfolding right before my eyes. The stage was set, now it was time to write the rest of the script.

Walking into the facility, my first encounter was with entertainer Byron Allen, who was there to interview Lisa for his show. His welcoming demeanor and genuine words instantly put me at ease as he congratulated me, and extended a warm welcome to LA. We captured the moment with a picture and him wishing me success. As this moment was happening, Head Coach, Julie Rousseau, and Assistant Coaches, Orlando Woolridge, and Colleen Matsuhara, entered the gym and introduced themselves. Rhonda made her entrance as a beacon of support. I eagerly anticipated the chance to thank her personally for believing in me enough to offer this opportunity. She reassured me this was my shot, reminding me to bring the same energy from the tournament that earned me this spot. And there it was, her reassurance once again ringing in my ears. This was my shot, a golden opportunity I had earned through persistence, hard work, and determination. If ever there was a time to believe, this was it. Mr. Allen's welcoming embrace, Rhonda's support, and the collective energy of the coaches-amplified me.

Led by the team's manager, I received a WNBA bag filled with my practice gear, warm-ups, a pair of brand new Nike sneakers, WNBA socks, wrist and headbands, and other garments, each piece a testament to the cap of this amazing moment. But it was the number "7" on the bag that struck a chord with me, matching my practice gear. The number represented the vibrancy of the experience. Symbolically, the number "7" meant luck and divinity to me. It also meant completeness, harmony, and creation. All of which marked my journey up to that moment. As I sat on the bleachers, I took in the atmosphere, awaiting the arrival of my new teammates. Each time a door opened or a sound echoed in the gym, I eagerly looked up to see who it was. Then suddenly, one-by-one my teammates started entering the gym. Lisa was the first, as she entered to start her interview with Mr. Allen. She came over and greeted me with a smile, a hug, and a genuine welcome to the team. Others followed suit, as they were entering the gym having conversations and laughter, practice gear on and sneakers in hand. I didn't have any personal connections with any of the players, I was familiar with Katrina who I've met before.

There was no time for settling in. I was escorted to the locker room, changed, and joined the practice. Within a short time, I entered the gym with my new team attire, ready to learn. The practice started with drills, walk through plays, and scrimmages. We had a home game in two days (July 12th) against the Cleveland Rockers. This was one of two practices I would have. After practice, I handed a binder filled with plays and was told to learn as much as I can. I stood there in shock at how thick this binder was, and how short of time I had to learn. I was used to learning plays on the floor, this was the first time I had to learn this much, this fast, this way. This was just like college, when the professors handed us the syllabus, and gave us five or so chapters to read before the next class in two days. Learning comes full circle.

After practice, I was formally introduced to Haixia, along with her interpreter. This meeting was significant because she and I were sharing an apartment. I couldn't wait to see where I'd be staying. On the ride to the apartment, I was told I was staying in Marina Del Rey. Some of the team resided in the same apartment building, conveniently situated around thirty to forty-five minutes from the arena, taking LA traffic into account. As we arrived we went into the parking garage of a multi-level luxury apartment building that sat on a beautiful marina filled with elegant boats. As we entered the private garage there were beautiful luxury cars and trucks filling parking spots, showing the mixed genre of residents living here. He handed me a set of keys that had keys to enter the building, keys to the apartment and keys to a Chevy Malibu that was conveniently parked in my own parking spot. Also attached was the key fob to enter and exit the garage. As we entered the lobby of a nicely decorated building, marked by a secured code required to enter. We caught the elevator to the second floor, doors opening to a nicely decorated floor reminding me of a four-star hotel. As the door opened to the apartment - a spacious two-bedroom, fully furnished. On the left, adjacent to the kitchen, lay Haixia's room. A living room with a beautiful fireplace. My room was off to the right, with a queen size bed, dresser, tv, and nice view of the LA sunset. We had a nice size balcony overseeing part of the marina. I felt very comfortable with my living situation. After dropping my bags off to my room, I instantly went for a walk to see the sights and I could smell the salt from the beach. Curious how far I was from the beach, I drove to the beach. I love being at the beach as the sun set and at night, so the timing here was perfect to take advantage of both. This is when I realized I was just minutes away and it was the very beach that got me here in the first place, Venice Beach. I walked until I got to the basketball courts where the Queen Latifah tournament was held. There were some guys playing full court, I stood and watched for a few minutes before taking in the rest of the sites. The beach was filled with people singing & dancing, skating, playing music, and juggling up and down the boardwalk. As I glanced over at the water watching the sun set, tears of happiness formed in my eyes, proud of myself for not giving up on my dream. After sitting on the beach for a few hours, I started getting tired. It was a long day of travel, introductions, and practicing. I was ready for what was to come.

July 12, 1998 - LA Sparks vs. Cleveland Rockers

The excitement I felt as I pulled up to the arena for the first time was indescribable. I could feel every nerve popping under my skin. As I walked through the tunnel, I saw some of the LA Lakers' players exiting. Shaq stood out the most because he had this huge truck inside the tunnel that seemed like the size of a bus with a sound system loud enough to fill the tunnel and the arena. He was dancing with some of the arena staff. I watched him for a couple of minutes before being guided to the locker room by one of the arena staff. Walking up to the locker room, I noticed the LA Sparks logo on the door. Stepping into the locker room, I found a familiar essence, not a culture shock but a continuation of my experiences with the locker rooms of the NY Knicks and the Detroit Pistons. For the NBA, it was a simple canvas. Individual wooden lockers appeared with purple plates with the first name and jersey numbers of players, a personalized sanctuary for each athlete. Each locker sat with a Lakers chair in front and inside included a small lock box on top and a large lock box on the bottom. Off to the back was the training area, showers, and a small refreshment area with food, snacks, and fridge with drinks inside. One side of the room had a large wall with erase boards with a Los Angeles Lakers logo on it, basketball courts outlined, and others were plain white areas. My locker was next to Blue. Blue was a forward from Florida, and she and I hit it off instantly. I pretty much got the just of the things from her, and when it was time to take the court for a shoot around, I walked out following her lead.

Walking onto the court from the tunnel, a surge of nostalgia came over me, bringing back memories of playing at Madison Square Garden. The essence of those unforgettable experiences seem to come back to life, as if the echoes of my history were playing out again. As we watched the Cleveland Rockers leave the court from their shoot around, I walked to half court, where I stood and looked at the Lakers Championship Banners and Hall of Fame Jerseys of basketball greats like Magic Johnson (32), Jerry West (44), Wilt Chamberlain (13), James Worthy (42) and many others. There were many people moving about the arena. Staff that worked the scores table assembled computers, mics, and sound systems. The media was setting up their cameras for the game, while other arena staff were walking the aisle of the seats. My gaze was broken by the sound of the coach's voice saying, "Bring it in." We walked through some plays, got some shooting in, and discussed what time to return to the gym for the game. After shooting around I got to meet the owner of the team Jerry Buss and son, Johnny Buss who was the teams President. They gave me a warm welcome to the team and mentioned they heard a lot of great things about me. It felt good to hear and I just smiled hoping I had the opportunity to live up to what was said.

Game time was 7 p.m., and we had to be back at the arena no later than 4 p.m. I returned at 3:30 p.m. because I wasn't used to the LA traffic, and to me on time was late. When I arrived, the half-time performer was doing her sound check for the National Anthem. I got to meet some of the floor staff that sat behind our team bench. I went back to the locker room and at this time some of the other team started shooting around. My adrenaline raced as we ran from the tunnel to the court for warm-up. The roar of the crowd gave me goosebumps and butterflies. Palms were sweaty, I felt like a deer in headlights. I only had a day to learn the warm-up routine and for the most part I just followed the lead of my teammates. I didn't know if I would play or not, either way, I would be ready even if I didn't know the plays. What do you know, there I stood with the court beneath my feet, called in for the first game of my WNBA career. I played 5 minutes and 41 seconds scoring two points, grabbing two rebounds, got my one assist, and a personal foul to fill my first stats. It was the most confusing 5 minutes and 41 seconds, only because I didn't know the plays, but I got through it. My strategy was to find the open spots, rebound, and show the coaches my skills. If I was running sprints, that time would never seem to end, because I didn't want the game to end and play longer, it went quickly. We were 3-8 prior to me joining the team and it felt good getting a win on my very first game with the team. 87-66, giving us a 4-8 record.

Clock Ticking against Me

With the clock racing against me, having very little practice in between games because the next morning we flew out to play the Phoenix Mercury on July 13th, then traveled back to LA on the 14th to get ready for a home game against the Sacramento Monarchs. I needed more time to learn the plays and gel with the team, but there wasn't much. There was either one day in between each game or those were usually travel days. Our schedule was tight. A lot of closely scheduled games. Unlike the privately chartered NBA, commercial flights flew us to and from our destinations, connecting us with eclectic travelers. We walked through the airports, waited at gates, and boarded just like every other traveler. We spotted and often had flights with entertainers such as actors, comedians, and singers. One day in the airport, we ran into and shared laughs with comedian Sinbad, and during our stay in Washington, DC, we ran into singer Brian McKnight as we entered the hotel. It was common to run into celebrities in LA. I got to meet and share laughs with Regina Bell who came into the locker room after singing the National Anthem. One day, Lisa, Blue, Jamella, and I all spent the day together; we stopped by Lisa's house and then went to the Forum for a celebrity basketball game. I spent a lot of time with Blue because we shared a room together on road trips. We often hung out with point guard Jamella and a few other players on road trips to go eat or sightseeing when we had extra time in our days.

I enjoyed traveling and being a part of this team. I gradually got used to Coach Rousseau's system when she was fired on July 30th from the franchise after a 7-13 start to the season. I really liked her passion for the game and hated to see her go. They immediately made Orlando Woolridge the interim coach, and my binder of plays got thicker with an additional set of plays to study. At this point, we were having a losing season, so Woolridge's coaching style focused on the players he felt most comfortable with and confident in, hoping to get us into the playoffs. He was just as intense a coach as he was a player. He pushed us, and I understood why. Like any franchise, the goals are to make the playoffs and bring home a championship. However, not even his system worked. The Sparks had so much talent. It confused me as to why the season wasn't going better. We got along well on and off the court, so that had nothing to do with it. Like any team, when things aren't going well, they look to the coach as to why that's not happening.

We still had a good amount of games left to go in the season even if we missed our opportunities to make the playoffs. I personally was looking forward to going to New York to play against the NY Liberty, Houston Comets, and Cleveland Rockers on their home floors. NY

Liberty for obvious reasons. These were my opportunities to play in front of my family and friends. I wanted the chance to play against the best team in the league, the Houston Comets. Our final game of the season was scheduled against them on August 19th. Facing off against the Cleveland Rockers on July 27th, brought out some of my friends from Cincinnati, Ohio who drove down to come see the game. Don't get me wrong I loved the entire experience of each team, but those games allowed me to invite my people to come see me play, and that felt good.

We flew into New York early August 7th. This gave me the chance to go home and spend a couple of hours with my family. Blue wanted to get her hair styled, so she took the ride with me to Queens. She met my family, and we got our hair done, and then headed back to our hotel in Times Square. Tomorrow, we would go up against the New York Liberty at Madison Square Garden. For this game, my mother, brother Vic, Uncle Eddie, Cousin Yvonne, Cynthia, and Monet, along with some other friends from the neighborhood and the basketball circuits, made an appearance. It felt so good having family in the stands, it was a long time coming. Not to steal away a great moment, but this was the first time since my sophomore year in college did I have my family in the stands to see me play. That's a big gap. The funny thing about this game was when I got in for the last few minutes of the game, I took off after the rebound, got a pass for a fast break, I was all alone for the layup and laid it up too hard missing a wide open layup. I couldn't do anything but laugh and hustle back on defense. I had jitters, I can't lie, and I didn't realize how high I was when I released it. I recovered by coming down and hitting a jump shot from the corner. In my 9 minutes of play, I grabbed a couple of rebounds and scored two points. We would lose that game 62-80, but it felt good playing pro ball at home.

At this point of the season, we had five games left to the regular season. I was in and out of the lineup a few minutes here and there, until I was temporarily taken out of the line up due to a big knot that formed on my shooting elbow that swelled up so big I couldn't bend my arm. This affected my shooting and sat me down for a few days. In street clothes one game, waiting for this knot to ease up, I became a cheerleader instead of a role player. I hated this situation because I had no room for error. This was the only opportunity I would have within these final games to hopefully come back next year, and I was sitting. At this point in the season, the coach was giving the reserves more playing time, and I was sitting there pissed. I didn't come here to watch the game; I came here to play. Coming in mid-season, then the coaching change, and playing behind five or six players who had been with the team since preseason made it exceedingly challenging to catch up. My goal was to come in and be that player to help contribute to the team and move us into the winning column more, but it didn't unfold that way. I wasn't sure what this meant for me after the season, but I would hold onto hope that I would be granted the opportunity to return for next year's preseason, allowing me to integrate with the team from the first day of camp.

We ended the season with a record of 12-18. Now that the season was over, it was time for me to pack up and head back to New York. Although I wasn't all that happy about my lack of production, I had no reason to hold my head down. I made the best out of the situation I was given. What I know for sure is, if I was given more of an opportunity to play, my skills would have shown why I was invited to the team in the first place. I'm very grateful for the opportunity, for the team welcoming me, and the friendships I built. I have no regrets, and I thank God for giving me a chance.

What Happens After The Game

What Comes with Being a Pro Athlete

After my return home to New York, I decided to take a few weeks off to relax, and live in the experience for a bit. I paused from actively playing, strategizing a new plan. Now that the season was over, the need for a job became apparent. As a rookie player, the salary for the season was set at $17,500, but being that I came in mid-season, I received a prorated amount of that. Now that I was home, my focus shifted to securing employment. That meant going back overseas, but until that happened, I needed to secure other sources of income. In the meantime, I decided to attend some tournaments happening throughout the city. Although my time with the team had been an incredible experience, financially what remained only covered my monthly expenses for the next four months. The reality was that the compensation of a professional athlete, especially as a rookie, didn't match the perception. Attending these tournaments allowed me to divert my attention from the challenges of transitioning back to a regular lifestyle. It was heartwarming to witness the strong support I had from people in NY. The congratulations and inquiries about my experience were truly uplifting. Many were familiar with my skills before joining the Sparks and consistently voiced their belief that I deserved more playing time. While I acknowledged their sentiments, the circumstances were beyond my control. Basking in the positive recognition I was getting from the community being an WNBA player brought, I began receiving invitations to participate in various events, often accompanied by honors. My accomplishments were highlighted in prominent publications like the New York Daily News, New York Newsday, and the Queens Profile newspapers. Among the notable events, I was invited to "The Arthur Ashe Athletic Association Third Annual Leadership Awards Breakfast," where individuals who contributed to youth development were acknowledged. The Central

Queens YMCA extended an invitation for me to be their Special Guest Speaker at their First Annual Family Day. I received an award from the U.S. Department of Housing and Urban Development on their "Recognition Day and Heroes of Public and Assisted Housing" Ceremony. I was named one of NYC PSAL All-Time Greats of the Game becoming the spokesperson was another significant honor. Further, I was celebrated as one of five outstanding women residing in public housing by the New York City Housing Authority, in honor of Women's History Month. The Southeastern Queens Rotary Club presented me with the Detective Keith L. Williams Hero of the Month Award. Boundless Sports also acknowledged my contributions with a Recognition Award.

The Girls Basketball Team of Wings Academy bestowed upon me a Contribution and Leadership award, while Humatradomes granted me the Women Humanitarian International Award. My involvement extended to speaking engagements at numerous youth sports camps and clinics across NYC and Long Island. A particularly remarkable experience was being showcased in "The Many Faces of Queens Women Photo Exhibition" by The Newsday and Jamaica Center for the Arts. The sense of pride and accomplishment that came from being recognized for my dedication to both sports and community was truly fulfilling. My mother played an integral role in ensuring that my achievements didn't go unnoticed in the community, and I owe her a great deal of grace for that.

Dissolution of Contract

With my first WNBA season under my belt, it was time to plan a new strategic approach for what was next for me. I learned quickly that securing a spot on the '98 squad did not guarantee a permanent spot on the team for the '99 season. My contract was for that one season.

What Happens After The Game

My stretch with the Sparks didn't leave the lasting impression for them to have me on speed dial for next season. Although I left LA feeling accomplished for getting there, I knew I had more work to do if I wanted an invitation back, and that meant I was going back overseas to stimulate interest within the league. Though having WNBA on my resume was important, it didn't guarantee me anything. Unfortunately, I hit a snag along the way. My agent and I started having differences of opinion when it came to building my brand. I wanted to capitalize on the invitations I was receiving for public engagements, as these were opportunities that could be monetized through brand association. My role as a sought-after attendee, spokesperson, and networker at various events compelled me to channel these connections into tangible opportunities. Regrettably, she didn't prioritize her time to schedule these events, prompting me to make the connections myself. I had trusted her expertise and support thus far, but her attention didn't appeared to be focused on other things and not on advancing my career. Her time elsewhere led to the delays or, in some instances, forfeiture of potentially lucrative opportunities. Contrasting viewpoints left us deciding to part ways, prompting the search for new representation. I knew I had a limited time to live in this moment, so the urgency to seize these moments became important for me. I had responsibilities, and the WNBA salary wasn't enough for me to sit on the sidelines and wait for others to act on my behalf. Having a professional title was one thing, but the need to act in desperation now that the season was over, proved less satisfying. It was personal conviction that a more successful season with the Sparks might have gotten swifter responses from her end. While it wasn't in my nature to repeatedly ask for help over and over again, agreeing to terminate our affiliation was in our best interest. Despite this parting of ways, I remained appreciative of her instrumental role getting me into the league. The ending of our professional relationship underscored shared accountability. I'm almost positive there were areas in my decision making that fell short to lack of experience; however, at the time, my focus was directed solely toward creating a brand for myself that outlasted my playing days.

Opportunities Come a Knocking

Until I secured new representation, I took matters into my own hands by scheduling event bookings independently. I was invited to numerous sports organizations to speak with their athletes throughout NYC and New Jersey. Among the notable invitations during this period, I assumed the role as a spokesperson for the NYC PSAL Championship games being held at Madison Square Garden. Furthermore, I earned the distinction of being recognized as one of the PSAL All Time Greats of the Game, a recognition of outstanding honor. This included speaking at schools affiliated with the girls basketball teams in the playoffs; collaborating with prominent figures such as rapper Mase, NBA player Rod Strickland, and streetball legend Pee Wee Kirkland. We attended radio interviews and other networking events representing the PSAL. Addition to these commitments, I found myself addressing the youth at NYCHA community events, as well as affiliated events held by the Police Athletic League (PAL) and Young Men's Christian Association (YMCA) of Jamaica, Queens. My reach spanned across numerous organizations and educational institutions. These ventures not only made me meaningful connections with remarkable people but also sparked a deep sense of fulfillment as to what I wanted to do with my career off the court. I took part-time employment that allowed me to work with youth in sports and recreation. It was a feeler for me to see if this was an area I wanted to explore after playing professionally.

I eventually tested the waters and accepted a part-time assistant coach position in September 1999 at Concordia College in Bronxville,

NY. The position provided a unique opportunity as I collaborated with a former NBA player who had recently assumed the role of head coach. I saw this as a good platform to get my feet wet at the college coaching level. This was a Division III level program and was in its rebuilding stage. Despite the challenging phase, these young women on the team exhibited determination, displaying a lion-hearted spirit and eagerness to learn the game and establish a winning program. During this time, I reconnected with a longtime friend, Ms. Haywood, who was a figure of substantial influence and well-respected in women's sports and was an agent at Bruce Levy Associates. At this point, I already interviewed a few lawyers and agents who wanted to represent me, but the connection wasn't there, and their vision didn't align with my goals. With Ms. Haywood, however, there were no ulterior motives except a genuine desire to see me secure another spot on a WNBA roster, which she knew I deserved. Our history stretched back to my high school playing days, where she had offered me a scholarship to St. John's University to play basketball. She extended her support, provided me mentorship, and training, as she leveraged her extensive network within the agency to secure me a contract to play overseas. With her experience representing current pro players and training athletes, her expertise resonated. Entrusting her commitment, I found a renewed sense of focus that enabled me to concentrate on getting in shape and my coaching responsibilities.

However, two months into the coaching opportunity, it came to a swift end. The head coach was fired! In his absence, I was presented with the offer to fill the vacancy. I weighed the options against my ambition to return overseas and decided that assuming this leadership role would be ill-advised. I knew my plan to seize an overseas opportunity, and accepting the coaching position, knowing that I would probably leave would lead to the disappointment of the players. They already had to deal with losing one coach, and I didn't want to intentionally put them through that just to have a job. With this realization, I respectfully declined the offer, choosing to prioritize my schedule with my overseas goals. I couldn't let them down like that. Returning to Queens, I did some basketball clinics and guest appearances for the YMCA, which quickly led to a part-time position with a YMCA branch out of Brooklyn. I would be able to sustain this position until something opened up overseas. With Thanksgiving approaching in a few weeks, this was perfect timing. I was just over two months out of the league, and all of this hustling to secure work didn't make me feel like a pro player. It was hard to accept myself as a pro player when all I had was a few thousand dollars in the bank. I just didn't feel like one. It was a bigger deal to others more than it was for me. They saw the title, but I was living the reality. I got pleasure from getting involved in community activities and that felt better than having the title. I had to figure out the balance of my life after the game, and not seem ungrateful for the blessing. It was very hard to do. The low pay scale left me feeling desperate. I would love the opportunity at another shot at returning to the WNBA for the 1999 season, but I had to honestly face the fact that with the low pay, I wasn't feeling too excited about pursuing this goal. Yes, it was a great opportunity, but if it meant hustling for work after every season, I didn't know if it was worth it?

1999 - Espoo, Finland

Although I still had the support and guidance of Ms. Haywood to continue my pro career overseas, the excitement of that idea was slowly fading. Christmas was approaching in December of 1998, and she convinced me to continue to give overseas another go, and soon after that conversation, she called me with an offer to play in Finland. There was an offer on the table for me to leave right after the New Year, contracted to play from January to March. They offered me $2,500 a month, for the next three months. My knowledge of Finland was limited to the fact that one of my WKU college teammates was from there; that was my sole connection to the country. Ms. Haywood handled the details of the contract negotiations, I accepted the terms presented, resigned from my position, and within the week, I was off to play for Tapiolan Honka in Espoo, Finland. As I researched the weather, I saw that the temperature could plummet as low as -4 degrees Celsius during their winter season. Recognizing this, I packed the heaviest winter gear I owned, as I was preparing for this almost 13-hour trip to Helsinki. Where I will be staying and playing in Espoo, is about twenty minutes away from Helsinki, which is the Capital of Finland. This flight gave me ample time to set a plan as to how to use this experience to get back into the WNBA next summer. Ms. Haywood, true to her commitment, presented me with an opportunity of playing pro basketball again. This marked the culmination of her support and my dedication, marking another chance for me to step back into my professional role.

Upon my arrival in Finland, the sound of people speaking in English excited me. The team's assistant coach greeted me at the airport with a big sign with my name on it. He welcomed me with a big smile and escorted me to my apartment that would serve as my residence for the next three months. Although this contract didn't come with a car, I found myself nestled within a convenient local area, twenty minutes from Helsinki, and within an area with a city-like atmosphere. Helsinki gave me a city vibe with lots of vibrant color buildings. The white snow cascading off the city lights made for a beautiful portrait. People moving about the street in Eskimo-type jackets, bundled up just right for the brick temperatures. It was dark outside at midday and that threw me off. The first thing I noticed was how fast Finns drove. The coach seemed like he was driving 80 miles an hour in his Volkswagen stick shift. Cars were speeding past us, just as fast as we were speeding past others. I learned quickly that this was regular for them. Sounds odd coming from a New Yorker where we speed for no reason, but they tailgated each other, which had me holding onto to my seatbelt and door handle. Within twenty minutes we pulled up to this small apartment area, which expanded for blocks. My accommodation was a one-bedroom furnished flat with all the necessary amenities. While my expectations regarding the cold were not unfounded, the degree of cold I encountered was beyond my range of tolerance. Coming from New York, our winters were nothing compared to being here. I've been to Chicago in the dead of winter, and this was colder than Chicago. Mountains of white snow lined the streets, but not until I stepped out of the car and took a closer look, what I thought was just snow, was actually layers of pure ice several feet thick. I thought I was walking on snow and sidewalk, in fact, it was ice topped with snow. My arrival coincided with the heart of Finland's coldest season, which lasted from November to March. I learned the difference in their daylight length of time. During these winter months, Finland not only comes with frigid temperatures but has limited sunlight, with daylight lasting for approximately 6 hours. Many times, dark skies blanketed me to sleep, and I awakened to it getting dark again. They called this their "kaamos-depression" because of depressive disorder that occurs in the autumn and winter. Some say it's a stigma, but I am going based on what the players shared with me. Needless to say, I didn't see too many sunny days. Daylight was from about 9 am to about 3:30 p.m. By the time I woke up most days, I saw about two or three hours of daylight. I walked to practice around 2-2:30 p.m., and it would start getting dark. By the time practice was over two hours later, it is pitch-black outside. That was something I couldn't get used to. People moved about their days normally, and in great spirits. I loved the Finnish culture and hospitality.

While adapting to the demands of the cold weather, my Finnish experience proved to be very exciting. The camaraderie shared with the team of young women I played with was so inviting. Delighted to introduce me to their family and friends, I also enjoyed their willingness to introduce me to the locals. They wanted to know about my life in America, and what it was like playing in college and in the WNBA. Many of them had their goals set to one day attend college in the States while others wanted to play in the WNBA. They too held the role of playing on the pro team while juggling full and part-time jobs to support themselves and their families, mirroring the challenges I deal with back home. I was fortunate to connect with my college teammate, Juanna, who lived not too far away from my location. I was able to catch up with her and meet her amazing family which remains a cherished memory. They made me this cake, without a doubt it is the best cake I ever tasted; to this day, I crave that delicious cake. I don't remember what it was called, but it was by far the best-tasting cake I ever had.

I was surprised to learn that Finland attracted a lot of American athletes. My teammates took me to a club in Helsinki, frequented by many Americans and athletes. I didn't run into anyone I knew, but I had the opportunity to forge new connections. With our demanding basketball schedule and it being so cold, I didn't get to hang out much. Plus, not having my own car, limited how far I went. Besides games, practice, and hanging out with a few teammates, more often than not, I found myself chilling at my apartment. I would often speak with family and friends on the phone, but for the most part, I read books, listened to music, wrote in my journal, and watched tv.

Temperature Shock

The cold weather was torture on my body. The gym was a ten minute walk from my apartment, but in the cold and blizzard snow and winds, it was more like thirty minutes. When the winds got really strong mixed with the snow, it was hard to hold my head up to see where I was going. Sometimes I would get a ride from a teammate, but other times I jogged to the gym, mainly to generate heat. Sometimes the wind was so strong it blew me to practice. Practices were traditional, nothing I wasn't used to, but the problem came for me when the coach took us outside to run on the track in 25-degree weather. Yeah, I had a big problem with that. That was pneumonia weather, and my body wasn't accustomed to that type of training. I pushed back on that. I tried it the first time to not seem difficult—outwardly, anyway. When I got sick after the first few days, I pushed back and asked for another option. Finland's 25 degrees was like -10 in the States, and with less daylight, the temperatures were even colder.

The weather started taking a toll on my body especially after practices and games when I would walk to my apartment with my paws open after showering at the gym. One day in practice I was feeling very weak and dizzy. I barely had energy to stand and walk, the coaches immediately took me to the hospital. I ended up spending the night fighting a fever. I was so dehydrated I needed several bags of IV, but aside from this "medical" blip, I felt good and joined practice after a day's rest once I was released. I quickly made changes, stopped showering at the gym after games and practices, and added additional layers of clothes. I started taking these vitamin tablets that dissolved in my water. This was the first time I knew such tablets existed. In the states I was used to the hard big pills, but these tablets kept me hydrated, boosted my immune system, and gave me energy.

The first few weeks I went through spells of boredom and loneliness when we weren't playing. I would often call family and friends from the states, but I had to keep that under control to keep from running up a hefty phone bill. Finland is 7 hours ahead of New York. New York's 12 p.m. was Finland's 7 p.m. Most of the time my free time was with people in the states work hours. So, I usually stayed up until 1-3 a.m. to call people in the States. One of my sisters on my father's side often called me. She is older than me, and we didn't grow up together. Before I left for Finland, we started getting to know each other. She brought my younger siblings and my father together to take me out to eat before I came to Finland. Our conversations brought us closer together. She actually booked a flight to come spend a week in Finland with me, which I thought was very cool. I was looking forward to her visit. For days, that's all we talked about. She really helped ease the loneliness I was feeling there because she called often and didn't mind the international rates. We were building a connection, and this felt good to me because I didn't have a relationship with the seven siblings on my father's side. He had shared their names, but I had no faces to go with those names. I did meet one sister when I was about 11-12 years old, but that was the extent of the communication. So, for she and I to have this time to bond felt special.

The season had begun for them in November. We played one game a week, and by the time I arrived, they only lost one game. We went on a winning streak through January and February. I averaged 18 points and 10 rebounds a game. I had to get used to the tight-fitting uniforms, but in the act of playing, I didn't even notice. This team reminded me of Sullivan and WKU combined. They wanted to run the ball as quickly and as often as possible, but when necessary had half-court motion offenses. Our tallest player was 6'4" and she was the primary ball handler. Her and I had similar games. She wanted to run the floor, attack the basket, and I did too. We both were strong shooters, and overall, the core of the team was strong in many areas of the game. Each player on the team brought a uniqueness to the game and everyone understood their roles. Everyone from the coaches to the players had the same goal, and that was to win a championship for the club and as a team we knew we couldn't do it without the other.

Some of them expressed the need to adjust to my game, but, in reality, I had to adjust to theirs and their rules. They constantly talked on offense and defense. The bench was active and just as vocal as the players on the court. No one complained about playing time. They were ready to contribute whenever they were called on. This made learning their system of play very easy. If I was ever out of place, one of them would guide me into position, or direct me where to go. Because this was so effective in practice, by the third game, I knew exactly where to be and what to do. I didn't sit much. I started from day one, and played all but maybe 4-5 minutes every game, depending on the score. As much as I thought I was in shape when I arrived, I struggled keeping up with them, but they played me into tip top shape. I was winded for the first week and a half, but what I wasn't going to be was outplayed. I had a lot on the line, and a goal of getting back into the WNBA. I needed to shine at this moment, so when the agency shopped me around to teams, they had everything they needed to get me a contract.

We rallied past teams, and these were good teams. We had top seed going into the playoffs and had three teams to beat for the title. I turned my ankle in the last game of the season and was having difficulty on it as we prepared for the playoffs. What felt like a tweaked ankle sprain, grew to me was having trouble bending and walking. I would get treatment on it, and that helped get me through practice, but at night when I slept, my foot would stiffen sitting straight up in the air, and it would take me at least 2 ½ hours to get it loose enough to put pressure on it to walk. I experienced this for a week straight until the pain got unbearable, and I knew something was wrong. Their doctors said it was a bad sprain, but this felt different. I woke up one day unable to walk to the gym and could not run on it. I placed a call to my agent, explained what was happening. I hated leaving the team, especially with us having a winning season and being two games away from the 'ship, but I couldn't take the pain anymore. They provided me with my return ticket back to NY, where I faced a dilemma of figuring out how I was going to pay to get my ankle treated. I thought the club would have covered it, but turned out, when I flew back, my contract ended. Here it was March 1999, I had the goal of going to WNBA camps with the goal of securing a contract with a team, instead, I was trying to figure out how to pay for my ankle surgery. I was above the legal age on NY to be added onto my mother's insurance and the only way to get this surgery done was to pay out of pocket, which wasn't happening. There went the WNBA season, especially with camps starting in May. I was right back where I was before I left for Finland.

I got letters from one of my teammates and assistant coach from Espoo writing to see how I was doing and to share with me the team that won the Championship, which was great news. I wish I could have been a part of that celebration. We really played well together, and I wanted to have that moment with them. Instead of celebrating a championship, I was sitting in my room with a swollen ankle trying to figure out how to get this surgery. The doctor explained the procedure required me to be on crutches for 6 to 8 weeks depending on how much damage he sees during the procedure, and additional two months minimum for physical therapy depending on how I heal. All I kept thinking was how did I get here again. I did everything I was supposed to and more. Why did I keep hitting these dead ends? I set goals, exceed them, only to find myself behind the 8 ball again. I got into my head. I started getting down on myself. I felt as if the world was working against me. I take two steps forward, only to find myself ten steps back. I dug into the pity party. Why me? This is just not meant for me. I was frustrated and losing hope. My mother said and did everything within her power to help me through this, but it wasn't for her to fix. I created these massive action plans, only to end up wondering where my life was headed now. Making it to a WNBA team this season was not happening. I had bills to pay, and my savings from

Finland would only take me so far. I felt defeated, and I couldn't lean on the one thing that always got me through my toughest moments, basketball.

Favors Remembered

In May 1999, I was figuring out how I was going to pay for this surgery I needed. My birthday was coming up, but I didn't celebrate much. Some friends took me out to celebrate and cheer me up, but I was bummed. To work out, I would often go to the Jamaica YMCA to exercise. One day, I ran into Kim who was a director in the youth department. I did a guest appearance at a Family Day event she held at the Y in November of 1998 for 50 kids. I was honored she asked, and she said they didn't have a budget to pay me, so I did it for free. If you know Kim, you know she is hard to say no to. While I was working out in the weight room she asked me what I was doing during the off-season. Kim is the type of person who loves helping others. As much as I tried to avoid the conversation, I explained to her my situation with my ankle and the surgery I needed. At the time, her and her supervisor Rachel were looking for someone to help them with Summer Camp. She introduced me to Rachel that same day, and I was hired on the spot. Being at the Y gained me some great experiences. I went from being an assistant within the program to becoming a full-time leader in a director role for the summer program. Rachel gave me the responsibility of screening, interviewing, and hiring the summer staff coming in. She also allowed me creative control of the summer training and summer program design. I oversaw the staff and gained new skills in this field. Because of the trust and extra responsibility both Rachel and Kim provided me, I tapped into new experiences that not only trained me for what they offered me there but also led me to become a program director at a higher level and work within the field for the next twenty-plus years later. At that time, once you are with the Y for 90 days, you get full medical coverage. This was perfect. All I had to do was get through the summer with this pain, and by the end of camp, I could schedule my ankle surgery. Little did I know that was their plan the whole time. Camp was over in August; I had my ankle surgery in September. Once I got the medical coverage I needed, I visited my childhood orthopedic, learned I had chip bone fragments and torn tendons in my ankle—way more than the sprain I was originally told. He clearly stated, if I kept playing, I would have caused permanent damage. He suggested surgery right away. I had surgery at a Long Island hospital, and it took about ten months to get back to playing condition. By then, it was the year of 2000, and I decided to retire from pursuing my professional career. Although I kept playing, it became something I did to stay in shape and compete as opposed to playing to make a pro team. Plus, at this stage, I was offered a position with the NYCHA that paid more than I would have made in the WNBA, and passing on this position meant giving up something permanent and I wasn't willing to take that risk. I had bills that needed to be paid, and having a job felt better than hoping it may come again later. It was a big decision, but I was kind of burnt out trying to pursue this pro career, and it just stopped being fun after a while. I was having more fun playing pickup and in tournaments, and I knew where my money was coming from every week. I set my sights on building my life up and figuring out who Michelle was *after* the game.

So, it was at that time in 2000 that the new journey began.

Who was I outside of the game?

What Happens After The Game?

They Saw in Me What I Did Not See in Myself

Talk about a miracle. Rachel and Kim were my miracle workers. I had to be vulnerable enough to open up to Kim, willing to say yes to the opportunity they provided me and accept that the Lord works even when we stop believing. This situation tested my strength, showed my weaknesses, and restored my faith. It also taught me how to give outside of putting myself first, because you never know who is in need of what I have.

From this union with Kim and Rachel, it led to other opportunities within the Y. Kim and I started the first ever Ladies Night Open Gym for Female Basketball players on Monday nights. This single court gym ran from 7 to 10 p.m. and was standing room only with women who came to play pickup basketball. Players showed up as early as 5:30 p.m. just to get their names on the list to play. If you weren't there early, you waited awhile before your game, depending on where you landed on the list. People tried coming in with their own five, trying to give themselves the competitive edge to keep winning and staying on the court because winners stay on, and losing teams were sent back to the sign-in sheet with the hopes of getting another game in. We had to cut the game from 15 to 11, counting by ones to give everyone a chance to play and get more games in. This was the gym of the who's who that was coming to play. One thing was for sure; you were guaranteed a good run every Monday.

We drew in a standing-room-only crowd of players coming from all over NYC, Long Island, Jersey, and, sometimes, PA. High school players from around the city came, as did college players and professional players, both WNBA and European players. This night got so popular the newspapers started showing up. The gym had agents, lawyers, doctors, judges, you name it. They didn't just come to play; this three-hour window attracted the great energy of women who wanted to be in the gym with each other doing something positive. Word got out fast, and we started attracting media outlets throughout New York, which led to me hosting my first Women's Basketball Tournament at 40 Park. We had games scheduled at both the Y and in the park because we had such a great turn out of teams wanting to play. This is when I found my mojo. I found my niche outside of just playing.

I had so much fun running ladies' night and my summer tournaments that the excitement of returning to the league dwindled. Going back overseas just didn't seem worth it to me. As much as I loved playing professionally, it was more hype than it was a living for me. I was in debt up to my eyeballs, and with bill collectors hounding me every day for payments, I needed to put my responsibilities first. Developing these three crafts gave me life. I was having fun, and I was getting paid to do it. Those six months developed the director and entrepreneur in me, and I appreciated the 1998 and 1999 Jamaica YMCA Family for giving me that shot. I would not have believed that being a director would manifest within me and would become my career for years to come. Thank you, Y Family. You truly gave me life!

Thank you, Rachel, Kim, Kaleek, and everyone in that era who played a part in this stage of my life.

Bracing for Retirement, 2000

Figuring out if retiring from playing professional basketball was my best choice or not was a significant decision and milestone because it would mark the end of an era and the beginning of a new chapter in my life. As a professional basketball player, my life had been consumed by the sport, as basketball was the focal point of my existence since the age of five. But as I stepped into the real world, I was left wondering what life would look like once I shifted from "the pro athlete" to playing for exercise and pure enjoyment.

The truth is retiring from basketball was a daunting experience, but it was incredibly liberating. For the first time in a long time, I had the freedom to pursue other interests, hobbies, and passions. I no longer had to sacrifice everything for the sport I gave so much of my life to. I could now explore different avenues and find new things that excited me, and I was in a place to do it from a clear mind and body, unlike how I left college and just took a deep dive into mess after mess.

Retiring also presented an opportunity for self-reflection and self-discovery. I gave myself time to figure out who I was and what I wanted out of life, a conversation I never sat still long enough to think about. I needed to create an identity comprised of new goals that had nothing to do with playing. I would use the discipline, dedication, and work ethic I learned from the game to transfer over into other areas of my life. Now, I would have to figure out what that looked like and prepare myself for what it felt like too. It meant clarifying my why and creating a massive action plan to see it through. It meant testing areas of my strengths, coming to terms with my weaknesses, and discovering opportunities that will pay me to build up both.

Of course, retiring from basketball also came with its own challenges. It was difficult to let go of the dream of being a WNBA player and the identity I'd built all of my life as a basketball player. I struggled to find a new purpose and direction in life without the game. After spending the majority of my life living the dream, I now had to figure out how to make the next half of my life focus on something completely different—while still using the skills learned. I felt lost, uncertain, and even depressed at times because when I had bills to pay, the pressure to find answers became the focus, and that alone added its own stressful levels that often blocked any new visions I was trying to create.

But as I walked this journey, I saw that I wasn't alone. There were many athletes who had gone through this transition and came out the other side stronger, more resilient, and more fulfilled. They showed me that life after basketball can be just as rewarding, if not more so, than life on the court. I started believing that I, too, would have a rewarding outcome. I knew the first part of my plan meant discovering what I saw myself doing every day that I would love just as much if not more than, I did playing basketball. It meant exploring my options and touching and seeing what I liked and what I didn't like. I was prepared to use each opportunity to learn new skills and extend my education. Importantly, this was my chance to volunteer in places that forced me to help others beyond my own needs, to give of myself receiving nothing but the experience of gaining knowledge in return.

To make the most of this transition, I reflected on my strengths, passions, and values. What motivates me? What brings me joy? What kind of legacy do I want to leave behind? I used these questions to guide my thought process first, and then help me to find new opportunities that align with those interests and values. Additionally, I had to get past this blockage I created by asking people for guidance and help. I had to assume the risk that came with it and accept that every "No" isn't a setback, and every "Yes" isn't a step in the right direction. It was up to me to filter through each and align them with the skills I wanted to develop.

At this stage of my life, I was emotionally sensitive, and my triggers of disappointment were on high alert. So, I was careful in my choices, and comfortable with who I put my faith in. As we know I often did things the hard way which delayed my progress, and I was now learning from those mistakes. As I grew to see the error of my ways, I started to work through those issues and learned that choosing who to ask was just as important as knowing what to ask for. This process taught me to be intentional with what I sought from people and the importance of doing my homework beforehand. I wanted every question I asked to land me the right yes and limit the no's. I grew to see that all things happen for a reason, whether I understood it at that moment or later. Some experiences led to growth, and others led to opportunities, and my faith was teaching me that what is for me will never be denied. This mindset helped me accept my decision to officially retire.

Officially Retiring from the Game

Basketball was my life since the age of five, and it will be a love of mine for the rest of my life. I have traveled the world and have been to many places several times. I got to meet so many wonderful people and experience different cultures and lifestyles. I got to compare America to Europe through first-hand experiences. I traveled to all 52 states in one lifetime. This is something I never imagined basketball would give me as a kid. My entire life, up until the day I stopped competing, was all about basketball. During my ball days, nothing could threaten my love for the game, not even my setbacks, but now, with retirement before me, the scariest part of this for me was answering the question, "What now?" Answering that question came with changes that seemed to threaten my identity, and I tried to avoid the reality that success as I knew it was no longer a living truth for me. At least, not as a professional basketball player. Here was another moment in my life where I did not have control of my mental health enough to believe I could get through this without stressing myself out. I didn't know what was harder: never playing again or facing the fact that I made it to the WNBA and would not be going back.

With my ankle surgery done, the healing process started, as did the rehabilitation. I already missed the 1999 WNBA season, with my ankle taking over seven months to properly heal-I didn't return overseas, and I still had three months of rehab left before I could step foot on a basketball court, meant I would miss the chance of trying out for a team for WNBA team for the year 2000 season too. I had a hard decision to make. This time, I would make it from a clear mind and understanding of what was absolutely best for me. *I decided to hang my pro sneakers up and pursue new goals.* The choice to retire wasn't driven by an inability to continue playing; rather, it was driven by a deep realization that I had lost touch with my identity, my preferences, and my sources of joy the game used to give me. New ventures outside the game were being presented; putting me in place where my interests, passions, and skills would need to converge to make life after the game enjoyable. At this point, I was feeling way more excited about the work I was doing in my community, and I loved the idea of weighing the options on the table to accept a career that came with receiving a steady paycheck. The speaking engagements I did, along with helping organizations run their sports camps and tournaments, inspired me to offer my own. After hearing about a position within the New York City Housing Authority and an upcoming civil service exam, I decided to apply for both. The civil service exam was a series of tests offered by the City of New York used to evaluate whether candidates have the training and experience required to perform a job. After putting in my application with NYCHA, I took the exam for the administrative line, passing it with a score of 98%. This put me high on the call list. Passing this exam offered a sense of security within city agencies, especially when it came time for city layoffs. Usually, if you were on this list, it was somewhat of a security blanket.

In the meantime, I started running small camps and clinics in my neighborhood at 40 Park for the youth, and that led to other opportunities that grew me from a part-time position I held at the Y to a full-time with a salary at the New York City Housing Authority. I started out working at community centers but quickly got bored because I wanted to offer sports programs, and these sites didn't offer the facilities for me to do that. An opportunity opened up with the sports department for NYCHA in Manhattan, and I jumped on it. Our team was made of four of us that ran various sports programs year-around for the residents of NYCHA throughout the city. This was the perfect opportunity to capitalize on my skills and develop new ones with the training it offered. I love this position because it offers variety, flexibility, creativity, and social connection. Until 9/11 terrorist attacks happened. Our main office was out of 250 Broadway in Manhattan, which was a few blocks from the World Trade Center towers. I don't know if it was pure luck or timing, but by 8 a.m., I was usually at my desk working. On this day, however, I chose to get going at 10 a.m. My mother had called me in a major panic, thinking I was in the city at the time of the tragedy. As scary as that day was, the months, years that followed weren't much better. This tragic day in history left working downtown a scary and unsettling thing to do. Months after the event, public places still faced many threats, which made New York a scary place to dwell. When we were called down to another NYCHA building on 90 Church Street for a departmental meeting, the train ride, the smell, and sight of these attacks gave me a real feel of the catastrophe that took place. Our meeting lasted about two hours, and within those two hours caused me to go straight to the doctor's office from the meeting due to breathing trouble which had me out of work for about a week. Until the department cleaned the entire building we were all placed in different locations throughout the city. When I got word we would eventually return to 90 Church Street for work, I instantly started shopping my resume. Unfortunately, I wouldn't get immediate interviews until after we were advised to return to 90 Church Street months later. Until then I stressfully rode the subway from the first to the last stop dealing with the countless bomb threats. The sorrowful feeling of working just blocks from all of the loss the city suffered, I found myself going to work fearful every day. I looked for every excuse to work out of one of the Long Island City warehouses in Queens, just to keep from reporting to the city, and so that I could drive to work, but we still had to report to the Manhattan office. With no way around working in the city, I decided to shop my resume even more looking for employment closer to home, and that's when a Sports Coordinator position opened with the Police Athletic League that was a five-minute drive from home. As much as I loved what I did with NYCHA, after 9/11, I developed anxiety taking the subway and working the city. I saw the challenge as an opportunity to take what my previous position taught me and offer it on another platform.

I continued hosting tournaments but under the umbrella of the PAL, and the demand it brought led me to start a not-for-profit organization called Pro-Response Sports, Inc which offered sports camps, clinics, leagues, tournaments, family days, and educational events. From 2005 to 2012, Pro Response Sports teamed up with NYCHA Resident Association to offer these services to the community every summer from June to August, which also led to me expanding my skills, being offered higher positions within my career, and allowed me to build an audience of youth who were able to use my platform to further their education and opportunities. At the time I was teaching them about my experiences, they were teaching me about life and the reflection of the adult I wanted to be for them. The logic I learned as an athlete doesn't always resonate with people in the real world that had no relations to a sport. In the sports networks I was a part of, we were responsible for each other, it came with a level of commitment, loyalty, teamwork, and togetherness; all which formed a team. In the real world, it was every man for themselves. It took me years to adjust to how cut-throat people were in corporate America. I was trying to adjust while staying true to my morals and values, thinking my genuine desire to see those around win would outshine the hate. I knew I couldn't mentor the youth I was connecting with if my intentions weren't pure. I learned quickly that our youth was being misguided and used for numbers and I wanted my work to represent them better than that. The game taught me many things, but at this point in my career, it was teaching me to invest more in *me*... and not the people who cheered in the stands. This was something I wanted to pass onto the youth I was teaching.

Everything I did from the moment I accepted that part-time position with the Jamaica Y served as stepping stones to what was to come. I found my niche, mastered it, and started building my career around it. Of course, I didn't see it at the time, but ultimately it began to make sense. The skill sets I was building allowed me to support my mother's community endeavors, be of service to the community I was raised in and got comfortable with the idea of retiring from the game. What I didn't know then, but well aware of now, is I was learning to leverage both my strengths and weaknesses, learning new things about myself every step of the way. It took me years to understand that things weren't happening to me, instead, they were happening for me. Every experience was completely different, but each taught me more and more about who I was becoming after the game. What I thought were failures and road blocks was actually me investing time into growing as a person and professional from what the game has taught me on the court, transferring it all to the game of life. One of the best teachers truly was my experiences and the one way of understanding that was never giving up on myself when life got really dark and hard. The destination was always to be successful at everything I did, and keeping that in mind taught me that the most valuable person was always me.

Relationship Odyssey:

The Depths and Dynamics

Relationships are tricky beasts. They can infuse you with light and air and make you feel you can conquer the world, and they can infuse you with darkness and confusion, causing you to question your beliefs and values. Add an unchecked past to the mix, and you could find your good relationship covered with the doubt, worry, and fear of past relationships. I have a past that led me to stumble in various relationships, but I broke through that cycle through my desire to understand who I was, what I needed, and how I would better myself for a good, solid relationship.

Innocent Crushes

Throughout my upbringing, I was blessed with numerous friendships, each filled with love and cherished memories that still resonate within me to this day. I remember during my elementary school days when I engaged in innocent relationships where we playfully called each other "boyfriend and girlfriend." Playing games like hide and seek transformed into a fun version of "hide and go kiss." Perhaps you're familiar with it—running away from the boys we weren't interested in, only to be caught intentionally by the one we truly liked and get a kiss on the cheek. At this age, it was nothing more than puppy love, but it was fun, nonetheless. At this age, most of the boys were afraid of my brothers so they dared to cross that line.

Junior high though was a lot different for me. I had two major crushes. One was Mark, a friend of one of my brother's. He who was a senior at my school during my freshman year. The other was Dame, who was my teammate on the school's basketball team during my senior year. Mark was a DJ like my brother and often came to the house to see my brother. I used to look for him at school and couldn't wait until he came by the house to see my brother. He knew I had a thing for him, but to him, I was just Vic's sister. Dame was one of the pretty boys of the school; most of the girls had a thing for him. I just so happened to have front row seats to his fineness every day through our connection playing basketball. He saw me as the homie, and I was good with our friendship. It was frustrating for me to even date in junior high. For one thing, my mother wanted me to stay a child, and for another thing, my brothers weren't having it. For any boys to admit their like for me meant they had to go through my brothers, all of their friends, and some of my teammates. Dating was safer in our crew settings when we would all go to the movies, amusement parks, malls, hanging in the neighborhood, etc.

In high school, I gradually began unraveling the intricacies of my emotions and understanding the difference between having crushes and developing meaningful connections. Just like now, I was very selective about who I spent time with and who I called boyfriend. Similar to JHS, in high school, we hung out within our crews and often built our crews around who we were crushing on and eventually would start dating. This was when parties for us were at our classmates' houses, and on the weekends, it was the hangout spot, too. I hung out with my friends from around my way and some of my high school teammates. Whenever I would hang out with my teammates, we arrived as an all-girl ball crew, towering over the other girls and captivating attention with our presence. We stood out effortlessly, showing both style and grace. Guys gravitated to us because we related to a lot of the things they liked, and we liked having fun. We frequently found ourselves dating friends of friends, and as a result, our social circles intertwined seamlessly. We enjoyed spending time together, both in our shared social gatherings and when they came to our games. The support they showed us added an extra layer of encouragement and made our friendships that much more layered. It was cute and cliquish. This was the vibe in our freshman and sophomore years. By the time we were juniors and seniors, some of us had that one guy we vibed with, called ourselves being in love and attached at the hip. I was dating a football player in my junior year, but his parents moved him and his family out of the city, and we broke up. He and I dated for a few months before his move. It was so sudden.

One day he was in school, and the next he was gone. Our last phone call was him explaining what his parents decided, and that was that.

I played the field for a while until I met Marvin, who became my first love during the middle of my senior year. I met him at the Doc Turner holiday tournament our high school team played in every year up in Harlem, NY. He was dark chocolate and had such a sexy smile, just how I liked them. After our game at the tournament, our team stuck around for the following game, so we took a seat in the bleachers, and it just so happened we sat right in front of him and friends. At first, I paid him no mind when he and his friends kept talking to us about how they enjoyed our game. But as he and his friends kept chatting with us, they were pretty hilarious, and our laughs ended with us exchanging numbers. He talked a lot about how much he liked watching me play and how much of a fan he was of my game. He went from a fan to a friend to my first love. We hit it off from the first phone call. We spent many a late night on the phone, him coming to just about all of my games, and when he met my mother, they hit it off at hello. He was my guy until I went away to Sullivan College. As much as we loved each other, the distance was rough for us. Well, for me. He always remained in my heart, but as I began meeting new people and enjoying the new friendships I was building, I eventually started dating other people. I didn't want him waiting on me, and against his wishes, I urged him to date other people, too. He was my first love and forever holds that place in my heart. I am grateful that we reconnected when I moved back to New York and remain friends to this day.

Balancing Ball and Relationships

Because of my basketball schedules, I never really settled down with one person too long. I loved the diversity I had in my life and enjoyed fresh starts and new experiences. Throughout my college years I've had guys I dated, but no real heart throbs like Marvin. For the most part dating was just a hobby for me after him, something I enjoyed in my down time. Just having that college fun and figuring out my feelings at the same time. I just didn't meet that one who made me feel like he was the one. At Sullivan I did meet a boxer who I vibed with but dating him eventually was too much drama. He had what he called his ex, but she claimed him hard, and with that came craziness. I met him through my college friends. He would often come over to our apartment complex with his friends to hang out with us. He was a cool guy, and he would often invite me to his boxing matches, which I enjoyed so much. Not until this young lady showed up at an event we were at off campus and was ready to fight me over him. First off, I am not fighting over no guy. Second, I knew nothing about her until that moment, as she stood there screaming, "We've been together for years, and he's not going anywhere." That's when I drew the line. I was in Kentucky to play basketball, not to fight over a guy I really was just having a little fun with. This girl was sending threats my way, talking about having her friends coming up to the college to jump me. I cut him off quickly. He was asked to tame his flame and stay away from our apartments. He tried to convince me they were over, but I wasn't there for that. I saw enough of that drama where I lived in New York and know very well how those situations can end. The message got to her quickly that he was a non-factor on my end, and she had no worries about me seeing him, and she backed off. The word apparently went to her, and she backed off. The last thing I wanted was to put myself or any of my teammates in harm's way for any reason. He made several attempts to reconcile, but I wasn't having it and nor were my friends. After that I chilled with dating and concentrated on basketball. I was new to those Kentucky streets and that drama definitely wasn't my cup of tea.

At WKU, the campus vibe was much different from Lexington. Due to the demand of my schedule with classes and basketball, I was ok with just having chill dudes. You know, those no-strings-attached understandings, the "You do you, and I'll do me, and if we feel like it, we'll get together and hang out." That worked for me for a while until I started dating one of the players on the men's basketball team. It started as friendly flirting and small talks and grew to us developing feelings for each other. We were good for a couple of months, but after some time, I couldn't trust him. Girls on campus began giving me major side eye, and then I heard he was hanging out in other girls' dorm rooms. When I caught him in my dorm room with two people whom I thought were my people, that was where I drew the line. I'm sorry, but there was no way he could explain why he was in a locked dorm room with two other girls, both of whom I knew very well. Talk about disloyalty on both sides. Having grown up witnessing my brothers and their dating escapades, I vowed, I would never be that chick fighting over no grown man, ever!

After going through the craziness with him, I just didn't have the patience for anything serious with anyone. I dated for fun, and if I enjoyed their company, we would hang out a few more times. Calling anyone my boyfriend didn't happen.

A Path to Self-Discovery

I found myself lost in thought often during my college years, reflecting on these different feelings I was having as a woman. I found it both interesting and confusing at the same time as to how I was becoming curious about dating a woman and how it was surfacing at this point in my life. My mother used to ask if me becoming attracted to women had anything to do with the disappointment I had from my father and the letdowns from my brothers. I never thought about it like that until she mentioned it, but after careful thought, that probably had a little to do with it, but I couldn't put all of that on them. I found it had more to do with me just having a better connection with women than I did men—a journey I would truly understand with time. I wanted to understand more about this unfamiliar attraction stirring up in me, leading me to want to explore parts of myself I had never noticed nor acknowledged before.

My first inklings of being attracted to women were subtle, often conversations and daydreams in the back of my mind. My first year of college, these thoughts sparked for one of my college teammates. It was different, something I hadn't experienced with men. My thoughts often wandered about her when I was around her, creating a newfound awareness of my own desires. It wasn't so much of the physical more than it was the attraction and trying to make sense of why her, why now. At the same time curiosity surfaced, fear did as well. The fear of judgment I thought I would face, not from her or my teammates, but from my family and those who would not understand. These thoughts weighed heavily on my mind day in and day out, leaving me to carry these feelings for years and never speaking or acting on it and instead just holding onto a crush that would remain a little secret until we met again down the line. I was so concerned with society's expectations while I was at WKU that I never had the desire to act on anything toward anyone, not even a conversation on the subject. Besides, I still had an attraction for men, but just never felt that deep connection with them. Plus, I didn't want to be stereotyped, and even my own preconceived notions about my sexuality threatened to cloud my new sense of self. I knew I wasn't the only woman exploring these feelings, but none around me lived their truth like they did at Sullivan and in high school. Those were the elements I could have easily confronted this identity, but at those times, I just wasn't in this same space of understanding. I sat, often wondering if people would see me differently, would my family accept this aspect of me. These questions gnawed at me, planting seeds of doubt on ever acting upon anything. I planned to just leave curiosity embedded within me and keep what I labeled as normal and accept my miniscule desire for men.

As time went on and the interest grew, I knew at some point I had to sit with the truth about myself that was developing. The question that gnawed at me was "Who would I release this truth to that I could trust to keep it quiet until I fully understood my identity in it?" And then came the realization that not everyone would embrace my truth, so why was I thinking so much about external understanding than I was about my own internal understanding? When I did finally come clean to my college crush my junior year of college, a weight was lifted off my shoulders. Not so much because I came clean to her but because I had someone to share this deep secret I held inside for years and not get judged for it. We both had something relatable to talk about. We were able to be honest with each other and became closer friends because of it. Although the crush didn't go beyond our friendship, which I was ok with, nothing but us stopped it from becoming more. Our friendship carried me into my first relationship with a woman who was way more experienced in the lifestyle than I, and although she cared for me, she was young and enjoying life with me, and with others, too, which led to only dating for about seven months. I didn't mind her moving on if that was her need; I just hated that she chose to cheat on me, making my first experience one that ended in heartache. Leaving me to question that world even more than I did exploring it. We were young and living in our own truths. Although the relationship ended poorly, years later, we would talk it out and become friends to this day, which is priceless for me. If I learned nothing else from the experience, it was that to always try to walk away in a good place if the situation warrants.

As I found myself in this new world, I knew how to find peace in it around my family. It was one thing to be comfortable in it in Ohio; it was going to be another in New York. One of my brothers expressed discomfort with my attraction to women, revealing his immediate disagreement with it, while my other brothers supported my decision. One out of three wasn't bad. My mother of course showed no judgment whatsoever; her question was always "will you give me grand babies?" As humorous as I found it, it was a relief that I didn't have to stand in this new way of life all alone, even if they didn't understand my decision. My brother's disapproval was heavy, especially the way he handled it with such disrespect. It was a reminder to me that the path to self-discovery is often marked by adversity.

The lifestyle I have chosen is and always was a place for me to understand myself. Once again, my decisions weren't marked by the likes or dislikes of others but by self-love. There was a sense of understanding I had to walk, an unspoken truth nestled within. This was a language of love that only I needed to comprehend so that I could be happy. This connection with self felt real, raw, and undeniably profound. One that needed to happen, so the choices I made moving forward was not being made out of fear or regret. Living for myself took on a new significance. I realized that in order to be truly content, I had to embrace my identity and desires wholeheartedly. This was an identity separate from the stereotypes I grew up believing and hearing that all female athletes were lesbians. Although many of us make the decision to live in this lifestyle, many do not, and either way is fine. We are not less human for our choices. Who we love no matter the sex is a personal choice, one of peace and one of desire. It is fair to say not everyone chooses to understand, and that's their cross to bear. Life is full of labels, unfortunately the world doesn't function without them. Similar to how as individuals we are labeled as numbers. Those numbers being the date we were born, the social security number that identifies us, and the date we die. Labels and numbers. I am a complex individual with multifaceted passions, not simply defined by my sexuality, numbers, or my achievements as an athlete. I am one of love, waking up every day finding my place in the world based on my own values, goals, and commitments.

I found myself on a quest to understand not only who I am every day but also who I need to be to live an authentic life. This mindset came with a yearning for authenticity, a desire to strip away the layers society places on me. Creating my own comfort zone became paramount, a place where I could explore my feelings, my identity, and my truth, without fear or judgment. I want to be seen for the totality of my being, not confined to a single aspect of my life. So, every day, I face the challenges that allow me to push past stereotypes, to break through barriers, and to educate those around me about the richness and diversity of living one's life's experiences to be happy.

Ultimately, my journey of finding my sexuality began with those initial thoughts of attraction, confusion, and fear, but graduated to that of self-discovery, courage, and resilience. It's about embracing my beauty, understanding connections, standing up to judgments, and owning space for myself where authenticity and love flourishes. When I see my future, I see well beyond what people think, and more into the soul of myself, the greatest I stand for, and my determination to embrace every twist and turn that lay ahead, that leads me to my superpowers and love.

Genuine Connections

I was about 35 years old when I began comprehending the intricacies of having meaningful romantic relationships. I realized the importance of shifting my perspective from viewing the people I dated as temporary to genuinely exploring profound and heartfelt connections. I wanted to embrace the nature of both the positive and negative experiences that shape trust, communication, and love. My goal was to evolve into a person who could fully understand and navigate the complexities of what true connections felt like without reservations. I wanted to be that person who trusted love and nurtured the softer side of what that experience entailed. I knew to get to this place I had to deal with some real traumas that I left unattended. I was ready to start working through what was holding me back and why.

I needed to confront why I was fearful of letting people close to me and giving my whole self to anyone. It was time for me to confront some past pains, understand how those past pains were affecting me presently so I can have more meaningful relationships moving forward. For me, it had to begin with one fact: I grew up in a family where effective communication tools were not readily available, and lacking those tools led me to the challenges I was having with fostering healthy interactions. This was a lot for me to unpack. I sat reflecting on how I experienced love and affection at home. Growing up, we laughed a lot, engaged in fun activities within the community and the household together, but beyond laughter, we didn't know how to express ourselves in empathetic ways that built strong nurturing connections with each other. My brothers are closer in age, so they related with each other more because of that. I was nearly a decade younger, and their maturity levels were way more advanced. They had more in common with each other as the years progressed, so their bond was different. Their conversations and experiences were different. So, I witnessed them become permanent fixtures because what I saw was their personal developments happening, and it was happening to them as boys and as men. I saw their relationships with my mother, I saw all of their relationships with other people, and then I was developing from their relationship with me. What stood out most to me were the patterns they engaged in and how those patterns were being passed onto me. I didn't quite understand what was good or bad, I just lived off of the emotions I was gaining from their character traits. I saw early how hard it was for my mother to raise three boys on her own, and when they got old enough to where she no longer had control over the decisions they made, our lifestyle changed.

I saw how protective my brothers were of me and my mother, but I also saw how much of an influence the streets had over each of them. Seeing these changes shaped my own behaviors, but as the baby and only girl child, the boundaries were different. I wasn't being guided and taught as they were, and I wasn't developing the way they were either. The disciplines I was taught and witnessed were shaped from a place of protection, but that protection wasn't always healthy. I saw how my family stood together when times got hard, but I also saw how hard times came between us. The biggest skill we lacked as a family was how to have healthy conversations. I would often witness how disagreements led to anger, anger led to shouting matches, and shouting matches resulted in distance that lasted months, even years. I would see my brothers argue and work through their disagreements by still doing things together, but I didn't see that same relationship when it came to how they managed their anger toward my mother. I didn't understand that. I didn't understand how they could hold on to grudges when it came to the woman who gave them everything within her being. I witnessed them have more love for people outside the home than inside the home. As a child, I was too young to understand that; as a teen, it confused me; and as an adult, I grew to understand how it traumatized me.

I didn't know the type of behavior that was being created until my beliefs around relationships seemed difficult for me. Forming meaningful connections with others has been challenging for me, as I've often found myself building protective walls that I would only let down when I sensed that the people around me had genuine intentions. I have difficulty trusting others and allowing myself to create space to welcome love and feel vulnerable. It took a long time for me to get to a comfortable space for this. I acknowledge that it is a process that takes time for me and is not very easy for others to maneuver. I had been exposed to patterns of behaviors that created so much confusion for me at an early age, and there was never a time when those confused moments were explained in a way that helped me control the emotions I felt to keep them from becoming my traumas. I became aware early of the impact that words have and how those words can trigger emotions uncontrollably. I didn't know that the pain my family was passing along to each other was inadvertently affecting me, becoming deep-rooted past pains that would show up in my future. From my mother, I saw how a woman addresses men, and I saw from my brothers how men treated women. I also saw how my brothers engaged with our mother and with me as their sister. I also got to see how men treated their girlfriends, just like I saw how men treated my mother. I have to say, my mother didn't date a lot of men, and I never saw one disrespect her, at least never in front of me anyway. The only men I saw disrespect my mother were my brothers, and I never understood how that was because they never let a man disrespect her in front of them, ever. So, as I got older and sat with this, I started to understand how the dynamics of their relationship stemmed from poor communication within the family. What we tolerated with each other was way different from what the rest of the world saw of us, but what we had was unhealthy. This wasn't about right or wrong teachings; it was about learned behaviors from them that happened in front of me, that became unsafe patterns passed down to me. I only went off of what I saw and was taught, at least until I gained an understanding that forced me to stop emulating what I experienced.

Being that my family members weren't good communicators and problem solvers, the presence of silence and emotional disconnect had a ripple effect, affecting each one of us in so many ways. Whether we wanted to play a part in how things were playing out or not, it was hard not to feel the effects of what was manifesting and recognizing what was really happening to us individually and collectively. I've witnessed my family not speak to each other for years due to disagreements, and I became a product of that behavior when me and my brothers crossed our paths of difficulty. I was repeating what came between some of them, and it ultimately became how I handled things, too. I found it easy to break free and just abandon conversations because our track record showed when things got hard, we were incapable of talking it out and moving on from it. Working through things looked and felt like ignoring it with the hope that it just goes away, but in many cases, it never did. It resulted in us losing sight of the values we were originally raised with and developing new ones that related more outside of the household than it did within it. I know now how those experiences between them weren't personal toward me; they were experiences they battled. However, then, that didn't stop those experiences from becoming my own.

As a teen, when my family would disagree, I often found myself feeling like I had to choose sides because I didn't know how to remain neutral. I loved all of my family, and it hurt to see the damage being caused and not having a voice to fix it. I didn't realize how witnessing such behaviors and actions numbed me from the inside out, causing me to silence my voice, accept disappointments, and lash out in other ways because I didn't know how to keep the peace at home.

I've learned to create awareness around the power words have, and when they are not used correctly, they can cause pain that carries over into years of lost time if never taught how important communication, compromise, and empathy is in building relationships. My most important childhood relationships were with my mother and brothers; as a teen and adult, those crucial relationships came from the people outside my family that I grew to bond, trust, and love. I didn't know that what I saw wasn't mine to build my life around and make them my beliefs and traumas, but where we were from, there weren't many people around to show and tell me different because many families had similar experiences.

With time and experiences, I learned to face these challenges and start healing from these traumas. I knew to grow through my past traumas that showed up for me as current triggers, I had to learn how to let go of what was for them and know that it wasn't for me. It all became mine when I made it mine, when I started creating my own emotions around their experiences. I also knew in order to break these patterns, my past had to be addressed, healed through, and let go of. For years, I learned to cope with the pain of not having my family around for many great moments of my life. Because I never dealt with that pain, I just harvested it, and those unhealed behaviors bloomed into traits of who I was. It showed up in my happiest of moments, and it showed up when I was angered, habits all learned that must be unlearned. I understand now, more than ever, that our parents pass down trauma they don't know they have in turn passes that trauma along, and the cycle just continues until the healing starts.

I acknowledge what was passed onto me, and I own how I show up in the world from it. I don't have any kids; however, my brothers do, and I hope they can identify it in their own ways, stop duplicating these traumatic behaviors, and heal from it to stop the cycle from becoming permanent fixtures in their children's lives, especially now that their kids are growing their own families. I knew when I was hurting people because when I did, I was hurting, too. I didn't know then how to turn that hurt into something good. I just knew how to live in it and make it work for my life. When I got tired of hurting, that's when I decided to stop living in the past and to stop letting that hurt show up in my current life. I didn't want to be that person who knew I needed to heal and didn't. I didn't want to be that person who, when triggered, knew it wasn't about the person standing in front of me but about the child who couldn't stand up for herself and was choosing to lash out because of it. I didn't want to be that person who traumatizes someone else because I was neglecting my responsibility to heal.

My goal as an adult is always to try to communicate openly and honestly, and to support those I care about. I want to be there during good and difficult times and celebrate each other's successes.

Not having the best relationship tools growing up didn't mean my family was bad, nor did it mean I was a bad person; it simply meant I had inner work to do so I didn't have to be that guarded little girl anymore. It became clear that I needed to comprehend the significance of genuine relationships and how much of a crucial role having people who genuinely cared for me in my life was. Learning how to trust people and developing the skills I need to feel confident within that I am choosing safe people are essential parts of my journey.

While I've had many positive relationships throughout my life, I've also experienced my fair share of negative ones. In particular, I cared for people within the confines of my emotions. I didn't allow myself to get too close out of fear of feeling insecure, powerless, abandoned, or neglected. Although I've been cheated on in only one relationship that I know of, it still took many years to recognize how my patterns of self-sabotage kept me from connecting deeply with people who genuinely wanted to love and care for me. Not growing up witnessing the full scope of what healthy relationships looked and felt like pushed me to ignore and accept things from people even when I knew better. In some cases, I gave misplaced emotions to people in my present when it was tied to people from my past.

The benefits of being a basketball player with a busy schedule made relationships simpler for me to engage in because I didn't have too much time to get invested in one person for too long. At least it didn't allow me to. I was able to control how deep of a connection I had with others and used my career as a barrier to put distance around my heart by focusing on my game. I felt safe in friendships; that wasn't the problem for me. It was matters that touched on my deeper emotions that scared me.

I own my past trauma of abandonment and how much that affected my career, my finances, and some opportunities presented to me. Because I had a problem trusting people when I entered unfamiliar territories, I didn't know how to decipher between those who had my best interest at heart and those who didn't. So, when my career as a pro basketball player started slowing down, and I wasn't traveling as much, I came face-to-face with the internal healing I had to do. I wanted to understand my emotions so I would stop blocking my blessings and be open to living a healthier life. It meant living intentionally so much so that I gained control over my thoughts, actions, and decisions. Now that I was living to address the child within, I was able to shift my habits and behaviors. I struggled with having self-control over my emotions, and that was what I had to repair. I was no longer willing to hurt my present and my future by not healing from my past.

At this point, my destiny wasn't about my past experiences anymore; it was about growing stronger and being more resilient regarding how I love myself. Yes, each person I built a connection with over the years played a unique part in my personal growth. I cultivated deeper understandings of myself and my connections with others. I lived in each experience with patience, allowing how I learn from mistakes to be my release and my reward.

Through this walk, I am understanding my relationship with myself first and foremost, and I've come to appreciate the complexity and importance of human connection. Whether positive or negative, relationships offer me opportunities for learning, growing, and healing beyond conditioned thinking. I am aware that it is not about being mad or emotional; it is about me understanding who that anger is directed toward and dealing with those emotions accordingly. None of my experiences was solely about other people; they were about me and how I wanted to show up in the world. I've met and engaged with some amazing individuals, and to this day, many still play essential roles in my life. It is about connecting with who I am, what I want, and what I need to fulfill me internally and then building strong, thriving, personal, and emotional relationships.

Throughout my personal odyssey, a remarkable revelation unfolded for me about how I believe the bond for my family slowly began to break. It dawned on me that our strength and closeness reached its peak during the time we shared a snug two-bedroom apartment in the squares. Within those walls, we shared beds, gathered around a single dining table, and huddled together in the living room, where a solitary television served as a focal point. Our family dynamics thrived as my mother had her own room, two of my older brothers shared another, and Jeff and I shared the living room couch. However, the equilibrium shifted when we moved to a larger three-bedroom apartment. The addition of televisions in every room and the freedom to dine separately gradually tipped the scales. Experiencing these two living styles showed me the significance of minimizing distractions that can create distance and hinder communication within a household. I have come to appreciate the importance of carving out family time, where meaningful conversations flow effortlessly and seemingly with activities like sharing daily meals can forge unbreakable and genuine connections. Such essential moments to me should not be compromised.

Today, there are so many distractions, and it is far easier to lose sight of what truly matters: family, love, communication, and staying connected. Despite many of my past turns of events, reaching so many new revelations has instilled in me a deep understanding of the value safeguarding these foundational pillars have. Rather than cherishing large spaces, I am learning to nurture the essence of bonding together and to minimize as many distractions as possible that may potentially threaten peace within the home.

Now, when it comes to my family, I don't blame them for anything. I chose to stop living in the past. It was a part of my makeup, but I am not committed to it being what makes up my life. My mother, my brothers, and I lived with the tools we were given, and often, if the proper habits aren't taught from generation to generation, the healthy and the unhealthy continue until the trend is broken. Each of us has to identify patterns within ourselves for the lives that we want to live and the legacy we want to leave behind. We, individually, get to decide whether we want to pass down behaviors filled with negative behaviors or whether we want to examine these behaviors and replace them with more positive and empowering ones.

I've learned the importance of setting boundaries and limiting how generational teaching shows up for me. I welcome new patterns of behavior that promote healthy habits, healthy communication, and healthy relationships. I understand I get to choose what that looks and feels like for me. I have the freedom and the willpower to surround myself with people who counteract my energy. I understand that self-care and self-compassion are vital to this process, as is engaging with people who promote the physical and emotional well-being I am committed to. I recognize that when my triggers show up that allows me to communicate exactly what I am feeling and work through those emotions rationally. I accept the ongoing process and challenges that come with this for the rest of my life, but the beauty is that I have healthier tools to make my journey more productive and fulfilling. My life is free from the constraints of unhealthy generational teachings, and I accept responsibility for what happiness looks and feels like based on who I am today.

The benefit of seeking out healthy relationships is acknowledging what healthy looks and feels like. That's growth. That's self-improvement. That's living.

Mind, Heart, and Soul

In order for me to get to the words I want to express in this chapter, I have to start it with this quote:

"Cancer can take away all of my physical abilities. It cannot touch my mind, it cannot touch my heart, and it cannot touch my soul."
Jim Valvano

This quote expresses exactly how I feel about my friend, sister, and now angel in heaven, Simone F. Courtlandt.

Simone was a light. She embodied strength, love, passion, and fight. She displayed a level of strength that I only saw from my mother. Simone and I had some characteristics that only we understood but drove many crazy. We often would be hurting but only showed our strength. We would often want to cry but held back our tears. We often wanted the people around us to be good, even if it meant we were uncomfortable. We often protected our hurts so others wouldn't have to feel our pain.

Simone and I met when we were kids. Her grandmother lived in the same building as we did in the squares, and she used to babysit me and my brothers. Simone came from a large family of sisters and brothers, so when they came to visit their grandmother, they always ran deep. Everyone knew when they were around. They came in together as a group and left together as the same group. After we moved from the squares, I would see Simone every now and then at basketball events in high school. It wasn't until I returned to NY in 1997, however, that Simone and I became good friends. Basketball was our common denominator, and a friendship developed from that passion. When I first reconnected with Simone, she was coaching a women's tournament at Elmcor Recreation Center in Corona, Queens; I didn't know it was her at the time, however. It was one of the first tournaments I went to see after moving back. I was trying to feel out the world of women's basketball after being away in college for so many years. I was trying to get familiar with the NY scene.

I came to watch but wound up getting invited to play against a team that Simone was coaching, and man was she competitive. I noticed how vocal and expressive she was as a coach. She didn't accept losing, and she didn't accept excuses from her players. I noticed this, and I wasn't on her team. I kept asking myself, *Where do I know this girl from?* Not until the game was over and she made a joke about me being the new girl coming in here kicking her team's butt did she remind me of who she was. It was quite a few years from the time we last saw each other again as young teens.

After a good laugh and the reminder, we instantly became friends. Our time was spent playing basketball together and on opposite teams, hanging out at her house playing cards, and partying. Simone was so private yet so outgoing, which I totally was able to connect with because I too was the exact same. Selective about our circle and what we wanted you to know about our personal life. Simone was so adventurous that she would have me try many things once. She and I had an attraction for each other early but realized we were too much alike emotionally and would drive each other crazy. We agreed we would be better as friends, and that is what we remained up to until her passing. Our friendship was genuine, and we respected each other. We talked about anything and everything. As close as we were, I still had to drag things out of her when she would go through challenges

233

because she was always displaying her strength to get through and her desire to work it out on her own.

Simone had her own style. She loved her baggy clothes, often reminding me of the late singer Aaliyah. She explored life. She embraced everything she did by going all out. When we decided to start bike riding for exercise, she purchased the bike, the helmet, and all the fixings for the bike to make it her own. When we started going bowling, she purchased her own ball, gloves, polish for the ball, shoes, and bag. When I introduced her to playing poker, and she saw my custom poker chips, she began to love the game so much she purchased chips, too, and a poker table so when we had games at her house, it felt close to the casino feel. I loved that about her. If she was going to do something, she was going to do it big or not at all.

For a few years, we would often talk about buying motorcycles, but first, we needed to learn how to ride. I was taking too long for her. One day, she called me to come downstairs and meet her in front of my building. What did I see when I got there? Her new motorcycle and her matching gear to go with her bike. All I could do was laugh with excitement. I was so happy for her. She did it. I admit, I was taking too long to go learn, and she was determined and did it. Until this day, I get my drive from her. I was always the type who had that "go big or go home" approach, but she took it to another level with everything, and I adored her for it.

In 2015, Simone would share with me the hardest thing she would have to endure: She had early stage ovarian cancer. Like most of us react when we hear the C word, we automatically equate it with a death sentence. I knew that moment for her was hard because again she was so private no matter how much she trusted you. As she spoke, I stared off through the front windshield of my car. I didn't want her to see the tears forming in my eyes, and I definitely didn't want her to stop telling me how she was feeling and how I could support her. As usual, she downplayed the process, but I knew her, I knew her body language, and I could see the fear in her eyes for the first time ever. Here was the most adventurous person I know, always ready to take on the world, and she was, for the first time ever, sharing with me she didn't have the answers but that she was going to beat this battle. I had no doubt whatsoever that she would.

Along her journey, we explored more, we laughed more, we supported each other more, and we valued each other more. Heck, I got her to go to a club for a party, and she hated going to clubs. As usual, she exuberated strength during her weakest moments, often choosing to fight the fight in silence to protect those around her. She rarely asked for help, so when she did ask, I would drop everything to be there. I would often get frustrated with her because she would isolate herself from me to keep me from seeing the changes chemo was making to her body. I would fuss with her to tears, letting her know I cared nothing about that, that I was her sister, and no matter what, I had her back.

We had one good cry one day about it, and she broke down and explained she was having difficulty dealing with it. I had no choice but to respect her journey and just be there when she called. I wanted to do more to support her healing. I prayed daily for God to spare my sister. She created a level of normalcy as often as she could. If she was up for going to the casino to play poker, we would gas up her car or my truck and go. She played paddle ball every chance she could with her friends PJ, Jackie, and Carlene. We had game nights at either her house or mine. She called me one day and said she needed a fun night, so we invited some friends over to my house and had a game night. I wasn't crazy about having people I didn't really rock with in my house, but for her, I made the exception. I wanted to help her through this process as much as I could. I in no way knew what she was feeling or going through. When I lost both my cousin Yvonne and Uncle Eddie to cancer, theirs took them so quickly there wasn't enough time to process what was happening. That's why I was so grateful that Simone was fighting and doing everything she needed to and more to fight this demon off from day one.

One day in the winter of 2018, I received a call from her. It wasn't unusual for our check-ins throughout the week. I made it a habit of checking in with her if I didn't hear from her first. On this day, she beat me to the call. I had just spoken to her a couple of days prior, so we were about due for this call. I answered the phone as I often did, saying, "What's going on, ladybug?" That is my term of endearment. I called a couple of people around me that I knew would make them smile. She let off her little giggle and said she needed to talk to me. It was good timing because I wanted to talk to her, too. I had ran into her brother on Far Rockaway Boardwalk about going to her house and her not wanting company and him telling me to do what he did and just roll up on her. I knew how fussy she would get if I did that, but it sounded very tempting to do. So, her timing for this call was perfect.

As I listened for her to tell me what she wanted to talk about, I began to hear her crying and sniffling, and instantly, my heart started racing.

"What's wrong?" I asked. "Where are you?"

I wasn't ready for the next few words to come out of her mouth.

"I don't have much time." Before she could continue, tears welled up in my eyes, and I fought back the sounds of me about to break down. She went on to tell me that her kidneys were failing, and chemo was no longer working, and she didn't have much time. She explained that she was at Sloan Kettering in the city. She gave the room info, and before she could finish her thoughts, I was already out the door on the way to the hospital.

I wasn't ready for this. I had just seen her a few days ago, and she was fine. She had stopped by my house with her dog Mojo. What was happening? Here it was again, a replay of my cousin's and uncle's conditions changing so fast. I had to pull over because the tears were blinding my view to see the road. It was a cold December day, so I opened the windows to let the cold air dry up my tears before they fell. I knew people were looking at me like I was plum crazy with all four windows down in the middle of winter, but I gave zero fucks. I just wanted to get to my sister's side and see what was going on.

I finally got to the hospital for what felt like a two-hour trip with NY traffic but actually took me 45 minutes. As I approached her room, everything seemed in slow motion. I saw some familiar faces standing outside her door, and I heard laughter coming out of her room, which slowly eased the tension that was running through me. I was actually confused. This was different from the call. Maybe I had the wrong room. A miracle happened, and she was misdiagnosed. Any of everything ran through my head to make that call turn for the better. As I turned the corner into her room, she looked amazing: skin flawless and a smile that greeted me. I tried to ease the tension with a joke and a compliment of how amazing she looked. The moments that lasted a few minutes of laughter soon turned into tears after she began to explain what was happening with her health.

I didn't start crying until she did. My eyes were burning so much from holding my tears back, and when she let go, I lost it. I couldn't believe what she was telling me. She looked fine, she was laughing, she was upbeat. There was no way this was true. I just did not understand. I sat with her for as long as she could and was at the hospital daily until she was moved to hospice. I didn't understand why they were moving her there. She was fine. She looked and was acting like herself. I couldn't comprehend what was happening. I had questions, lots and lots of questions, but nothing was more important than spending quality time with her. It seemed like yesterday we were just turning up for her 50th birthday celebration. She was so happy, doing her two steps, taking pictures, and just enjoying being loved on. We had so much to do. She had so much living to do. This couldn't be real.

I struggled for days without proper sleep. Crying throughout the day. Playing back moment after moment, hearing her laugher in my head. All I could do was talk to the Lord and ask him to give her more time. To make her whole again, to bring her home to the family and friends who loved her. As thought after thought kept me up all night, the sun came up, and time ticked, and I finally got the call from Carlene that Simone was settled into hospice, and I immediately went right up there.

Again, she looked fine. I could not understand why she was there. By the time I got to her, some of her family from out of town and a few of our basketball sisters had arrived, too. There were so many of us that they rolled her out to the lounge area so we all could spend time with her together. We laughed, reminisced about old basketball stories, and talked about how much fun we had at her 50th. It honestly felt like a gathering she would have at her house over a good card game or a game of Pokeno. None of us wanted to leave her side, but we saw she was getting tired. It was an amazing time. It was a beautiful time.

No one would have convinced me that I would get a call the next day telling me her health was beginning to fail her. She was in and out. I wanted to be by her side. I gave it a day in respect to her family who wanted time with her, but I couldn't just sit at home. I needed to be with my sister. I needed her to know I was there for whatever she needed. She was resting most of the day, but when I walked in her room and said, "Hey ladybug," she turned her head to look at me and gave me a little smile. The difference a day and a half made. How could this be? She was alert, laughing, and talking with us then. How was it that now she was barely alert and not talking? I kept asking why they moved her from the hospital; she was doing better there. I didn't understand. As I held her hand and talked to her, I desperately wanted her to get up out of that bed and tell me she was fine.

Instead, I sat and watched my sister rest. As it began to get late, I went to give her a kiss and whispered to her that I would be back tomorrow. She opened her eyes so big and let out a moan as if she didn't want to leave. I reassured her I was coming back tomorrow morning, and she just looked at me as I walked out. That moment meant everything to me. Her letting me know she didn't want me to leave caused me to lose it when I got into the hallway outside of her room. I was up all night again, waiting for daylight so I could head back to the city to sit with her.

When I arrived home, I had to take some Tylenol PM to get rid of my headache and to try to get some sleep. After finally dozing off, my phone rang at 7:09 a.m. with the dreadful news that my sister had left us at 6:53 a.m. That numbing feeling hit me at first, and then I lost it.

On this day, December 23, in 2011, I had to put my cat Tiger of 15 years to sleep. To lose two best friends on the same day hit me so hard.

Thinking about the both of them, I balled up under my covers, held my cat Nike, and cried myself to sleep. As much as I tried to prepare myself for that moment, I just wasn't ready. I felt a piece of me leave with her. She was one of the strongest people I had ever known. I just knew if anyone could beat this beast, it would be her. I wasn't ready to let my friend and sister go. Who would I go to for my Red Flag talks? Who would I go to give me the Real? Who would I go play poker with? She was just an amazing and blessed person. All the way up until her burial, she was looking over us. On the day of her funeral, it was a partly cloudy and cold day, and maybe it was just me, but the day seemed very mild when we came out of her service. It was partly sunny in Jamaica, Queens, but as we headed toward the cemetery, it was getting cloudy as if it was going to rain. You would have had to be there to believe it, but the moment we gathered at her burial site, the clouds parted ways, and the sun shone. I never witnessed anything like that in my life. We looked up in the sky and knew it was her way of letting us know she was welcomed by God to be the angel she was here on earth.

It was so hard to say goodbye to the shell of my friend and sister, but I forever live with the presence of who she was in life every single day. When I seek strength or need wisdom, I reflect on our talks, recall the advice she often gave me, and gain my power from all the years of watching her battle a disease that would take her life. No one will ever replace the person I had in her. She left me with so much. I know she is protected and welcomed on the other side. She confirmed that for me with an experience I will hold sacred, for it was special. Her memories live on through so many people she left behind. She was loved so much and still is.

Ball in heaven, Simone. I hope to see you when I get there.

Forever In My Heart…

In Memory Of
Simone F. Courtlandt
April 14, 1966–December 23, 2018

The Right Kind of Love Manifested

When I first wrote this chapter, I started from my emotional past from parts of me that was still healing and making mindset shifts. I spoke from the situations I was living through. So, I am making the adjustment and choose to speak from a place of manifestation. I want to speak into existence the love and nurturing I want to give off and attract. This is important to me because I just don't want to focus too heavily on all of the past lessons more than I want to focus on my present practices.

Before I go too deep into my healing process, let me give you a little back story. Not until I retired and began to settle down on how much the sport had me on the go did I start to focus on stability. When my travel schedule changed, and I was no longer on the road as much, the shift to find someone to settle down with became essential. Now, I just needed to work on new habits, such as being present more frequently, planning more time doing "couple" things, having check-ins in person and not over the phone, and sharing more of my physical time and space. It was me learning to adjust to traditional styles of relating outside of the on-the-go routines I was accustomed to. It was me respecting their ways and my routines and finding happy mediums beyond what I was accustomed to. The transition from a travel-heavy lifestyle to a stationary one challenged me the most, and it took some time for me to get used to a new routine and establish a sense of stability. This also allowed me to explore what I truly desired within a relationship and what qualities are most important to me in a partner.

Before retiring, I never really sat down and had to do this before. It wasn't about the others adjusting so much from my routine; it was me learning what I sought in another person and how much of myself I had to shift from and to.

One of the benefits of having more time at home is the ability to build deeper connections with others.

For the first time, I got to experience yearning for a companion because I had time to focus on what genuine companionship is without traveling and playing being the focal point. It was and still is important for me to remember that finding love and building a stable relationship takes time. I developed patience with the process, keeping an open mind that the work is not overnight. Plus, I had to be committed and willing to put in the work required to build a lasting connection with someone special, and with this came a new level of trust. I practiced being honest and communicative about my needs and desires and being willing to consistently compromise and work through challenges I never had to face.

Before I can go into what I want, I must first start with self-love. Self-love is what love is built from. In my forties, I found myself asking a question I had never considered before: "Michelle, what does a profound and fulfilling relationship truly mean to you, especially when it comes to creating the basis that draws in loving relationships?" Every day, I practice nurturing Michelle with compassion and kindness. I embrace my worthiness and value from within so that I am creating a solid inner peace and love that radiates from the inside-out. I am learning when I genuinely love the authentic parts of me, it radiates the true essence of who I am and who I want to be. Embracing qualities about myself that I love, like, and want to improve will allow me to attract meaningful connections and be someone else's meaningful connection.

What Happens After The Game

The self-love I honor myself with empowers me to set and maintain healthy boundaries, which allows me to create an environment harmonized with love and respect. This feeling reciprocates itself in a way that brings me joy. The solid emotional foundation I am building within is equipping me with emotional resilience that helps me prioritize my ability to give and receive love. This gears me to not only attract love but attract the right kind of love. My day starts with developing a sense of self-worth that enables me to recognize and avoid people that are unhealthy and not aligned with my needs. Placing this value on myself opens my heart to receive love from a safe, vulnerable, and free place that builds my courage to walk into who I deserve and be ready for the interaction without fears.

I noticed the shift in my life and mindset once I made this transformation and gave self-love the power it deserves. By loving myself first and foremost, I am allowing my experiences to be authentic, courageous, and worth pursuing. I honor the fact that I am open to quality relationships because I no longer settle for less than I deserve. When you start making the right choices about being the best version of yourself, it cultivates a deeper love noticed by those who align with the same energy. The way I love myself establishes the foundation for how I express love to others and the depth of the meaningful connections that stem from it. I want to be a magnet for love in its purest forms, and I want it to transform my life. Now that I am pouring love into myself, I am truly self-assured about how I approach relationships and embrace the confidence it gives me in healthy ones. I get to choose those meaningful connections, just like I get to avoid the ones that come with emotional turmoil. I am equipped to handle rejection, setbacks, and conflicts that may arise without bounce back and with a move-forward attitude. This level of confidence is helping me relinquish my need for perfection or approval and embrace my authentic self. I get to create a safe space, and I get to thrive in it.

The healthy patterns I am setting are helping me set the stage to be happy with and for the people in my life. Because I understand that my well-being is my responsibility, I prioritize my happiness and growth around it. I no longer put unrealistic expectations on myself or others. I function from a solid framework built in self-love and exercise patience that my individual experiences with people will evolve differently over time. This benefits and influences how I relate with others. To love and accept others comes with understanding. It's working through struggles and insecurities. It's approaching relationships with empathy, kindness, and compassion. I have the ability to inspire others by creating how love affects and ripples off me.

Getting to this level in my life has been very difficult. It meant me sitting with myself for a few years before I could feel comfortable even wanting to date because I want my outcomes to be different. I want the cycle to change, and I want the expectations of who I was in relationships to mature. I am aware that I attracted what permeated from me. That aspect alone meant I had to evaluate my love within and commit to nurturing my own happiness and well-being.

In my own experience, I am learning to trust myself with being loved and giving love. I trust myself to find the right people to love. It requires a lot of honesty and healing because both are necessary paths to grow. With age comes wisdom. With contentment comes growth. All of those limiting beliefs that held me back in various areas of my life, I release and replace them with more empowering beliefs. I am worthy of receiving love. I am worthy of giving love. I am in love. Love for me is limitless and self-imposed. I manifest love in abundance in every aspect of my life. I break free from any and everything that sets me back from the aligned spiritual essence of love. I turn my attention to the voice that provides clarity, guidance, and a healthy sense of purpose. I align my life with my desires and prioritize my life with emotional stability and resilience. By feeding my needs I am able to navigate willingly allowing relationships to be formed from a place of wholeness and maturity.

At this point in my life, the person I will settle down with is the person I've been through good, bad, her worse, my worse, and we survived it all stronger than we went in. I've walked what temporary looks and feels like; now, I want to experience lifelong bonds, and I believe that connection is God-sent and God-approved. I am a believer that life is happening for us to meet the perfect time in the perfect way.

I look forward to being vulnerable and open, to share thoughts and feelings without fears of judgment or rejection. I look forward to sharing my space with a partner where we both are seen, heard, valued, and desired. I know there are many layers to love, and with each layer, I lead with prayer and faith. I am living a life toward healing and wholeness, and I am manifesting love in every area of my life, starting with self-love.

Achieving Success

Success is more than obtaining a high-paying job, a big home, and a luxury car. It's more than just climbing a ladder to the top. What if you get to the top and realize that you may have a lot of *things*, but what you lost on the way up is your*self*? Success can mean accomplishing goals, but it can also mean loving yourself so that you can pursue your greatest dreams and have the confidence to believe you *can* achieve them. To understand what success means to me, I needed to research myself, to see the multi-faceted person I was and how all those facets could be used to design the success plan catered *to* me and *for* me.

Defining Success on Your Terms

The adage "Give it all you got or don't do it at all" resonates deeply with most fields of business. The quote captures the essence of commitment, the unwavering dedication required to reach our goals, and the significance of persevering through challenges. It is a common human tendency to admire the success and achievements of others, often yearning for a similar life. We see people who have reached the pinnacle of their endeavors, basking in the glory of their achievements, and we cannot help but feel a twinge of envy for their elevated status. Yet, we often overlook the arduous journey it took us to arrive at such a remarkable position. In the pursuit of understanding the concept of success, it is essential to reflect on how we define this elusive term. What does success truly mean? It holds diverse interpretations as its meaning is not the same for everyone. It is a concept that transcends a one-size-fits-all definition but varies as it is deeply rooted in individual perspectives, values, and aspirations. What may be considered a pinnacle of achievement for one individual may hold little significance for another. The beauty lies in the diversity of interpretations and the multitude of paths that lead to personal fulfillment. Take a moment to contemplate and define what success signifies in your life, for it is this personal understanding that shapes your journey and aspirations.

In the past, I sacrificed time, my money, and my health to achieve this idea of success, but this ultimately led me to major burnout. I used to tie success with my professional achievements, such as having "pro athlete" after my name, or reaching a high-ranking position, earning substantial amounts of money, and garnering accolades and gaining recognition. I also tied success to how much work I did to make the bosses *like* me, as if this would ultimately elevate me to the success I craved. While I believed that these measurements determine the tangible outcomes seen from external markers of achievement, the real benchmark for me identifies success as the pursuit of personal growth and self-improvement. Making this shift in my perspective, cultivates meaningful relationships, finding inner contentment, and nurturing a sense of purpose, valuing these aspects above those conventional markers used for determining success. Central to this perspective came the vital qualities such as happiness, fulfillment, balance, and overall well-being.

As an athlete with years under my belt, I grew to understand that success is not guaranteed, and it was my unwavering dedication that set me apart. The commitment to training, practice, and self-improvement became ingrained in me from level to level, driving me to push beyond my limits. I will admit, there were times when I got too comfortable in my career and did enough to stay in the fight. There were many a day when getting back in shape felt like work instead of fun, and I made excuses. Those excuses got me poor results. One thing for sure—when your craft becomes an excuse, people stop believing in your dedication even if they see the potential. Even the most dedicated athletes face moments of laziness but when you see how much you stand to lose because of it, you change your work ethic and get back on your game.

I faced immense challenges and obstacles when my mental health started taking a beating. Those were the moments that something deep within me started losing my love for playing. This was major for me after college. What ignited me to keep going was the shame and guilt of quitting on myself. I knew within me was a powerful internal force residing, and it served as a constant reminder of my goals. From all of my hard work awaited more to be done beyond the trials and tribulations of adversity. When I fought through the worst, refusing to succumb to the allure of giving up, the results of my hard work allowed me to see my potential way more than any defeating feelings I felt. The taste of victory was sweeter because I never lost hope in myself, even during those temporary setbacks. The culmination of countless hours of working out in the parks in the rain as a child, to the long weekend practices during my junior high and high school years, which helped me enjoy the sacrifices I made then to excel at the college level, and the relentless pursuit of making it as a pro player into the WNBA even when I wasn't drafted. The elation that accompanies achieving each goal reinforces the idea that giving it my best was not in vain but rather an essential ingredient to my success. I have reached a point where I no longer feel inadequate by the fact that I didn't have the opportunity to play years in the WNBA, achieve All-Star status, or secure championship titles and MVP awards. While it would have been amazing to attain such accolades, I take pride in the fact that I made it that far, considering the countless women who vied for one of the limited spots in the WNBA. I did that and I damn proud of myself for that 1998 season. I gained invaluable wisdom, acquired qualities such as discipline, perseverance, and determination that extended beyond my pursuit of those specific achievements. Those lessons enabled me to recognize my strengths, confront my weaknesses, and unlock potentials in myself I didn't know existed.

Behind the curtain of my success lies a story of relentless dedication and unwavering commitment. Through years of committing to the sport I love, I learned so many valuable lesson from the countless hours, days, weeks, months, and years I invested into the game that not only shaped my character but also paved the way for tangible success. This journey has been defined by the culmination of sacrifices I made for my life's work, transcending my dreams into reality. It was also defined by my unyielding determination and belief in my capabilities. I may not have gotten all the steps right, but even when the setbacks, the skepticism, the discouragements, and even the naysayers were all enough to quit, I kept going, and that boosted my confidence and began my transformative experience. That part of the journey in itself helped shape my character, molded my mindset, and instilled in me a level of resilience that transcends my life to this day.

For me success is measured by the positivity I can bring to other athletes, the communities I venture into and by the legacy I leave within my footprints. I draw inspiration from understanding more of who I am every day and when I struggle with that, I find solace in my faith. The depths of my self-awareness has influenced my life in way that speaks to the better person I strive to be to myself and to others. That to me is my greatest success.

Self-Validation Is Success

For far too long, I allowed the opinions of others to drive the direction of my life. I would often find myself concerned with what people would say about my career choices, its direction, and outcomes. I felt an incessant pressure to always want to do the right thing and shine within my career. I see now I was seeking approval instead of pursuing my dreams. Because I was one of the ones who used the game of basketball to make it out of the hood, playing college ball, and going pro, it seemed that all eyes were on me. I felt as if living under constant scrutiny made me hyper-aware of how my life was perceived by others. People used to share with me how proud they were of me and how many people looked up to what I was doing with my education and playing basketball. I was looked at as one of the staples within my community, and it was ok for me until my pro career didn't have the longevity that I thought it would, and then I retired.

My primary goal was to make my family, friends, and community proud. Ironically, I prioritized meeting their expectations over pursuing and living out my own. However, I have come to realize that the problem did not lie with them; it was my own tendency to put pressure on myself to have it all together, attempting to fulfill their expectations—a recipe for disaster, to say the least. Seeking validation through the satisfaction of others was scientifically impossible.

Another part of my transformation occurred when I switched my focus from caring so much about the thoughts and wishes of others to asking myself, "What is it that I care about?" "What do I want?" and

"What will truly make me happy?" This is not to disregard anyone's opinions, but I have reached a pinnacle point in my life where I genuinely can care less about the expectations of others. With a newfound sense of peace settling over me, I realized that whether others accepted me or not, I am content with who I am. If my authenticity and decision making for my life disturbs anyone, I kindly suggest you move on and find peace within yourself. I am no longer bound by the need for external approvals.

I love that I can move according to my own will and purpose. My personal happiness is the measure of my satisfaction, and I find peace in this way of thinking and being. Adopting this mindset has brought me so much clarity. I have embraced living for myself and aligning my thoughts and my actions. By making this change, I have reclaimed what I had previously relinquished. I humbly accept that the burden lies solely on my shoulders; my past shortcomings came from a lack of knowledge and now that I know better, I can do better. Now that I am armed with this new level of awareness, I strive to be fully cognizant of my existence. As I observed my mother's selfless acts throughout my life, despite her own better judgment, it pained me to witness how people often took advantage of her kindness rather than truly value her ability to give. Her generous heart taught me the importance of helping others when possible. However, I now understand that possessing a giving heart cannot come without personal boundaries set on my terms. The difference lies in setting my own terms and establishing personal boundaries. With this newfound knowledge, I am committed to doing better, honoring my own needs while still extending a helping hand within the limits I have set for myself.

Getting to this place was a challenging endeavor, as it entailed a path of darkness and solitude. It required me to make sacrifices that required me to let go of not only my old beliefs but of those individuals who made me an option while I made them a priority. It is amazing how quickly people change when I start saying NO and put my well-being above their reliance on me. I came first over their dependence on me, and as I finally began to grasp how I moved forward with my life, I was liberated.

When we establish boundaries that make others uncomfortable, the identity that was once aligned solely on their desires vanishes, and the potential for mutual nourishment and growth starts to flourish in every area of our lives. This realization also prompted me to walk away from a twenty-plus-year career as a program manager/director. I grew weary of being reduced to a mere number, longing for a more fulfilling existence in my body of work. I wasn't able to notice these toxic behaviors within me or my inability to set boundaries because I hadn't yet confronted the triggers that led me into those troubled waters. I had one-sided outcomes because I had a one-sided vision.

Cycles and circumstances remained unchanged until I acknowledged them. At this point, the obvious thing I had to do was release old habits and embrace a heightened awareness, allowing me to evolve into new versions of who I could be. I came to terms with the fact that certain individuals may no longer have a place in my life. Either they will choose to leave, or I would make that choice. Learning this, I firmly placed the responsibility square on me and me alone.

This latter half of my life is solely focused on how my footprints can impact me and those I come in contact with. The snapshots of what was will never measure up to the rolling reels of who I am becoming right now. The person I am becoming is only accepting things based on the canvas I want to paint, not the old black-and-white version of what appeased others. I undervalued myself for so long, and the unapologetic me is manifesting my winning season. I won before, but I am winning now through the lens I can see through without the ok or approval of others. Without regret, I didn't have the courage or know-how to achieve this. I can now live with my decisions and love myself even more for making them. Only God can judge me, and that's the only judgment that matters.

I love the fact that I am in a position to use my life experiences to mentor and inspire others. I remember when I was totally against telling my story, again, worrying about people's judgments. I am glad I came to terms with the power of words and, when used correctly, how they can make the difference not just in my life but in the lives of others. Each one of us possesses a relatable story; it is just a matter of how we choose to harness it to establish positive connections with others. I was being very selfish in thinking I would keep all of this to myself. I was not only hurting myself but hurting others.

I am a true believer that I will gain more by sharing my experiences than I will by keeping them to myself. Of course, there will be things I hold onto and cherish dearly, but I willingly share what I can offer with winning expectations in mind. My beliefs lie in paying knowledge forward, just like things were passed onto me. When someone blesses me, I seek opportunities to bless others in return. I am big on values and beliefs. That is why I constantly revisit mine and ensure I live in my truth. I am clear that my values are the principles that guide my behavior and

that my beliefs are the ideas I hold to be true. Guided by my values and beliefs, both are shaped by years of experiences, background, and the people I chose to keep company with.

Don't Wait for Someone's Permission to Get Started

Affirmation: I am confident to know that my journey is about my GO.

From the moment I started working, I moved from job to job, seeking something a job could partially fulfill. My very first job was at McDonald's on Jamaica Avenue in Queens, NY when I was a senior in junior high school. I had just got my working papers at the age of 15, loved their chicken nuggets, and thought what a perfect place to start. I started out making chicken nuggets, go figure, moved to fries for a day or two, and then to the cashier. Big mistake. Putting a 15-year-old on the register was like saying, "Give as much food for free to your family and friends as you want." I wasn't crazy about it, but I did hook a few people up. My biggest hookup came the day before I knew I was quitting. A couple of my family members came to get some food, and for $20, they got about $60 worth of food. I mean, I cleared the entire food holder. Whatever was under the lamps, they just about left with. I hope Mickey D's don't come for me for their $40. I loved the job for the experience it gave me and the fact that some of my schoolmates worked there too, but I hated the rude NYC customers whose bad day became my headache. It was this job where I knew I wasn't cut out to work front and center like that, but at age 15, that was most jobs. When I left there and applied at Key Food in Rochdale Village Big Mall, they put me on the register, and I dealt with more crazies. The only time I didn't have to deal with people's rudeness was when I worked at Popeye's by my high school on Guy R. Brewer and Baisley Blvd. They had me on biscuits. That job was so boring. I lasted about two paychecks, and I was out the door. I will say, those fresh out of the oven biscuits with butter and jelly hit the spot on many occasions.

A job was a job then. It wasn't about me doing what I love. It was about getting that sneaker money and that extra money to play Pitty Pat at lunchtime in school. My mother often brought my clothes. Taking these jobs gave me firsthand experience of what a little independence felt like. Making a little money and what I did with it was my choice. I didn't make a lot because I never stayed too long, but it kept me from asking my mother for money all the time. I had a sneaker fetish, so the majority of my money went to that. I knew nothing about saving and couldn't care less about it. However, I wish I was taught to be more financially literate because these little lessons early could have set healthy habits. My family didn't discuss money matters. It wasn't something my mother learned growing up. She knew survival and made sure we all had what we needed on a daily basis. One thing is for sure; if it wasn't taught to our parents, it probably wasn't taught to us. Like many kids, I often heard the phrases like "Money doesn't grow on trees," "...working to make ends meet," and "...living hand to mouth." To me those terms describe times when money was tight, but we wanted for nothing, and we didn't have that feeling of doing without. That is as far as conversations about money went. I had a savings account with a debit card when I went off to college, but my mother set that up for me. I was never shown how to open an account myself. So, any money I saved went under my mattress, in a pair of sneakers, or under my pillow.

In every job I had, I did what I knew: make money and spend money. What I also learned was what jobs I would and would not do to make money. McDonald's, Key Food, and Popeye's weren't lifelong careers; they were experiences, and experiences are there to teach us something, right? During my first year in college in 1992, when I was in Kentucky at Sullivan College, I took a job at Lane Bryant. I lasted two days before I quit. I wasn't fit for retail. I was not going to keep picking clothes up off the floor that people selfishly kept dropping. I would fix a table and make it presentable, and it only took one person to come and make it look like I did nothing. I was over it. Again, I was bored and unfulfilled. This job, and others like it, taught me that I was the type who needed to be challenged, and my interest needed to be piqued. I was not cut out to do things just to do it. I eventually applied for a job at the local Salvation Army, where I was in charge of the gym. Now this I could do. I ran scrimmage games, taught kids how to play, and engaged in some play at the same time. This job allowed me to interact with the people doing what I love. This was my comfort zone. This would be my outlet whether it was a job or volunteer work.

After the Salvation Army, every job I pursued had me gravitating to sports, which was no surprise. When I left Lexington 1993 and moved to Bowling Green, KY, to join the WKU Lady Toppers, our schedules were so busy with school and traveling I didn't engage in working until the season was done. That was an NCAA rule, anyway. I was on a full basketball scholarship, so my primary needs were met— room and board, meals, and books. Anything outside of that was on us. Nobody explained that part in detail to me and my mom. When they say full ride, we thought I didn't have to come out of pocket for anything. Unfortunately, no matter how many game tickets were sold, I still had to call home for money. Clothes, toiletries, and other things weren't a part of the package. It especially got frustrating when we would travel and visit local malls and outlets, and I had no money to buy a pair of socks if I wanted. I did have the debit card with cash my mother put on it, but I used that for food and essentials from month to month. I did *not* feel good. We got a meal per diem, but if we spent that, it cut into our meal purchase for that day. That was annoying. Why take my broke ass to a mall in these cities if I couldn't shop? That's like handing me a bag of money and telling me I can't spend it. This frustration built along with the constant calls home asking for money. My mother always deposited money monthly into my checking account, but it wasn't enough to keep up with the lifestyle I was tempted to create.

When that first credit card came in the mail that I didn't apply for, I immediately ran to my dorm room and activated it. It was a small balance of $500, but it was enough to now go into a store and walk out with something. As good as it felt, I didn't realize the monster I was creating. I knew I could afford the card. With the monthly deposits my mother made, I could cover the minimum payment. After a few on-time and extra payments, rapidly, the limits increased, as did my balances. I did not apply for these cards, they just came, and once they saw I could manage the first $500 card, others followed quickly.

I had no experience with having cards in my name. I used my mother's cards a few times back in high school to rent cars, but I paid for the cars when I returned them, so I didn't have to worry about a balance. I had no knowledge about how credit cards worked or what was expected of me. I just knew the problem was I had very little money on these road trips, and the solution was these new cards with large limits. By my junior year, I had about five credit cards with a minimum of $1,500 limits. My sneaker and clothing game was solid now. I had these things prior, but this time I was paying for them, not calling home all the time. I had a plan. At the end of the season, I would get a job and pay them off, well, at least down so I could keep using them. Giving a broke sophomore college student credit cards with high balances was a disaster waiting to happen. What I didn't know was this is what these credit card companies were banking on, me paying them interest from the debt I was building. For the first year, my mother would help me keep up, but by my junior and senior years, I was out of control. Those summer jobs during the off-season helped, but by my senior year, I had about six cards. I told my mother about three of them, but the others I was excited to have but too embarrassed to admit I had. I maintained control of my spending. In 1996, my debt got out of hand when I moved to Cincinnati, OH, and called myself being independent and able to handle whatever life threw at me. When I moved to Ohio, I worked at odds-and-ends jobs to pay bills and hang out with friends, but I had no idea where my life was going at that point. I was running from one crazy self-created experience to another. I knew I had to work to keep my apartment, car, and food, and to have gas in my car. Not until I got into a car accident did things go crazy. The injury I suffered from the impact had me out of work for a few months with no money coming in.

Bills continued to come in and get behind, but because I had to finish therapy before the car accident case was settled, I had no money to pay the bills. I took the money I did have and caught up on some bills, but that didn't stop my car from being repossessed one week before the settlement. My mother held my rent down and sent me money for food. Back then, my rent was $350. Half of my credit cards were in collections, and I lost the jobs I had. At that point, I knew I had to face the fact that moving back to NY was my only answer. I had very little money, no car, and no solid plans for my life. The summer of 1997, my mother rented me a U-Haul, and with the help of some friends, I loaded that truck up with my cat Tiger, and we drove 13 hours straight to Queens, NY.

I didn't see any job I did as a solid or serious career, because I still had so much basketball left in me, I missed competing even after the poor decision I made in stepping away from the game. The fact remains that I love playing basketball, and that was what I saw myself doing.

Charting the Course of Ownership

Let me be real, the journey to becoming an entrepreneur is a long, grueling, lonely, stressful road, especially when the leap starts a little later in life. At the core, every entrepreneurship takes an exhilarating commitment to a specific vision. It is a path filled with challenges, triumphs, and countless opportunities for personal and professional growth. It starts with identifying a problem or an opportunity and envisioning a unique solution or innovation that can make a difference. Inherently, it involves taking risks, stepping outside of my comfort zone, challenging the status quo, and embracing uncertainty. The quest for knowledge and growth is never-ending. I adopted a perpetual learning mindset and sought out opportunities to expand my skills, knowledge, and expertise. Then it's turning ideas into reality, which takes discipline, execution, and tenacity. It's not an overnight process; for me, it's taken years, and those years came with overcoming obstacles that seemed never-ending. I thought because I didn't figure out my business ideas and the money to fund these ideas, my visions were dead, but that was far from the truth. I learned to flip how I was defining failure to understand those were opportunities for me to approach my vision differently and refine my strategies. I always saw failure as me doing something wrong, but it's really about adapting to what needed adjusting and having the willingness to pivot.

A big part of those pivots was building a robust network of like-minded individuals, mentors, advisors, and potential collaborators that would challenge my thinking and provide support during my highs and lows. To preserve my dreams, it meant changing my circle. I wanted a circle that consisted of people who had the same ambition to own something, and I found myself walking with a much smaller circle. It took a high level of commitment, and it wasn't for the weak and definitely not for the fearful. I thought I had the strength to reach that level of commitment, but my fear outweighed everything and blocked my visions. Fear slowed my process—but so did people who made me question my journey and distracted me, which is why it was vital for me to tighten my circle. To get to success, you need fewer detractors, so as I began to build that circle of people, the fear lessened. It was also important that I make sacrifices if I wanted to become a successful business woman. Making those sacrifices would allow me to streamline all areas of my life: physical, mental, financial, spiritual, emotional, social, occupational, and intellectual. Let's look at my love of sneakers (financial) as an example. I had a habit of buying sneakers. I love a fresh pair of kicks. I used to shop for sneakers every pay day, and oftentimes in between. Not because I needed them but because I loved them. It was a habit I had since I was young, and it just grew year over year as I made more money. Oftentimes, when I would find myself overthinking, I would find myself at a shoe store looking for a temporary fix. Not until I started educating myself about money and planning for retirement did I start calculating how much closer I would have been to retiring comfortably if I would have purchased more Nike stocks than I did Nike sneakers. This led to me evaluating my spending habits as a whole. The reality was I wasted more money on liabilities and had no tangible assets. Every pair of sneakers I bought, cars I leased, sunglasses and watches I splurged on, none of it accumulated to any kind of wealth for me. None of it. I spent the majority of my life making someone else rich while I was living life poor. The more I spent on carless purchases, the more I gave away years of hard-earned money that did not work for me.

And it wasn't just about the money I spent but the money I would set aside in my retirement accounts. I didn't heed the advice of those who recommended that I maximize my annual contributions to my retirement accounts when I first started working. Although I had automatic monthly transfers of a few hundred dollars into my savings and checking accounts, I frequently dipped into these funds instead of investing the money and allowing it to compound. It's a damn shame all of my years of education and not one level taught me this. Reading financial literacy books taught me this and taught me this in my late thirties and not while I was in my twenties and had time to really make all of the money I earned over the years work for me. This is why learning about ownership took me longer to process because by the time reality hit me about my ignorant money mindset and habits, I was approaching forty and scared to take risks in fear of losing the savings I had. My habits made me more comfortable with material purchases than investing into solid assets. Every time I went to start a business, I got scared because I knew my common sense about money needed changing, and that's when I started reading as many books on the subject as I could find. I used to go to the Barnes and Noble by St. John's University on Union Turnpike and load up on business and financial literacy books.

During COVID, I started learning about the stock market and how to capitalize there, too. I was on overdrive, but I had to slow down because I found myself gaining knowledge but not applying it. When I finally got to a space where I was ready to see how much I knew, I realized I had to work on my mindset. Learning all of this information was nothing if mentally I didn't have the confidence. I found myself one decision away from walking clear off the path because of what I had to give up to see my vision through. Not only is sacrifice required but so is the work that goes into believing in one of the many ideas I had, choosing the right one, and forging full speed ahead. It gets hard and stays hard. Even after the hard work seems done, there is always more. For years, I was committed to the idea of becoming a business owner, but my mindset wasn't aligned with the process. The thought of giving up shopping for clothes and shoes weekly, vacationing three times a year instead five or six times was torture, but when I made a list of what I wanted my life to look and feel like, I realized those things kept me mentally and financially broke and began changing gears quickly. A profound realization hit me when I calculated the hypothetical value of Nike stocks if I had invested in them fifteen years ago until today. This eye-opening moment served as a catalyst for transforming my perspective on money and prompted me to make significant changes in my financial mindset.

If no one has ever told you, you will often find the only person you have to turn to is **you**. When you embark on your journey, it's important to remember that not everyone will understand your vision, but here's the crucial point many often overlook: You require a constant stream of encouragement and positivity to fuel your progress. This is the time when much-needed support is required and, it is wiser to distance yourself from all negativity rather than subjecting yourself to the influence of naysayers. People who believe in your potential and cheer you on are the best people to be around. Usually, these people are on the same ownership journey as you or have already achieved what you are after. Their unwavering support will empower you to overcome obstacles and keep moving forward. The path to success is rarely straightforward, and doubts may creep into your mind. In those moments, you need positive reinforcement to reignite your passion and determination. Having people flooding your space with their doubts, their fears, their ignorance, and their lack of vision and drive can push you ten steps backward if the noise infects your thoughts. There are certain individuals who I hold a special place in my heart. However, when it comes to discussing my entrepreneurial aspirations, I have made a conscious decision not to share them with these beloved individuals. Rather than truly listening to my aspirations and dreams, they tend to project their own visions onto me. In such situations it becomes crucial that I protect my dreams and nurture them in an environment that fosters support and understanding.

The very individuals who label you as selfish, crazy, or distant will witness the fruits of your efforts and suddenly seek to benefit or join you on your journey, eager to "walk the walk" alongside you when it's time to reap the rewards. This is usually the point when most of the work is done, and they want to revel in the finished product, dismissing the hard work it took to arrive at success.

They deem you *selfish* because now you keep them at arm's length and are not being who they want you to be for them. I call this *the golden round*. The golden round is the moment when you know your hard work is showing and paying off. This is that stage when people appear from nowhere and want to be a part of what you've been building and now want to invest in you. This is the stage when the money and time you no longer need suddenly becomes available. This is the part when people expect discounts just for knowing you and feel you owe them for that reason. This is the part when the majority of your support comes from people you don't know because the people you do know want something for nothing. This is the part where you grow a thick skin and meet people where they are. Don't take the noise personally and keep the faith. This is when your vision starts revealing the version of yourself you need to be to level up. People show you who they are based on your hardest roads. Those who walk with you at the hardest times are the ones you ride with.

Whatever you do, don't give up. Keep going and remember why you started the journey in the first place. I am not saying to turn your back on people because they are not aligned with your path. What I am saying is stay true to myself; this is part of the journey you get to control, and it is what will drive you to continue as an entrepreneur. Not everyone will believe in you. Sad to say, but many will not. The key is that you believe in yourself and that alone can take you further than anything others can deliver. You get to control the narrative.

Learning Who to Lean On

Journaling and prayer had their places in easing my burdens and made me take a deep look at life beyond myself. *Teaching me to accept challenges not as defeats but as opportunities to find alternate paths to triumph became my perspective.* Even if it meant embracing the reality of using a cane for the rest of my life, I learned to approach that truth with gratitude. Coming to terms with the distinctions between being injured and being disabled, and understanding my purpose in facing both, has become an ongoing mission for me. Meaning, despite which one I am faced with, it is important for me to contribute to life on purpose regardless of setbacks and limitations. Yes, it means doing things differently, and even thinking differently, but it doesn't mean stop trying to work my way through it. Is every day a battle? Absolutely, but this will not defeat me. Of all the things I've been through, this will not be what wins. There's not a single day where I don't feel pain, but I continually dig in my reservoir of strength, resilience, purpose, and hope to make it through the day better for the next. I've become mindful of what I say, what I choose to think about, and my intentional choices. Words hold immense power, and I awaken each day with the conscious choice of using words that will align with the positive outcomes I desire from this experience. Some way, somehow, I will reclaim my life. Even if that involves shifting the focus away from myself and onto others, finding peace in my heart. This book serves that purpose for me. The potential impact it could have on others as well as myself fuels my determination.

What Happens After The Game

When I tell you angels come in all shapes and forms, I lived it to be true. I discovered my accountability partners through this experience, radiating the right energy for all the right reasons. It's only fair that I pass that forward. My faith remains steadfast, praying that the insurance company acts justly at all times, and that my attorneys continue to prioritize my case, recognizing the urgency it holds in my life. I'm immensely grateful for Tam Tam, my brother's girlfriend, whose wisdom keeps me on a healing path. Her unwavering support and guidance carry profound intentions. Often, the faith that others carry can be transferred, leaving a lasting healing impact beyond the initial conversations. Both she and Carlene, despite how frequently I reached out, always answered. The rock that Carlene has been for me throughout the last couple of years of this process is a testament to her compassionate heart. My aspiration is to mirror the positivity that I receive from others. They stood by me throughout this journey, a kindness that, regrettably, I can't say applies to many I've been there for. Thankfully, those troublesome relationships have faded, and I am emotionally at peace about it. It remains true that life's most demanding tests can upend relationships that weren't meant to endure. Gratefully, I ceased pouring energy into those unreliable connections and redirected my focus toward the people whom God has blessed me with. I concentrated my efforts on those deserving of my attention, while releasing the others in my prayers. I needed to change more than I needed them to change. These moments were my awakening, my lessons, my reality to see, and stop making excuses for people. *I had to stop being a call away for people who were sending me to voicemail.*

The Spark I Needed to Offer This Book

In 2020, when the onset of the Covid-19 pandemic led to lockdowns, I embarked on resuming the process of giving voice to this book. The stories and experiences I've been recording in journals throughout most of my life began to coalesce into a coherent narrative during a motivating phone call with my childhood friend, Kesha. She persuaded me to share my story, and I discovered that recounting my truth was a form of therapy that prevented me from relinquishing hope in the life I was grappling to perceive in the present moment. Pouring my thoughts on paper has always been my way of releasing, allowing myself to feel, and learning more about who I am. With the gradual loss of sensation in my right arm and hand, I faced uncertainty about how I would manage to document everything. The prospect of typing it all out seemed exceedingly time-consuming. Taking Kesha's advice to heart, I began articulating my thoughts into a recorder and using software on the computer to transcribe my spoken words. I spoke at length, generating fifty chapters of content across three separate Google drives and amassing experiences that could potentially fill at least three books of notes up to the current date. Once again, life demonstrated its knack for turning challenges into opportunities. *I knew this book needs to be written not just for the healing of the little girl in me, but for the brilliant woman I am destined to be.*

Among my writings from prior years, I rediscovered my aspiration to become an entrepreneur. In 2017, I had filled a composition book with ideas about wanting to invest in real estate, opening laundromats, and reviving my sports organization focused on nurturing female basketball players. However, the injuries I sustained in 2018 forced me to put these plans on hold, intending to strategize once I improved my health. By 2020, I had plummeted so deeply into a sense of defeat that achieving those goals appeared more unattainable than ever before. The test has now evolved into a quest to attain those ambitions, even in the face of limitations on my abilities. I strive to maintain the perspective that these injuries, while persistent and sometimes worsening, are ultimately temporary. By 2021, the prospect of real estate investment began to seem feasible, thanks to a connection I forged with a real estate agent through a social group on Facebook. She illuminated pathways that made it appear achievable, until I underwent another significant surgery that same year. This was followed by two more surgeries in 2022. The more determinedly I tried to forge ahead, the more the vision seemed to be put on hold. At this juncture, the doctors began discussing the possibility of permanent injuries, potentially rendering me permanently disabled or immobilized in certain areas. The topic of surgery resurfaced, this time concerning my back. Growing weary of feeling like a perpetual subject of experimentation, I found myself at fifty years of age, standing at the precipice of numerous opportunities, and the last thing I wanted to entertain was the notion that my life was coming to an abrupt halt once again. It was in this context that my accountability partners emerged, offering a renewed sense of hope and purpose.

Accountability Partner #1

Allow me to explain the concept of an accountability partner. An accountability partner is someone whom you form a mutual agreement with to support and hold each other responsible for achieving specific goals, tasks, or commitments. For me, my accountability partners embodied encouragement, motivation, and a shared sense of responsibility. My accountability partners emerged from diverse backgrounds, including strangers, newfound friends, and a few family members. Among them were four key individuals: Marsha, whom I met during covid over social media during the covid-19 pandemic. As a real estate agent, Marsha assumed the role of holding me accountable for my aspiration to build a real estate portfolio. Our talks required weekly check-ins. During these discussions, we delved into education and plans as investors within real estate. This consistent exchange suited both of us perfectly, as it enabled us to address challenges head-on, adapt our research methodologies and strategies, and provide one another with candid feedback. Marsha's presence served as a motivational force, urging me to transcend the limitations imposed by my circumstances and explore innovative pathways to achieving my goals. Through this alliance, we extended mutual support, tackled problems collaboratively, and brainstormed ways to bolster our respective weaknesses by tapping into the strengths of others. The crux of our partnership rested on our shared desire to witness each other succeed.

Accountability Partner #2

Next, I crossed paths with Mrs. Myers through a social media group focused on career support. I reached out to her seeking guidance on navigating the obstacles I encountered in my career now that I was plagued with all these limiting injuries. I needed help with seeing the other side of how I could discover ways to do what I enjoyed even if it meant doing it other ways. Right from the start, her energy exudes positivity. Similar to Marsha, she offered unwavering support. I was able to talk through various scenarios, and importantly, to *stay committed to the dream*. A friendship formed from her ability to support and my ability to mirror what she was pouring into me with projects she was working on.

The interactions were characterized by a dynamic exchange of uplifting ideas, as well as our roles as trusted resources for one another. We were able to help recognize the creative and passionate facets of each other's persona, specifically in relation to building up youth, our passions and ideas, and communities. Through our discussions, I underwent a small transformation, peeling back layers of doubt and uncertainty. This process enabled me to shift my perspective from focusing on what I couldn't do to envisioning what I was capable of achieving, *realizing the resilience within that refused to be silenced.* The encouragement she provided acted as another catalyst for me to keep working on this book. I was able to embrace my vulnerability and discuss the difficult aspects of my journey from my past until right now. The potency of my journey ignited a desire within me to share it, and furthermore, be as transparent as I never have before.

Accountability Partner #3

My third accountability partner came through the process of reconnecting with my faith, and this was inspired in an informed way by Tam Tam. Tam Tam happens to be my brother's girlfriend.

She possesses a remarkable ability to perceive life through the lens of thoughts, beliefs, and the spoken word, and connecting it all through manifesting these into reality. Our conversations are geared toward heightened sense of awareness—not just in what I believed, but also in the manner in which I hold those beliefs. Her insights prompt me to be mindful not only of what I desire, but also of how I articulate those desires and the faith I invest in their realization. Every exchange with her becomes a lesson in choosing my words thoughtfully. She encourages me to discuss my case with a perspective centered on the desired outcome, rather than fixating on the mechanics of the people managing it. This approach has allowed me to navigate around external influences that may attempt to overshadow my personal convictions, which I know through prayer can indeed come to fruition.

Through Tam Tam, I learned to incorporate these principles into my daily life, ensuring that *how I move is aligned with my vision for the future*—starting with the way I think. The extent of her commitment fills me with deep gratitude. Her intentions are genuinely pure, driven by an earnest desire to illuminate paths for others, mirroring her own illuminating journey.

Accountability Partner #4

Another of my accountability partners was my therapist. The initial therapist I worked with taught me the significance of embracing my emotions and addressing the ways in which my injuries were impacting my thoughts and feelings. He started me on the path of understanding where my fears arise from, facing them, and living past them. He started helping me cope with my injuries and the fear of not being able to do the work I knew and love again. Our sessions were proving to be beneficial until the arrival of the Covid-19 pandemic. I received a call from his office notifying me that he would no longer be seeing patients.

Subsequently, I found another therapist who, coincidentally, bore a resemblance to the mother of one of my ex-partners. This resemblance initially triggered a response within me that I had to navigate around to keep her as my therapist. Nevertheless, she helped with providing the much-needed support I required concerning my injuries and their toll on my mental well-being. Our sessions delved into deeper territories. She unearthed the weight of the losses I experienced during the period of my injuries, the uncertainties surrounding my aspirations of becoming an entrepreneur due to my injuries, past triggers and traumas from childhood, and the reasons behind my recurrent encounters with individuals who left me disappointed. She guided me in understanding the type of people I tended to attract and illuminated the connection between those patterns and unresolved aspects of my life. Importantly, she highlighted how the lack of support I had often felt throughout my life was closely intertwined with the decisions I made, and how addressing these issues was pivotal in aligning my life with my true desires. Speaking to her brought about a sense of relief, as I felt unburdened and free from judgment when sharing my thoughts and feelings. Her support and active listening provided an invaluable space for me to be heard. While she was compensated for her guidance and insights, it was the unfiltered feedback I received that prompted me to examine and view life through a healthier perspective. Speaking to her brought about a sense of relief, as I felt unburdened and free from judgment when sharing my thoughts and feelings. Her support and active listening provided an invaluable space for me to be heard. The unfiltered feedback I received prompted me to enter a place of vulnerability and take responsibility for all of the decisions and outcomes that filter my life. I accepted the good, the bad, and the ugly, and most important, I celebrated my wins because I had way more of those than I had losses. I just concentrated too long on the losses and missed winning moments. Our sessions reaffirmed, to use *being my loudest cheerleader as a reminder to me who is number one. She equipped me with identifying the distinction between "safe" and "unsafe" people and used these dynamics as tools to recognize them throughout my life.*

As a Whole, My Accountability Partners Gave Me...

They grew to hold immense significance in my life because I intentionally prioritized reaching out to them and embracing their support. I have no room for any more life altering setbacks, at least within my control. A unique sense of vulnerability developed between us, something I hadn't permitted with anyone else during this challenging period. They didn't owe me anything, and yet their genuine presence during this time and space provided the crucial push I required to commence an inner healing journey. What truly sets my accountability partners apart is their unwavering care, driven by a sincere desire to help when they stood to gain nothing from it. They originated from an authentic place and consistently remained there. *Forgiveness allowed me to write this book. Taking responsibility is what led me to publish it. These ladies helped me with that process.*

Mental Health Awareness

Facing my mental health challenges is a very real ordeal, and I speak from a place of truth. Many people fight with internal battles that are often more difficult and silent than anyone can fathom. Personally, I'm engaged in a constant struggle between my inner and outer selves. However, I firmly believe that mental health challenges can improve with the right support. Just as we can direct our minds to think negatively, we can train them to think positively. This is a path walked by many and triumphed over by some. It takes a great deal of courage to acknowledge the genuine emotions stemming from mental health challenges, to connect with those struggles, acquire the tools to overcome them, and then relentlessly practice every possible method to combat them.

I submerge myself in inspirational literature, uplifting music, sermons, motivational speakers, daily affirmations, and constructive self-talk. But no one can rescue someone from that internal space better than the person affected. For years, my mind played tricks on me until I looked in the mirror and reminded myself that *behind the curtain of my success lies a story of relentless dedication and unwavering commitment.* The progress I had achieved and the abundant contributions I have yet to make to the world has yet been realized. *Some will say my basketball career was the catalyst of my life,*

274

but honestly, I believe the experiences that emerged from what the sport provided will emerge from the publishing of this book and the lives I believed it will impact. Resilience holds immense power. *The bravery required to outgrow the impulse to give up is profoundly rewarding beyond imagination.*

I don't think that anyone can ever anticipate or fully comprehend anyone else's internal fight. Even when we attempt to detail them, others may not truly grasp the depth this goes. It converts into a huge self-battle, which we can conquer through the determination to fight, growing through every obstacle hurled our way in an attempt to conquer us. Prayer holds tremendous strength, as the aspiration to live one's best life takes precedence. Deep within each of us resides a victor, a conqueror, yearning to emerge from the shadows and demolish those unbreakable barriers.

The realization that I may have wasted too much time sinking rather than swimming. I am resolved to avoid being the wealthiest person in a cemetery, having hoarded my potential instead of sharing it with others due to fears and acts of growing pains. True richness extends beyond mere monetary wealth. The wealth I strive for originates from utilizing my gifts, sharing them with the world, and making a positive impact through every purpose bestowed upon me by a higher power. It's about the journey and the legacy. I want to be a blessing while I am here and well after I am gone.

Defining the Goal
Part 1

I reached a point where I needed to offer myself a sincere apology for being my own harshest adversary in the realm of my wealth creation process. While I had granted myself permission to work diligently and strive for financial success, I realized that my relationship with money was far from positive and nurturing. For a significant portion of my life, I found myself trapped in survival mode, perpetuating the rituals passed down through generations within my family. These ingrained patterns were also taught to me by teachers who all came from a good place. What they didn't understand was that what I wasn't taught about life to come held me in bondage.

Allow me to explain.

In my mid-twenties, when I filed bankruptcy after college, I knew my relationship with money had to change. I wrestled with the possibility that I was unable to make good decisions when it came to money. I knew very well how to spend it but lacked the skills to multiply it and create wealth. When I looked at myself in the mirror, I saw "mistakes" staring back at me, and that was a harsh reality. In front of a judge in a Brooklyn courthouse, I stood as my hired bankruptcy lawyer spoke of the debt I accumulated from my college years into the year I left school. I never saw money as an easy thing to make or come by. I watched my mother my whole life go to work every day, working hard as the main provider of the household only to get talked into a retirement pension plan that sold her short on what she could have earned if she accepted the right buyout. Because she listened to the wrong guidance within her union, she cheated herself of tens of thousands of dollars that would have put her in a higher financial bracket. Her relationship with money was minimal but enough to take care of her family and manage regardless. She worked for over 40 years, through rain, sleet, and snow, to survive, sacrificing whatever she had to in order to make our home solid. If you only knew poor, feeling a step above where you came from made her feel like she was doing very well for herself. She knew what she was surrounded by, and her surroundings consisted of other single-parent women who were working hard, too, to make a home. We weren't born into wealth but witnessed her hard work and dedication every day. Financial literacy beyond the basics wasn't taught to her; therefore, she taught us what she knew: how to survive.

So, when I dreamed of becoming a star basketball player, it was to do what I loved and to make things easier for my mother and family. I also told myself as a teen that if I made enough money my mother wouldn't have to work so hard, my brothers wouldn't have to hustle, and they would have time to come see me play. The thought of her spreading her two-week vacation days out into 14 weeks of three-day weekends instead of taking a one- or two-week vacation all at once like most people do. This allowed her to have Fridays off and extended her weekends to three days during the summer months when I was out of school. As I aged through high school, what I believed to be true about money is it owned my mother's time. She worked harder but not smarter. It controlled her entire life with very little freedom and created no ownership for her. She rented all of her life, that's all she saw, and that's all she knew.

I inherited this thinking and didn't realize how paralyzing this way of life was until I went away to Western Kentucky and saw some of my friends, alumni, and coaches in big houses with hoops in their backyards. Taking team pictures on a yacht of one of the alumni whose house was massive, and the yacht was docked behind their house on a lakefront. This was the first time I saw what wealth and ownership looked like. Here we were, taking pictures on this beautiful boat, and to them as owners, this was their lifestyle. Ever since then, I focused my life on making money and having this lifestyle. Even if the boat just sat docked, I wanted a big house, nice cars, and a yacht on the lake. These visions were huge coming from a little girl from Jamaica, NY. There, instead of large homes, we lived in stacked in tall brick buildings. Instead of a yacht in the lake, we had the local pool. I never knew such living existed until I saw it in person. If this was the American dream, I wanted my piece of the pie. I just had to figure out how to get it. Women's basketball wasn't going to do it at that time. These families had wealth because they created ownership. They had successful businesses that would be handed down through their families, thus establishing a legacy of generational wealth. The importance of the ownership they possessed lay in their commitment to educating their families on how to harness and preserve this wealth, ensuring its continuity within their family. It was clear that working hard for years at a job like my mother did wasn't going to level us up to that status. That type of living came with ownership, ownership in assets and not a bunch of liabilities. I wanted to know what I had to do to get to wealth. My problem came with not knowing the right questions to ask these families about money or that I could even ask at all.

Where I was from, you just didn't ask adults about where their money comes from. So just like my mother, when I stepped in the real world, with college being over and money needing to be made, I looked for jobs, hoping one would afford me such living. I worked hard, leveled up within my careers, but wealth was not being created. I was just continuing the cycle taught to me because although I had a college degree, my financial literacy was still at an ignorant level. This process was frustrating because here I was in the room with some of the wealthiest people I ever knew and didn't know how to engage in a conversation about money and building wealth. I just didn't know how to start these conversations. I didn't know what to ask even if I knew who to ask. For years, my thinking cycle was that; I knew ultimately I would figure it out, but first let me apply for this job.

I focused more on chasing money than I did on educating myself about how money worked. I spent years letting money hit my hands only for me to immediately give it away, and it became clear after filing bankruptcy that I needed to set tangible goals, and how these goals would play out was based on how well I could improve my relationship and mindset about money. I'm embarrassed to write this, but I also know the importance of being transparent when I talk about the long process I went through to train my mind against what I'd grown up seeing money as and, instead, create brand new outlooks and learn around them. My journey became about "How do I change my old beliefs to encompass the life I really want?" It's good I had my mother's blueprint to start with to know what that side looked and felt like, but to keep from staying behind the times, I had to make a shift and fast. To have these epiphanies in my twenties would have been great, but to reach my forties and have to make this shift was a totally different experience. My a-ha moment came in 2013 when I heard an entrepreneur speak about building wealth for my age group, and he said, "If you want to stay broke, keep going to work for somebody else. If you want to accomplish wealth, start creating ownership." BOOM! That was it. Then some years later, I read Robert Kiyosaki's book *Rich Dad, Poor Dad*, and his breakdown of the four quadrants. That's when three things clicked for me. One, if I couldn't control my finances, it would be difficult for me to get rich. Two, to get to the right side of the quadrant, which was ownership and wealth, was my goal. Three, to increase my wealth, I would need to invest in assets. Seems simple, but it's not when your teachings are built on the minds of employees, and you lack the knowledge and skills for the process.

I wanted the freedom Mr. Kiyosaki wrote about, the lifestyle of that college alumni family. Now I didn't know much about either of these individuals' real walk to their journey of wealth; I was just witnessing the results. However, it was important enough for me to figure it out, and for me, it started with trading in novels that got me through those train rides to work for financial literacy and self-development books. I knew building my emotional confidence up, getting past my fears, and developing my mindset were great places to start.

Many of us live in the pretense of the power we give money over our lives. That old-school conditioning of going to work, paying the bills, collecting a pension thirty-five to forty years, to only be too worn out to reap the rewards from decades of hard work. I haven't officially retired yet, and I am already worn out mentally, physically, and emotionally because the more I made, the more that was required and, ultimately, demanded of me. That adds up to wear and tear that consumes the mind and body.

When I worked in Manhattan for NYCHA in 2000, I would walk two blocks to Barnes and Noble, sift through book after book, and purchase anything that jumped out to me from the books' descriptions and authors' success. I bought at least 3 to 4 new books every payday. I loved the self-help books that came with workbooks because I used those to assess myself as I read. I discovered that making building wealth my sole pursuit was not viable as my primary focus—building my knowledge was. Learning how to manage and leverage what I had would move me from being someone's employee to being a business owner. I learned quick that it wasn't about how much I made but how much I kept, how productively it worked for me, and how I could use that knowledge to help others do the same. Because I was thinking money first, I lacked finding my true motivation that would ultimately attract the money. It took me years to figure out I was working backwards. Furthermore, despite the valuable knowledge I was gaining through extensive reading, its true worth remained elusive until I took action and implemented a well-crafted plan. It was at this point a whole new level of fear began to manifest. I had become so accustomed to the security of having a job that the prospect of venturing into entrepreneurship filled me with apprehension. Becoming a business owner meant I had to sacrifice the lifestyle I enjoyed to settle for the lifestyle I needed, and I didn't fully embrace that process. I just wasn't mentally there yet. I wanted an easier way without giving up things, and that kept me on the hamster wheel. Those thoughts of taking the leap, failing, and struggling again haunted me so badly that I doubted my ideas and my abilities to execute them successfully, and I shelved my dreams. Truth be told, I lacked self-confidence and doubted my own capabilities, despite actively utilizing the same skills and abilities in my current positions that would be essential for successful ownership. The numerous books I read provided me with a wealth of knowledge and allowed me to formulate multiple blueprints. However, when it came to putting those plans into action, my execution game was overwhelmed with fear. That fear loomed over me for years, hindering my potential until working for someone else just didn't light a fire under me anymore. When this occurred, it was time to apply what I was learning, and that meant taking a leap. Born from that leap was my first investment in 2009, Pro Response Sports, Inc. (PRSI), an investment created from different ideas and visions, which offered small parts of my vision as a coach, sports consultant, speaker, mentor, educator, and author. While the vision is still a work in progress, I find solace in acknowledging the small victories that come with taking the first steps. The biggest victory to date is publishing this book, and my proudest victories are the events I held for my community under PRSI. Deep down, I always possessed the inherent capabilities. What I truly lacked was faith in my ability to confront the challenges, grow through them, embrace discomfort, and persistently persevere on the journey. It was, and still is, so important to know that this work is an ongoing journey, similar to the lifelong journey we take to grow and develop into who we dream of being.

"If you want to know how you feel about yourself, check your bank account. And if you want to know how much you value yourself, check your savings account."
Dr. Venus Opal Reese

Defining the Goal
Part 2

At the age of 14, I obtained my working papers and enthusiastically applied and got hired at the McDonald's on Jamaica Avenue. Whatever I earned, my mother let me spend how I wanted. Whenever I would get my checks, I would go to the local cash checking store to cash it, or I gave it to my mother, and she would deposit it and give me the cash. Oftentimes, I was so eager to spend my little check and didn't care about the fee the cash checking place charged. I was upset with FICA for taking so much out. I held the job for a couple of months but ultimately left because it interfered with my basketball schedules.

That moment would have been the perfect time to have learned about money. The one crucial lesson that's apparent was the lack of financial education provided by the education system. Despite their assistance in helping me obtain my working papers, they supported my entrance into the workforce, but there was a glaring absence of guidance and knowledge regarding financial literacy. Thus, I acquired early knowledge of all the factors that had the potential to keep me financially unstable and lagging behind in life—SPEND! From the very beginning of my work journey, I held aspirations of driving a luxurious car and wearing stylish clothes. However, the essential teachings on making my hard-earned money work for me were conspicuously absent from my youthful development. It became evident that there were systems in place to encourage spending at my school's store, but there was a notable void in my education that would have taught me to plan, save, and someday invest my earnings wisely.

I wasn't taught, but read later, that was poor man's thinking. In retrospect, I realize that I should have focused on leveraging my money to create assets and enable those assets to generate even greater wealth. By adopting a strategic approach, I could have grown up with a better outlook on money, consistently generating passive income that would have provided the pathway to achieving financial stability and ultimately paved the way to financial freedom.

Did you know that schools were sorted and designed to classify kids and prepare some for college and the rest for work? The term "factory model school" is seen as a metaphor for schools that were "in a sense, factories, in which the raw products (children) are to be shaped and fashioned into products to meet the various demands of *life* and it was the business of schools to build students according to the specification of these factories" (Wikipedia). To sum it up, schools were designed to create workers, and that business model still stands. Some may say that schools don't want us to learn about money. It paralyzes our potential and puts limitations on how big we can actually dream and be. I'm not going to lie; school made me scared to make mistakes. My potential was evaluated early by pass or fail based on percentages. If I didn't make the grade, then I risked being left behind. So of course, to keep from being the kid who got left behind, I made the ranks by being well above average, but that fear always remained when it came to taking tests and building the right dream. It made me scared to make mistakes and take risks. Although there are multiple answers to every question, I still had to stay within the lines of what was taught if I wanted to excel. As a kid and young teen, this may fly, but in the real world, until taught differently, you remain a product of your environment. That belief kept me scared to leap forward for many years, and if it wasn't for me seeing the world and reading books I would never find in school, I would have died with my dreams.

In high school, my basketball coaches Asch and D.A. at August Martin drilled into me that I could go to college for free playing the sport I love and that an education would give me options beyond what I was made to believe. I created cycles of financial instability that made me complacent about my appearance and got me comfortable with seeing my life as no more than an employee. Repeatedly, I was told that as I advanced in my studies and acquired more degrees, my earnings would correspondingly increase.

The courses I enrolled in provided insights into various fields of study and the career opportunities associated with said degrees. However, I can hardly recall those classes emphasizing the crucial aspect of harnessing that knowledge to create something truly my own—an avenue through which I could establish and grow as an entrepreneur. As I went on to earn two degrees, instead of me thinking *mine*, I was thinking *someone else's*. That isn't all of their fault. I take responsibility for that, too, because I should have boldly stepped out of my comfort zone, asked more questions, and read books beyond what the courses required I read. I could have joined some of the campus groups to challenge my thinking and learning and help me see life beyond a lesson plan handed to me. All my life I was taught what to learn, but it would take adulthood to teach me how to learn.

Real talk, there came a moment when I had to stop blaming the system and take responsibility for my own destiny. I realized the importance of envisioning and manifesting my aspirations beyond the limitations presented to me. Yes, it meant unlearning a lot of information, and again, I learned to lean on people leading creative thoughts to help me broaden my visions. I was only taking what I was taught all of those years and carrying it, but I didn't realize that I had inherited a system designed for me to become an employee and stay an employee. The boss in me had to meet and engage with the others bosses around me to see how leaders are really made and opportunities were created. In my community, the closest people to being bosses were drug dealers running the hood. Even my teachers and leaders in the community worked for higher-ups and were employees themselves. The corner store wasn't owned by my people, the big supermarkets we shopped in weren't owned by my people, and the stores I bought my clothes in weren't either, so the reflection of success wasn't much mine. We held big positions, but our names weren't on the front of the buildings. When I worked as a program director, coach, and executive manager, I felt like what I saw growing up, an employee holding good positions...within someone else's company.

Developing a healthy mindset and relationship with money was a gradual process that spanned years and requires a lifetime of nonstop learning. It involved acquiring knowledge and insights, unlearning preconceived notions, and dedicating additional time to cultivate a positive and balanced perspective on financial matters. I don't care what anyone says, it is impossible to build wealth if you do not have a healthy relationship with money. Remaining trapped in survival mode perpetuated a sense of scarcity, which limited my ability to see beyond immediate circumstances. I was plagued by short-sightedness, though I had it in me to be a successful boss and business owner. I was constantly concerned about making sure my basic survival needs were met, and because of this, I did not have the mental bandwidth and emotional resilience to pursue the long-term goals I had to start businesses due to mounting fear. Plus, I had to learn to separate my wants from my needs. Meaning, those weekly sneaker purchases had to come to a halt so that I could put my vision before material things.

My first foray as a business owner came in 2009, when I began Pro Response Sports, Inc., which was originally started to run basketball tournaments and leagues in my community of Jamaica, Queens. It started with me running a women's basketball league for six teams, then me running a 3-on-3 tournament for residents within South Jamaica in 40 Park, then onto tournaments for players within the community from age 8 to 24. I then combined all of those events with running instructional clinics and camps in conjunction with the New York City Housing Authority Resident Association. This allowed Pro Response Sports, Inc. to develop partnerships throughout NYC with local civic associations, health insurance companies, local banks, and organizations that were able to educate and become resources for the entire community. This was my first boost of confidence that I could run my own business. My mission became buying a building to house an athletic facility. I would get offered a position as program director, which got me the space, but it wasn't mine like I wanted. It was a start, however. Becoming a program director allowed me to offer sports and educational programs funded and housed by neighborhood organizations. I had the best of both worlds for a few years, and I had reached a peak when the executive director tried to make me choose between my community work and holding their position. Because I wouldn't compromise on helping my community, I resigned and moved on.

Even with the success PRSI had, I was getting burnt out because I was working a full-time position at York College as an academic advisor, assistant women's basketball coach, referee, and sports consultant while also running the summer basketball league for South Jamaica Houses from June to August every weekend. I was exhausted and had to make the hard decision to commit to the job side of things, again, finding a place as an employee and not the boss I wanted to build upon. Why? Because these positions were how I made a living and covered my healthcare costs. Until I was able to build my program, I allowed program directing to become my comfort zone. My financial stability came from working for someone else, and because it took up so much of my time, I couldn't develop my business ideas. As months of this turned into years, I fell back into a comfort zone I knew would temporarily make me happy.

It wasn't until my last position as program director in 2018 that I decided that I wanted to lean more into discovering who I truly could be as an entrepreneur. I was tired of working long hours for companies that didn't care about my well-being and were more concerned with how they could use the likes of me to build up their numbers and care less about the well-being of the people they were serving. It was about money and numbers and them keeping their mortgage paid and jobs secured at the expense of our community who needed options, opportunities, and resources that would essentially get them out of their circumstances and meet their goals. I wanted to and needed to be a part of projects that made a difference in people's lives without it sacrificing my sanity and personal life, too. At this point in my life, I was no longer in survival mode but prioritizing my learning to invest in myself and create goals that helped me build assets and not live on liabilities. I wanted to be in rooms and at tables with people who talked about money, showed me how to make it, and took the fear out of me investing in whatever I wanted to achieve with the right tools to be successful. I knew I had to make changes in my mindset, lifestyle, and surroundings to get to this place. Yes, it meant ending toxic relationships and being ok with spending time with myself until I figured it out. I was committed to this process for however long it took.

I found strength in my earning potential from my years of giving other businesses my time, energy, expertise, and hard work. I also found confidence in my abilities to make all of those businesses I ran successful from what I gave it. I knew I left it better than I found it through the members I served and the joy they got from my leadership. With that, I knew the leader I wanted and needed to become because of them. I had to come face to face with my strengths and weaknesses. I already knew I could make and manage millions of dollars for other companies. Now, it was time I figured out how to do this for myself. I had to break myself down to unlearn everything I was taught and develop understanding of business development and ownership. It meant facing my fears and going after the dream anyway. It meant letting go of that limited survival generational learning and creating a new normal that looked and felt like a self-image of independence and emotional, spiritual, and physical trust in my ability to create the multi-millionaire mindset. I did the work on changing my mindset, and then it was time to manifest that relentless work ethic to operate from the opposite spaces of fear, lack, and doubt.

I understand that solely working hard will not lead to wealth and may instead result in financial limitations. I also recognize that holding a job is within my capabilities, but staying in my comfort zone alone won't gain me success as an entrepreneur or amass financial freedom. I did all the right things for years, but my poor survival energy repelled money from me. Survival got me an education, a job, and even debt, but my attention and intention on becoming a millionaire by what I know would take me from being the capital to providing the capital. Becoming a Black woman multi-millionaire would be my freedom, and I was letting that light shine for me. I am open to receiving this blessing, and it is my divine right to do so.

Healing was the hard part, and it was grueling, but I know I am the answer to a lot of people's prayers, and I want them to find me so that I can make a positive difference in their lives through my services.

It is one of my hopes for this book…for you. My reward is for you to read this book. Your reward is to figure out how the information between the covers relates to your goals and dreams, use that information to fulfill your goals and dreams, and then pass that information on to be a service to others.

Welcome to my multi-million-dollar transformation.

Bankruptcy

My childhood, like many others in the world, was simple. All I had to do was be respectful and do what was asked of me, be a great student, keep the house and my room clean, don't lie or steal, to name a few things. As a young adult, I learned to step into the first phase of my independence, applying the values my mother taught me and learning how to apply those teachings, make sound decisions, and be a model citizen in a world that was mine for the taking as long as I had a clear vision of what that looked like for me. Learning to stand on my own and make sense of my identity was a whole challenge. I didn't know who I was outside of needing Mommy's guidance and support. You learn fast that nobody owes you anything, and anything worth having you have to work for.

The difference between feeling grown and being grown are polar opposites. Being a grown up comes with responsibilities that seemed easy to a teen who had Mommy spoiling her. When you start thinking you're grown, life *really* happens, and that transition from *I need* to *I have* to provide becomes real. Many people will say they reached adulthood when they were in their early 20s. On the real, I didn't feel like a responsible adult until I was almost 30. I thank God that in many situations I had my mother there, as she bailed me out of situations I would have crumbled and burned in without her. Her being there was a crutch until I began to understand the importance of standing on my own and providing for myself.

When I filed for bankruptcy in my 20s, that was my first eye opener that I wasn't as ready for the real world as I thought. I had to stand before a judge and take responsibility for money I couldn't pay back. Looking back, I cannot believe I had over $70,000 in debt minus the loan from a vehicle my mother was a co-signer on that I didn't want to mess her credit up by including student loans that could not be included in the judgment. When I walked out of that Brooklyn courtroom, I was embarrassed and relieved. However, I was more driven to not cross that bridge ever again. It's nothing like feeling so irresponsible and careless. I sat for months wondering how I let it get out of control and when I understood it happened because I had poor knowledge about how money works and how to develop healthier habits as I begin to rebuild my finances. The blessing of it all was I was able to start from scratch. No debt except for my car payments and the insurance. This was my second chance to do better and be better, and I made a conscious effort every single day to be mindful of the spending habits. I became diligent about paying bills well before they were due and saving money, but there was so much more than that. My goal then was to never be in front of a judge ever again. That to me was primary goal. The second goal was understanding how credit worked. After committing years to those things, anything after that to me was extra. Not until I got my first job with a retirement fund did I learn about IRA's and ROTH accounts. Here I was a few years out of college and not one course I took prepared me with knowledge about these important tools. NOT ONE!

Yes, I took accounting classes that taught me what columns debit and credit items went in, but none of them broke down how these formulas worked when it came to real life and not business. Not until I met a financial advisor when I played with the Sparks did I learn how to buy a stock. She purchased a few shares of Disney for me. It was a $1,000 investment that I eventually sold a few years later. I didn't know to buy and hold the stock and let it work for me over the years. I withdrew the money to use toward a down payment for a new car, something I didn't need to do at the time. If I had kept my stocks, in a little time, I would have earned the same thousand dollars and still been able to keep the investment. Ignorance is a costly thing.

When she left soon after setting me up with that account, my "stock market education" ended. It wasn't until my mid-30s and took a job at York College that the "education" returned. One of the provosts sat with me and discussed how to diversify my retirement plan for the money that would automatically come out of my bi-weekly wages. Even then, it didn't click with me to learn more about investing in the market. It wasn't something I was ever taught or made to feel it was an urgency for me to learn. My motto was make money, save some, and pay all my bills well before they were due. Another reason why I loved the American Express card was it taught me discipline of paying off whatever balances I acquired every month, and when I was able to apply for credit again a few years after filing bankruptcy that was one card I couldn't wait to get approved for. It took a while before they gave me a card, but I learned how to utilize cards like Capital One, who helped me build back up my credit and move up the ladder to get approved for the AmExes of the world.

Learning about financial economics is something everyone should take upon themselves and learn. Everything I initially learned came from my own research and buying tons of books about financial literacy. Yes, learning from mistakes was the first lesson, but learning how to not go backwards was being proactive in my learning. Reading books is one thing, applying what I was learning was another. I started listening to people when they spoke about money, and I learned how to ask the right questions to the right people. This took me years to develop. My money lessons started in my 20s, graduated into my 30s, made a lot of sense in my 40s, and became sound practices from then on.

When I was at an investment recruiting meeting with a friend who was trying to get me to join his team of financial advisors, part of the presentation discussed how money really breaks down. He asked me what I loved spending money on and of course I said sneakers. He asked me what brand? I said Nike. He asked me if I owned any Nike stocks, and I said no. He immediately asked how many pairs of sneakers I owned, and I said hundreds. He laughed and apologized for his laughter, but also said that whether I joined their team or not, he would help me see money differently by just what I shared with him. After the session, he and I sat together so he could show me what he didn't want to say in front of strangers. He showed me the price of a Nike stock. He averaged off the cost of my sneakers by what I told him. He then multiplied 250 times the price of the current Nike stock and showed me what I could have invested into an asset. He then said how the stock price increases in time, and how none of the sneakers I own held value. Even if I sold them, I would not get near what I paid for them. He was right. If I had invested in the stock over the sneakers, I would have a nice cushion. After that meeting with him, I drove home in silence thinking about what he shared with me. The moment I got home, I pulled out a notebook and my computer and started from age 20 to age 35/36 and on average calculated what the stock price for Nike was at my age of 20 and what it was at that point, and let's say, I would have done very well into the hundreds of thousands of dollars of ownership. From that moment on, I started seeing my money differently. Now it took me a while to break old habits of not buying so many pairs of sneakers, but I started saving more. I wasn't knowledgeable about how to go about buying stocks or knowing which to select, but I knew it was something I needed to take seriously. As much as I knew this information to be true, learning about investing wasn't an urgency. I still had some traveling and living to do. I always felt I had time, until time and age caught up with me. I used money I had saved for ventures at the time I was supposed to put back and never did. I kept money in banks but didn't invest it. I didn't learn that keeping my money in a bank was financial suicide until I was in my 40s. That's when compounding interest conversations were being had. I started attending investment group events more as a student to how money works than for them recruiting me as an affiliate marketer. I cared less about convincing people to join and sell products and more about understanding how to make my money work for me.

I read books like *The Compound Effect* by Darren Hardy and *Rich Dad, Poor Dad* by Robert Kiyosaki. Both books blew my mind. After reading Kiyosaki's book, I was on a straight path to ownership. I wanted to learn how to buy everything as assets. I wanted to know what that meant. The more books I read, the more I began to understand how I fell into bankruptcy in the first place. Besides never being taught money management, I never had healthy talks about money most of my life, which resulted in me making poor choices and not knowing how to make my money work for me. At that time, I needed to have more talks about money and where to put start putting it. It meant moving beyond holding money in traditional banking and thinking bigger and better.

Reading all these investment, mindset, and financial books taught me more than I ever learned in school at every level. The most productive math teaching in elementary school was basic math. After that, the rest was never used in my opinion to relate to real life. By the time I learned about real estate, investing in the stock market, moving my money out of banks and into investments, I was reluctant about the process without losing it because it wasn't invested properly. After the stock market crash of 2008 and 2015. I didn't have any confidence in putting it in the market so I just kept it where I knew I could control it, in my bank accounts. When I did start investing and graduating my money into the market, it did well for years, and then the COVID-19 pandemic arrived, along with a new Democratic president, and the market tanked, sending my account into a downward spiral. I tried financial advisors who I hoped would teach me as they invested my money, but learned quickly they weren't there so much to teach than they were there to convince me why my money should go where they can make money too. That's when I took it upon myself to invest my time into learning where my money should go. It is more of a fearful process now because I am in my 40s and closer to a retirement age; however, I am not able to because I have to make up for lost time when I moved money around years prior and never put it back.

At this point, life for me is more about living and creating meaningful experiences that will develop me financially. I understand so much now and with YouTube University at reach, I don't always have to pay someone to research what I can research myself. Over the years I've learned the importance of ownership, creating assets that pay for liabilities. Starting businesses that serve my purpose filled life and not creating businesses chasing the bag. All of my life I did things best when they meant the most to me and I had to get back to that. I chased the bag for years and it provided more things than it did assets. Now my mission is living a productive life and making well thought out decisions. I know what hardship looks like, now I want to experience the reward of those experiences. I'm led by my Faith and my Trust in my higher power that anything he has in my life as long as I do my part he will guide my heart and journey. Failure is never an option. Even when mistakes are made, lessons are formed, and creativity is produced upon intelligence. I regret nothing and embrace what's to come. I'm not chasing the bag; I am chasing my dreams.

What Happens After The Game

Below, I share with you lessons learned through my journey of bankruptcy, and I hope these lessons help you *before* you find yourself embarking on a similar journey.

Filing Bankruptcy

After all the late fees and interest multiplied, trying to pay down over $50K in past-due credit card debt one by one seemed impossible. I couldn't manage because the creditors kept adding on fees, even on top of extra payments I was making. It would take me years to catch up at the rate of making the minimum on some and doubling up on others. Working two jobs, I still could keep up. My car payment was $155, and my insurance was $65. Of my $2200 a month before taxes, half of that went toward the debt. The rest, food for the house, and leisure which I wasn't disciplined to not have a life. After slowly paying down some of the debt, the stress led me to ultimately consider filing for bankruptcy. Although making the payments, the bill collectors were calling my house at all hours during the day and night, threatening anyone who picked up the phone. Usually, those threats affected my mother because these people had no filter. It got to the point where they were threatening to come to our door to get their money. Of course, when they crossed *that* line, I dared them to, even told them I would be waiting on them. It just got bad. Not being able to answer the phone was nerve-wracking. That alone made the decision for me. The more I paid, the more they called demanding more. I had to reach the painful decision of filing for bankruptcy. I first did my research on the process and the aftermath of filing. After countless conversations with my mother, I moved forward with the process. Standing in front of a judge and listening to a lawyer represent my poor spending habits was embarrassing. I was relieved to have the option of starting over, but this, to me, was the worst of the worst. Hearing the judge grant the bankruptcy was a rude awakening for me. It was the wake-up call I needed to do and be better with the decisions I made in my life, not just financially but as a whole. My life from 1996 to 1999 was the reality check I needed to take matters of money and life decisions seriously. There was no more calling on Mommy to bail me out. I got into debt trying to relieve her of having to send me money in college and called myself creating independence, but ultimately, I made some decisions that really changed my life for good and for bad.

Although I was in college on a full basketball scholarship, with room and board, books, meals, and all team expenses paid for, having pocket money, and purchasing daily essentials wasn't part of the agreement. Although those major expenses being covered saved me big time, I was still a broke college athlete. So, when those credit cards came in the mail without me even applying, it was easy money. Believe it or not, nothing in my college curricula spoke to or warned me about credit cards and debt. Everything to this day, I learned about money came from trial and error and reading books that were not part of my college syllabus. The real life education I needed about survival in the real world wasn't even part of conversations. Nobody prepared me for what was ahead of me when I entered the workforce: finances, real-life responsibilities, and what the American Dream really equates to and who it is designed for. There is the system designed for those to succeed, and then there is the system designed for people to fail. If you are not asking the right questions, in the right rooms, or at the table with people living successful lives, potentially, the outcome is struggle before success. At least, that is my experience. That does not have to be for this generation because there are enough conversations, both public and private, encouraging self-education and being proactive and not reactive about life. I learned quickly that the more something threatens my vision, the more I want to create a plan to conquer it.

The Lessons of Filing Bankruptcy

The first lesson I learned is if you expect schooling to teach you about money, be prepared to struggle! This is not aimed toward any teachers, because I know many who want to include financial literacy within the curriculum, but the school system would not approve it. Rather you stay misinformed than informed and with an employee's mindset, rather than a BOSS.

To keep from making unnecessary mistakes when it comes to money, here are some tips I want to share to help you avoid the long-lasting effects filing can make on your financial well-being. Although filing bankruptcy provides a fresh start from money mistakes, if you can avoid it in the first place, that will be an essential element to improving your financial mindset moving forward. I am not a financial expert, and this is not financial advice. These are tools I practice daily in making smart money decisions. I am still a work in progress and constantly learning every day.

1. Building a healthy relationship with money should be at the top of your list. Money plays a vital role in our lives. It has a big impact on the choices you make, the opportunities you have, and your overall well-being. Having a positive mindset that can support your long-term success is the respect and balance you want to help you make conscious, effective money decisions. Think of it like this the better your mindset with money is, the less financial stress you can have, the more control you have, the likeness of you setting realistic goals, you can avoid financial setbacks, and your approach budgeting, saving, and spending with a mindset of building assets instead of liabilities. Your intentions with money become clear and purposeful.

2. Tithe and donating monthly is so important to attract good energy with money.
3. As you earn, pay yourself first!
4. Educate yourself constantly in ways that empower you to make well informed decisions with money. Whether you are making money or not, it is essential to equip yourself with practices that prioritizes your money experiences.
5. Making money is one thing, learning the importance of managing money is another. Understanding key concepts of budgeting, saving, investing, and minimizing your debt as much as possible.
6. Develop strong money management habits by creating realistic budgets that work with the income and expenses you have.
7. Prioritize your needs over your wants and budget monthly for each. Be mindful where your money is going, but never stop enjoying the money you make. This should be something you celebrate, not dread.
8. Make saving a habit. There are many ways to save whether it's in a high yield savings account and/or investing in the stock market, pay yourself first! Set up separate bank accounts for every important need in your budget: emergency fund account, monthly expenses, tithes, vacations, taxes, college, etc. Having percentages of your earnings automatically deposited into these accounts on a monthly basis will keep you from missing the money and spending it before you decide to send it manually.
9. Learn the difference between Credit and Debit: learn the basics of credit scores, reports, and how they all impact you financially. Learn the different types of debt and the importance of how using other people's money can help you create wealth.
10. Learn about interest rates, and how they play an important part in how much you borrow, how much you pay back, and how long it takes you to pay back. Learn the risks involved with

accumulating high-interest debt and the ramifications high rates have if you mismanaging these debts.

11. Always plan for the future. It may not seem important when you are young and blowing through money, but as you age and responsibilities mount up, whether you chose to started using compound interest to build upon your retirement fund or decide to invest into a retirement plan, have these goals and outline strategies to keep them funded with your long-term goals in mind.

12. There is nothing wrong with consulting a financial advisor, counselor, or a mentor, the important thing here is know where your money is going and why. It pays even more to know how to invest your own money and if you choose, be able to have conversations with who you are giving the responsibility of managing your money. You should know where your money is going, and what making those decisions will do for you in both the short and long term. Your investments should align with your financial goals whether a portion is to buy a house in two years, fund a child's education, or get married and have retirement plans based on the lifestyle you want to live. Make this a ritual, not an option.

13. Gain a basic understanding about taxes. The principles and terminologies. Learn the importance of tax deductions, credits, and tax strategies that can keep you on the advantage side of filing.

14. Keep your finances organized and within reach. What you keep is just knowing how long to keep your financial records.

15. Living within your means can be the difference between avoiding debt and accumulating it. Avoid acting on impulse, which can save you so much money.

16. Stay up to date on your current events. Listen to financial news, sign-up for financial groups emails that inform you of economic trends, and legislative changes. These are all tools to help you know when, where, and how to invest, and manage your money.
17. Celebrate financial achievements, no matter how small, recognize your wins and reward yourself for reaching milestones along your financial journey.

The Time Trap
Unraveling the Brainwash

Choosing to do something for a significant portion of your life can make it challenging to discern the need for change. Imagine this. You dedicate the prime years of your life, from 25 to 65, devoted to work, only to realize your overall lifespan may reach only 75-80. What does that imply? It implies that you spend a staggering 40 years as an employee, only to have a mere 10-15 years of freedom. Reflect on that for a moment. By the time you finally reach a stage where you can savor the fruits of your labor, you might find yourself too old and potentially too drained to fully relish it. The thought of that can bring about a profound reflection on how and what those prime years are spent doing.

Now, imagine learning in your late 30s that this information existed but you not only learned it over 15 years later than you could have started, but had to spend another five or so learning how. If you have the chance to set your money in motion and let it work for you during your 20s, 30s, or even touching early 40s, would you plan differently? I hope you would, especially if it would grant you the ability to relish an extended period of freedom, enjoying more years of unburdened financial constraints. For more freedom and life, would you exercise every possible resource available to create your own wealth doing it your way? Or would you settled for life created for you in a JOB you really don't like, just to live Just Over Broke? I think about it all the time. If I knew then what I learned to understand in my middle years, I would have planned differently. It isn't about having regrets more than it is about knowing, digging deeper in those books in the library rather than sticking solely to curriculum outlines.

I cannot stress enough—learn how to invest, teach your family how to invest, and make your money work for you. Investing manifests in many forms, offering numerous avenues for potential growth. It may involve venturing into real estate, navigating the stock market, establishing a business that generates income irrespective of your physical presence, acting as your own financial institution—Do it! Learn! Surround yourself with people who are getting it.

Today, learning tools are so readily available. The invention of computers and search engines leaves us with no excuses not to build the life we want. It boils down to wanting it or not. The hundreds of books I bought and read are now on our phones, tablets, laptops, and desktops. Google and YouTube alone are two platforms I find fascinating. Once you have a clear understanding of what you seek, the process of finding it can be streamlined to its most straightforward methods. Finding people who are aligned with your goals and streamlining their strategies becomes the norm instead of the exception.

Countless individuals strive to conceal the knowledge of achieving financial independence through self-built wealth. The economy thrives on a labor force comprised of a bunch of employees. However, the IRS tax codes are tailored to favor business owners, granting us the most advantageous tax benefits. Ponder on this: spending a lifetime as an employee only to face excessive taxes.

Businesses are designed in a manner that allows the person doing all the work to pay more taxes than their boss. Consider this scenario: an administrative assistant earning $50,000 annually may end up paying more in taxes compared to their boss, who earns $250,000 per year. How? DO the research. I can make it easy for you and explain why that is, but if I do that, you will not dig deeper into why this is an important task for you. Once you acquire this valuable information, make it a priority to share it with as many people as you can. Trust me, keeping this knowledge to yourself makes you no better than the people who didn't teach it to us. Spread the wealth and empower others with the same insights. If your desire is to become the boss, build upon your creativity. Gone are the days of thinking like the student who waits for teachers to guide them. Start living like person who filters what the educational system failed to provide.

The Snowball Effect

"The greatest glory in living lies not in never falling, but in rising every time we fall."
Nelson Mandela

Through trial and error, I learned that the secret to leading a gratifying life was mastering the art of problem-solving while simultaneously minimizing the number of problems I create. Some may be minor and can be easily resolved, while others are significantly more intricate and demand a substantial amount of energy to work through. Having the ability to solve problems without turning my life upside-down takes skills that I learn everyday as I navigate through life. Certain problems prove challenging to evade, but minimizing the impact is where I start being proactive in my understanding. Learning how to anticipate potential issues, mitigating their impact, and taking proactive measures to improve outcomes became instrumental in my self-development. Increasing my awareness and thought process allowed me to take effective actions to improve my results. To do this, I use the 3 C's of Decision-Making:

- **Clarify**—clearly identify the decision to be made or the problem to be solved
- **Consider**—think about the possible choices and what would happen for each choice and consider the positive and negative consequences of each choice
- **Choose**—choose the best choice

In using the 3 C's, I began to understand how a series of events (the cause) creates specific results (the effect), for better or worse. This enables me to bring clarity to the choices I make prior to making them. Simply, it's recognizing that every action elicits an equal and corresponding reaction, regardless of its extent.

The older I get, the more I understand to take responsibility for my life and how my actions play a part in the outcomes. For me it starts by changing my thoughts and allowing my thoughts to give me the power to create moments of small corrections. These small corrections help me execute healthy habits and build a life of substance.

Now, when I make decisions, I am instantly aware of the potential consequences of my actions. I ask myself, "If I make this decision, will it give me the outcome I want? If not, can I live with the outcome I receive?"

When I began to make changes in my life, I played in my head the pros and cons of working for myself. Some of the pros were my ability to create financial freedom, the flexibility I would have to customize my vision my way, the success I would build, the people I would help, and the limitless knowledge I would have to attain my dreams. The satisfaction that comes with feeling the confidence that gives me permission to grow in the most intentional way is liberating. The inspiration that comes over me by the pure thoughts of exceeding levels by breaking barriers that I blocked years prior filled me.

But I couldn't write a wonderful list of pros without acknowledging the risks and the fears that are triggered. One cannot measure being an entrepreneur based solely on every positive outcome. The fact remains that the cons that exist are real. Business ownership is a stressful process. Anyone who tries to tell you differently is not being truthful with you. There is that fear of failing and losing every cent you put into it. There's the fear that people will not like what you are selling them. It's the possibility of running out of money or not making all the right decisions at the right time to stay afloat.

While all those things can potentially happen, *everything* can all happen, including the pros, and the business will be a major success. I remind myself often that all it takes is one idea to spark a vision that can make an impact on my life and the lives of others. What I don't want to do as a business owner is create a snowball effect of thoughts and actions that sabotage the experience before it happens. That was a part of me that needed to change. Developing that habit delayed my dreams, but now my drive is to get started. Staying knowledgeable in my field became a top priority and left no room for failure. I can either plan to succeed or plan to fail. The choice is mine, just like the choice is yours. Many people fail because they give up on their potential to figure it out at all costs.

Part of my "figuring it out" comes from getting started regardless of where I am in the process. Just Start! Reading helps me strategize what I am doing now and prepare for five years from now. I set a goal to do something every day that will lead me toward the results I want. It's asking the right questions to the right people to get me to my goals. It's constantly educating myself to stay on top of my game. It's operating well above my means and believing in my capabilities enough to make the right decisions at any given moment.

Yes, things will seem unstable at some points and will require extremely long hours. However, when it is hours I am putting in toward a dream I believe in and want more than anything, I am not looking at the clock. I am tracking progress. Once my goals are reached, I am now ready to become repetitious with the process by duplicating the vision and making it available to the masses.

I know I have the confidence to be successful in business ownership, and I am willing to obsess over it. All it takes is one idea and the inspiration to execute it that will change my life forever.

Study People Who Have Achieved What You Want

Life is hard enough as it is and with so many successful people and ventures that exist, why reinvent systems if we don't have to. There are reasons why books are made, and stories are told. We either learn how to use other people experiences and techniques and apply them to achieve our own goals or take the long road start from scratch and use the next ten years to create what could be done in two or three years. Why make life harder than it needs to be?

I want to become a successful speaker and mentor to student athletes. I know that there are many who are doing it and have done it and made a great living at it. So, my technique is to learn from these masterminds. The biggest advantages I have for studying successful people in this area is learning from their experiences and mistakes. What better way to build a business than off the valuable insights of what works and what doesn't based on others efforts in this field. I want to know their mindset, their habits, and the strategies they use that helped them achieve success.

I have an appreciation for Tony Robbin's high energy and interactive seminars. His ability to motivate and speak before millions of people around the world focused on the power of mindset and personal development is amazing. Using his system and making it my own among the audience of young minds is one of my speaking goals.

I am also inspired by Les Brown, a motivational speaker and author whose powerful speeches on overcoming adversity to achieve success is not only healing for me but also helps me tell my story from a place of obstacles to a place of overcoming.

Then there's Brendon Burchard, who speaks from a place of coaching high-performance habits and routines that builds clarity, achieves goals, and focuses on developing the entrepreneurial listener.

Lisa Nichols' stories about her challenging environment, including poverty, abuse, and having low-self-esteem speaks to a wide culture of people who needs to hear someone who advanced with the will to succeed and developed her brand based on letting us know we have the power to create the life we want despite our circumstances.

These four motivational powerhouses took their experiences and put them into messages that encourage others to take action toward their goals. That's exactly what I want to do. Take bits and pieces of each of their gifts, make them my own, and inspire others to focus on their strengths, face their fears, emphasize self-care, and to prioritize our well-being as we pursue our dreams. They're doing it. They have the future I want, and I will utilize their mastermind to help build my brand. Again, why reinvent the system, just customize it to match the success I want to achieve and thank them along the way for showing me how to do it. I'm confident, one day someone will feel the same way about me.

Unveiling My Inner Self

Affirmation: I am confident in the woman who is staring back at me.

One day while journaling, I asked myself, "How many times have you looked at yourself in the mirror and said, 'I love you' and was 100% happy with who was reflecting back at you?"

That moment occurred in 2015, and as soon as I asked it, I realized that the hardest thing for me to do was to look in the mirror, be honest about who was staring back, and accept how I needed to love and appreciate more of her.

Don't get me wrong I love so many things about myself, but I realized at that moment I had some major work to do on my self-expression. I wasn't quite fulfilled within my career, my relationship needed improving, my family dynamic still had been damaged for years, and my approach to life was totally unbalanced. I had a long list of goals and plans but had very few major items checked off because I got comfortable with where I was in life although I wasn't fulfilled or satisfied with where I wanted to be. I wasn't in touch with stretching myself when leaping got extremely uncomfortable. Realizing this revealed that I didn't have it all together as I thought I did—talk about the WOW factor or that a-ha moment. There's nothing more uncomfortable than discovering that my definition of happiness was being sacrificed for external "things" and not internal satisfaction.

The hard truth came by acknowledging that I was working in a career that left my glass half filled. I went to work every day, leading teams of individuals and serving thousands of others hoping to find relief in my desire to serve. I needed the tools to learn how to balance what I had and where I was going without acting ungrateful for what I achieved. As leadership roles require, I had to be accountable for myself and all those whom I signed in and out for at all times. With that thinking, I was working backward. I put the job and others' needs before my own and wondered why the work I was doing was not fulfilling me. Again, I was repeating behaviors from college, when I would put the emotional sadness of my family not being around before my own happiness. This was no one's fault, not even mine. It was just another level of my life where I was changing, and I needed to understand what that change consisted of. This level had me wanting more and seeing new visions for my present and my future.

I became a case study within my career. My wake-up call came when my time away from work wasn't my time, and I didn't know how to set boundaries to have a healthy personal life without feeling like I was complaining. My days off weren't days off, and vacations weren't vacations. There was always a constant need for me to lead, even when there were others capable of leading but wasn't ever challenged to exercise their ability to do so before me. The emails never stopped. I would go through hundreds of emails during the course of a day, and by morning, there were hundreds more. This often meant I would wake up two hours earlier than I needed to just to minimize that email list before I got into the office because I knew stepping into the building came with its own needs. I figured if I minimized missing urgent emails I could focus on my staff and patrons that warranted my attention.

Demands were always high, someone always needed something, and everything was urgent to everyone, even when it wasn't. When something didn't get done, fingers were pointed at me because I was in charge. There was a new list of to-dos that included my workload and the work of a manager who finessed her responsibilities onto me revealing more of what she wasn't capable of doing even in her position. Always a group to try to please and always that group that can never be pleased. The worst part was that no matter how much of myself I gave, it was never enough to catch up with the demand. Professionally, I wanted to do whatever it took to make sure my t's were crossed and my i's were dotted. Mentally, I wanted to manage it all productively, but physically, I was depleted, and this is when I knew something had to change. I felt my soul being sucked out of me with each day that passed. What used to be exciting and fun turned into me questioning who I was becoming and whether I wanted to continue down this road. I was given responsibilities and worked like my name was on the building.

Advancing within my career year after year was always a great accomplishment. Every experience taught me so much about leadership, ownership, business management, community, and using my creativity, which was everything I saw designed for me. However, it had also shown me how much I minimized my own needs to satisfy the majority.

I read all kinds of leadership and self-help books to understand and put new practices in place to help me create balance while keeping my sanity, too. I was searching for answers from my readings, from the work I did, and from others, only to discover that the answers would only come from God and me. I loved what I did on my climbs up the ladder, but I was unhappy with how much energy people were taking out of me along that climb. I led with the mindset that I was shaping and changing lives for the better, but I didn't see that I was consenting to not being content with my own. I endorsed this line of work for another five years or so before I made the decision to leave the field altogether. Deciding how I gave my services would be built on my terms. I needed to rebuild myself, starting with making healthy choices that gave me healthy results. This wasn't just about my professional life; this was about my life as a whole.

Mentally, I left my career a few years prior to this self-discovery. Physically deciding enough was enough in 2019. Two major benefits that came from holding such a profession for over 15 years were one, I realized what I always knew—that I am more than capable of being my own boss and can still add value to people's lives; and two, I was great at building businesses from grassroot stages, which solidified to me that I was equipped with the tools. I just needed to become as successful as an entrepreneur as I did as an employee. A third benefit was that I knew no matter what profession I shifted to, my gift was to work with people, so I needed to learn a different approach to leading and giving. The journey of my life came as it should have and just like my career as an employee, my journey as a thriving business owner will come with lessons I learned along the way of do's and don'ts and wills and won'ts—all done from a place of growth and not hindrance.

This came from a perspective of setting and sticking to boundaries, accepting the roles from a place of growth and not self-judgment, and getting back to loving the work I do. It also came from learning how to receive scrutiny without taking it so personally, learning how to celebrate all wins, and not putting so much pressure on myself to have all of the answers. I recognized my need to shift my mindset so intensely to recognize judgmental zones of people and methods for dealing with them. This meant listening without taking anything personally. It meant understanding without always wavering. It meant taking the good with the bad and waking up the next day to a fresh start. It also meant accepting scrutiny with professionalism so much so that it registers as information and receiving the message at which it is intended without me adding unnecessary emotions to it.

Once I learned this, I began to reward myself with positive thoughts, feelings, actions, and results.

This shift showed up greatly in my personal life as well. Instead of "tolerating" things, I set boundaries and met people where they were. Accepting this growth showed me what I was accepting in my personal life, and this recognition started creating distance from people to whom I'd given power to that didn't deserve space.

I like to keep people around me who don't tell me what I want to hear. Instead, they tell me the truth. I can take it. However, what I don't have room for is disloyal people. I can handle hard-nose talks, and I respect knowing how you feel first rather than hearing it from others first. Once I lose trust and respect for you, it is easy to remove the negativity from being around me. That to me is a conscious state of being in touch with my actions and correcting it. There's good, there's bad, and then there's reality. An important part of being in touch with who you are represents the energy we allow around us. If something shows up in my life that disturbs my peace, I've learned tools to reject it and move on. Owning my power and peace are two gifts I can control, and what I cannot control I give it to the powers that be. I speak peace over my life, and that's where my self-judgment lies. That has everything to do with me and no one else.

A Change of View

The confidence I possessed at the age of 40 differs from the confidence I now hold at 50. At 40, it felt like all the pieces of my life were falling into place. I held respectable jobs, earned well, owned a nice vehicle, and resided in a beautiful, secure home. My financial situation was stable, I could travel at my leisure, and opportunities were abundant. Managing the external aspects of my life came naturally. However, the internal facets, such as love, connection, and my struggle to trust others, posed challenges. The inability to trust the intention of others stands out as my most profound insecurity, impeding my efforts to let others into the depths of my heart experiencing meaningful relationships.

This challenge has persisted since my pre-teen years. Instances of abandonment, stemming from my father and brothers repeatedly breaking promises, fostered feelings of inadequacy. This led me to believe that I wasn't sufficient to the men in my life—that their lack of effort in being the positive male figures I needed meant I fell short. As an adult, my objective was to pinpoint these defining moments, acknowledge their impact, and focus on overcoming them. However, letting go of these moments from the past proved to be more complicated than it seemed. What took me several decades to comprehend, dug up the nature of my triggers and their origins. Once I pinpointed those pivotal moments, I had to confront my past by acknowledging where the trauma continued to manifest from and then take control of it.

Throughout my twenties and early thirties, I had a recurring habit of attributing my triggers to the world around me, mainly because I hadn't yet grasped their nature. During those years, I was deeply engrossed in traveling and playing basketball, leaving me little time to confront and examine my emotions. I found solace in immersing myself in the game, my lifestyle, and my apparent ability to conceal my pain and issues – or so I believed. I managed to veil my inner struggles by viewing each experience, interaction, and moment as transient. Consequently, my mindset revolved around safeguarding my heart, soldiering through each instance while only offering small pieces of my true self, all within the confines of predefined norms.

The most unfortunate aspect of aiding such unproductive patterns was that I assembled barriers that prevented people from truly understanding the authentic me – the version of me that yearned for closeness and affection, qualities that might have been reciprocally shared on a deeper level. I presented a front that seemed solid enough, yet unwittingly undermined any potential for fostering enduring connections plagued by fear. This fear was rooted in my dread of experiences, sorted of disappointments that had characterized my journey from childhood to early adulthood. In this process, I was unknowingly crafting a more resolute, but less favorable version of myself – someone likable and lovable on the surface, but ultimately non-committal in many situations that made room for deep connections in loving others. My words presented with actions would present a commitment, but the barriers I built managed to be my safety nets.

Don't get me wrong, I was open to forming connections, and I even had some genuinely great relationships that blossomed into healthy and meaningful friendships. There were moments when a handful of truly remarkable individuals succeeded in breaking through the barriers of my guarded demeanor, granting them the privilege of witnessing my vulnerability. Despite the challenges, the effort put into nurturing these relationships was unquestionably rewarding. However, it's important to note that this openness didn't come effortlessly. While the outcomes were valuable, my ability to fully embrace vulnerability remained a constant struggle. Whenever I sensed even a hint of losing emotional control or found myself in unfamiliar territory, my instincts kicked in. I would instinctively retreat, raising my emotional guard as a protective shield against potential unforeseen pain.

This defense mechanism stemmed from my past experiences and the feeling of constantly being disappointed. It wasn't a conscious behavior, but rather an automatic response that had taken root over time. While I recognized the worthiness of some of these relationships, I found it challenging to override this instinctual response to retreat and protect myself, even when it was clear that such defense mechanisms were hindering the deeper connection and growth that could be achieved through vulnerability. I learned I couldn't be vulnerable within relationships because I really didn't have a deep understanding of what healthy love and bonds consisted of.

When someone laid it out plainly for me, it became evident that during my upbringing, I observed relationships operating on the foundation of individual wants and desires, seeking to love others based on what makes me feel loved personally. However, the crucial understanding that authentic love involves embracing and valuing the intricate aspects of someone's identity and their unique yearnings for love from others. This goes beyond imposing my own preferences onto them; instead, it involves appreciating and reciprocating the forms of affection that resonate with their essence. Not only did this make sense, it explained what I needed to do to get relationships right. We all know the concept of love languages. Taking that test popularized by Dr. Gary Chapman in his book "The Five Love Languages", helped me understand what resonates for me from others, and the importance of understanding the expression of those I cherished. Genuine connection and healthy communication is led by understanding and not reflection. This was a game changer for me.

This taught me that it wasn't that I didn't want these connections. I was more than capable of giving and receiving it, I just needed to understand how to fully engage and trust myself to understand these hesitations by gaining the knowledge that provides healthy emotional tools. This lesson would come once I retired from playing basketball professionally, sit with myself, invest in learning, and start shedding layers that acted on automation, and needed to be reprogrammed.

Subconscious Impacts

Because I did so much traveling and meeting so many people, there were very few moments I choose to set aside time for a single person to fully provide everything I needed all at once. I was comfortable with constant variety and change; that felt safe for me. I was comfortable with the barriers I put for myself. I struggled to live long in happiness without always having that constant fear of being disrupted by a negative event. Growing up in the housing projects, were R.I.P. was a constant phrase used. The crack cocaine epidemic of the 80's and 90's spread rapidly, claiming lives left and right, along with people who hustled. I came to understand that a portion of this tragedy stemmed from inability to properly cope with the loss of a dear childhood friend named Darnell. We were inseparable during our junior high school years, playing basketball daily, sharing laughs at school, and nurturing a deep friendship. Darnell acted as my protector, fending off boys who showed interest in me and even threatening those who tried to disrespect me. Our friendship accelerated when we both made it onto the basketball team at I.S. 8. Each day, before and after school, we'd meet up at our schools basketball courts, whether to practice our shots, play a few games, or walk into the building side by side. He was the one who tried to make up for the times my brothers promised to come to my games, and never showed. He was the one who would say, "I'm your big brother. I got your back."

Years of camaraderie were shattered in mere moments when I arrived at school one morning, only to find Darnell missing from our usual meeting spot – his life snuffed out the night before. That devastated me, our team, our school. He was full of life and so funny. Always smiling and just an overall good person. He was more than a friend to me; he was my confidant, the one who chased dreams alongside me, and helped me develop my game and confidence. A companion I shared daily laughs with and looked forward to meeting up with every day. I found myself lost in a sea of emotions, uncertain how to navigate this grief. Although our school and community united in coping with his loss, it was the first time I had lost such a close friend, someone my age, someone deeply intertwined with my heart. I was mad and confused at the same time as to why at the prime of our lives, when we were having so much fun enjoying life, he would be taken from us. School was different after his loss, playing basketball with him was different, approaching the school building was different. From then, I started believing that every time something great would happen, something bad would follow. It was hard celebrating highs, especially as our winning basketball season went on without him.

In hindsight, years later, I began to see that failing to confront the loss of Darnell set me on a path of this type of thinking. I spent a year dwelling on his loss dwelling in fear, which hindered my capacity to draw in positivity, after challenging events. I didn't know I was training myself to expect the worst before considering the best, a pattern I learned later in life my mother tends to do too. I often wondered subconsciously if I got it from her, and it just showed up in other areas of my life.

It is worth highlighting that during this phase, my life got extra focused on being the player he and I always aimed to be. Despite how I had the tendency to foresee negative outcomes after major tragedies, when it came to the game, I had the habit of unfolding the best out of myself, which I of course was my safety net.

This was a part of my past I had to confront so that I can remove that disconnect I was making between good and bad experiences. I was glad I was able to confront this because that's when it allowed me to understand where the thought started, deal with the healing needed from that moment in time, and understand the barriers I created from these behaviors.

At 50, I understand the value of relationships and how important it is to be good within yourself in order to grow with others. The patience I have now comes with clarity like I've never had before. My space is my peace, and my surroundings are chosen carefully.

Who We Are without a Title Attached to Our Name

Without a title attached to our name, we are guileless human beings. But, who are we? Titles often play a large role in defining our identities and shaping the way that others perceive us. We tend to feel lost or uncertain when we are stripped of labels, as they provide us with a sense of belonging. At the end of the day, we are individuals with our own unique experiences, thoughts, feelings, and desires. We have our own personal journeys and relationships that are all molded by the world around us.

However, it is important to remember that our worth and value goes far beyond any title or label that we may possess. At the core of who we are our values, beliefs, and natural character. These are the qualities that truly define us and make us unique.

But beyond these surface-level characteristics, who we are at our core is much more difficult to define. Some people believe that their true selves are eternal and unchanging, while others believe that we are constantly evolving and growing. Regardless of where you fall on this spectrum, it is clear that we are all more than just the titles and labels that society places on us.

Title or no title, we are afforded the freedom to discover and embrace our true selves. Imagine living a life where you are not bound by the expectations or limitations that come with roles or prestige. This can be both liberating and challenging, as it requires us to take responsibility for our own identity and to find meaning and purpose in life on our own terms.

Titles and labels do have pros that can be helpful in providing a sense of identity and purpose. They can give us a sense of belonging and direction in life. However, the cons of that comes with that can be limiting and confining, preventing us from wandering and penetrating who we really are destined to be beyond role playing.

So, who are you without a title attached to your name? That answer can be complex and multifaceted, full of potential and possibility. We are all gifted to grow, change, and discover many things about ourselves, and it is up to each of us to determine who we want to be and how we want our lives to play out. I don't know about you, but I plan to live my live being the best version of myself without being bothered by the titles and labels attached to my name because at the end of the day the real title I love and will carry without questions is "God's Child."

Don't Make Decisions Based on Your Emotions

"Don't make decisions based on what you're going through now, make them based on where you want to be."
Unknown

Like they say, when you know better you do better. For me, when I got tired of giving my energy away to circumstances, I decided to make some critical changes. No doubt life is filled with emotions that are a significant part of life. How we practice our values has a way of showing up at the most emotionally tested times. I've been in so many situations where my emotions have clouded my judgment, leading to me making impulsive and harmful choices that took me a good period of time to recover from.

I found that my emotions show up the strongest when it comes from the actions of others and my relationship with money. I learned many valuable lessons from both that have taught me to sit in my emotions before acting.

I am the type of person who does not like to argue or get into confrontations because once that bear is poked, you get what you get. When it comes to disagreements, I am open to hear your side, always will share my side, but what I will not tolerate is disrespect. We can agree, and we can disagree, but two things for me will not be tolerated in those moments, blatant disrespect and putting your hands on me.

One or both of these will release a level of anger that the Gemini in me will not hold bank her anger on. I know like anyone else when emotions are high things can be said that create regret later. I've learned that not having control of my emotions gives someone else control over me and can result in saying hurtful things that can and will damage the relationship to a point where repairing it seems almost impossible, if not impossible.

I had an ex who used her words to hurt people. I saw her in action with others and not just me. I used to speak with her often about the power of her words and how her frustrations make it hard for people to logically communicate with her and difficult to recover from. For me, these were red flags. I would constantly believe that when our time came to disagree that I would do everything I could to refrain from reacting to her, but she was the type of person who kept going until she got a reaction from you. If you let her speak until she got tired of talking, she would try other methods until she got the reaction she wanted. That to me was a dangerous characteristic of hers because once she got a response out of me, she was now ready to calm down and move on like she said nothing. I learned quickly that this was her lash-out level and a way to use what I say against me to respond to what she kept driving for. I am very good at knowing when too much is too much and creating distance by taking a walk or a long drive to put time between us. I knew if I fell into her traps it would only work against me more.

But this one here was different. She had no chill. Creating distance fueled her more. The strongest thing ever. So, when I learned to let her just talk is the moment she decided she was going to put her hands on me. Now, this is where I draw the line. At this point I am not going to ignore my own needs to satisfy her mental instability. You get one time to put your hands on me and that is when you lose me. In that critical moment she thought that reaction was cute. It was the last day of our relationship. I packed my things with the intent of never returning and had to call the authorities to get some of my belongings back. The icing on the cake, however, was watching her lie to the authorities, damage some of my things, and put me in a position where I could have gotten arrested from her meaningless behavior. I was in a state that didn't care about locking another Black person up, nor did they care about how much I stood to lose when it came to my career. At that moment neither did she. One thing for sure and two things for certain, I felt if she could pull something like that once, she was capable of attempting it again.

For me, I knew unlike the first time I caught myself from really knocking her out, the second time I will not grab your hand and walk away. She would for sure catch these hands and there will be a ten count. Me being mindful of my strength over hers I decided to follow my gut and walk away from the relationship. There was no coming back for me.

I witnessed verbal and physical abuse as a little girl. Although I wasn't the one being hit, I felt those punches just the same. I knew then that I never wanted to give nor receive that kind of pain. Another reason why adults need to be aware of the ways they express themselves around kids. Without proper understanding of what this kind of trauma did to me I could have easily become a believer of such abuse or learn early that such behaviors are not acceptable nor excusable. It was, and still is, about personal growth, mental growth, and developing coping mechanisms that help me to show up resilient and equipped to handle life's challenges in ways that help and reward me. This part of the journey isn't about others more than it is about my need to be better in my decision making.

It is important and crucial for my overall well-being to constantly work on how I communicate and how I allow others to communicate to me. Skills such as active listening, empathy, and assertiveness, to express my feelings and needs in a respectful and effective way is so very important to me. I choose not to engage in any relationships that do not respect these boundaries. I want these healthy communication skills to help me build stronger and more fulfilling relationships with others, and lead to a happier and more fulfilling life.

Have Confidence in Your Abilities

Your words and thoughts are power. I can't elaborate more on how much that statement is true. You can talk yourself out of your blessing if you are not careful. I walked into every game with the win attitude. I didn't care if I was going up against the best teams in the nation, I approached every game with that "I can't be stopped" attitude and "we got this win" approach. I used to get irritated when I had teammates go into games like we lost before we got off the bus or out of the car. Usually, these were players who didn't have much confidence in their abilities. To this day, if I hear a player talking themselves out of performing at their best or out of winning the game before it even starts, I get annoyed. Imagine if you recorded your conversations for 48 hours straight. How many of you think you'd be shocked at how you convey yourself? Forget about the person you are talking to and their conversations to or about you. Focus on what you are saying and how much of what you may be saying can be self-sabotaging. I challenge you to put extra emphasis on everything that comes out of your mouth for the next 48 to 72 hours. Then, I want you to document how much of your message was thinking that will hold you back and how much of your thinking will push you toward the life you want.

I used to go into my relationships with the utmost confidence that this one is the one. That I was going to invest my time, positive energy, and attention to making the relationship work if this person turns out to be the one. Then soon as the person starts presenting what I call "red flags" I start sabotaging the relationship with my thoughts. Way before words came out of my mouth, I started checking out. Once I started doing this, I defeated anything positive that could potentially come out of that relationship. Now, some of my red-flag sabotaging was valid, signaling I needed to get the hell out of that situation and quick. However, there were a few that I could have given honest time and healthy communication to, but I allowed myself to check-out.

This was true for some careers I chose, too. Everything starts out amazingly, staff is clicking, everything is productive, and I let the bad energy or a supervisor change my focus. In this scenario, this supervisor was abusing my ability to do the job, taking credit for my work, missing important meetings, leaving me to fulfill her job responsibilities, and giving orders in areas she wasn't skilled in. Over the course of three years, I went through the "check-out" process. I kept telling myself I know how this will end. I said to myself, when people begin to see her shortcomings she is going to turn on me. Not only did this happen, because I knew the security she had in her job, when it became obvious she was taking advantage of me and other people were doing her work, she began to nitpick at things to make me look incompetent. I tried to talk to her and establish fair boundaries for us both. Her insecurities started coming out and she would make up situations. At this point, I told myself it was time for me to go, I told one of my staff ahead of time everything this supervisor was going to do before it was done, and I was right every step of the way. Now part of me told myself I was out, ready to move on, and this woman was going to come after me. Rather than trying to fix the situation I created a scenario in my head, spoke it out loud and watched it play out. I manifested my destiny giving her control I had all along but didn't use my experience to my advantage.

I allowed my thoughts and anger to control the scenario, checked out and decided to start making plans to move on. Not only did my thoughts control me, my actions showed what I was thinking, and I put her in position to get rid of me before I could resign. She was spiteful because she knew the work she was going to be left with, but also to get ahead of the question "why I was leaving." To this day I don't regret how that situation played out. It allowed me to grow past my situations and build bigger. I was no good to myself thinking and acting the way I was. I was only hurting myself, not her. I had the option to stay, but I already told myself I was ready to move on and for me, once I make that decision, there's no looking back. I thank God I grew from that type of thinking, but that was just one situation, I had a habit of doing this with many things in my life. It took this specific situation for me to see how much I influenced that outcome, not her. I could have turned noises into my power, but it had a reverse reaction all controlled by me. That beating people to the punch type of thinking. That, I will make the decision before you do. Giving away my power and my positioning.

I am thankful that I've grown past my own self-sabotage. I've learned to stand firm in my beliefs and decisions. Some things aren't our fault, and they just have to happen. However, the things I can control I had to own and understand and learn from. It is definitely a good time to have this hard truth when history repeats itself, and what is my truth follows me. To know that, and to understand that comes with growth. Not only have I practiced listening to my thoughts, but also I watch what I say. I found my thoughts are more in my favor when I am encouraging my thoughts to lead me to the life I want. Doing so brings in the right people, situations, and outcomes. I can care less of the criticisms of others. I have no problem listening, but if that criticism isn't to make me a better person and relinquish me a better outcome, I receive it as noise and press on. Because not all criticism is constructive, a lot is toxic noise that is said to break us down not build us up. Knowing the difference between the two is a craft I have to admit, is one of my prized gifts. It took me some time to get to the point of not taking things so personally. Now, I can receive it as it pertains to my life and toss it away when it doesn't. There are three phases of truth. There's the truth, what we individually believe to be true and other peoples truth. We get to teach people how to treat us, but importantly, we must treat ourselves better than anyone.

Judge Not, but You'll Still Be Judged

Point blank period, we cannot live the life we were meant to live if we spend our time judging the likes or dislikes of others. I don't know about you, but I just won't! When I look back on the times I judged how others moved, dressed, spoke, carried themselves, behaved; I had no choice but to explore why that was a part of my thinking. Why was I so focused so much on others when I had so many imperfections that I needed to tend to? Why did I think my perception of others deserved time and thoughts in my life? I had to explore this because I disliked watching others do what I was guilty of but seem to get extremely annoyed witnessing it. It's amazing how vividly we can see the actions of others and bypass the scope of our own behaviors.

They say with age comes wisdom. Well, that works for some, not all. It was such a natural behavior growing up; people did it religiously. I blended in with what seemed like the norm. Why? I'm sure you can agree it is natural human behavior. No rhyme, no reason, and absolutely nothing to gain from it. Just time spent focusing on distractions of self. It's mind boggling to the things we do and say just to blend in with the likes of others at the expense of others. But let's face it, it's all well and good until the shoe is on the other foot. The nature of cause and effect. The effects of me judging others caused me to also be judged. Often it's the company we keep that judges us the most.

What Happens After The Game

We all find ourselves as someone's target many times throughout our lives. It is impossible to be liked or admired by everyone. All it takes is one person in a crowd to stir up a conversation that drums up an audience of followers looking for attention. There is nothing I hate more, and I do mean *hate* more than imperfect people listening to and engaging in negative banter at the expense of other people just to avoid their own deep issues. Sadly enough, I witnessed this more from either people I called friends and family, or from people who did it to others they called friends and family. The older I get, the more it bothers me. Ultimately, the same people who share in these conversations are the very ones who returned the favor in rooms I was not in. Like they say, the people who show up in front of you are the same people talking about you when you are not around.

In my pursuit to understand how I work and why I work, think the way I do, I found that the moments in which I judged others, it was my goal to take the attention off of my imperfections and shortcomings. Judging others allowed me to dismiss my weaknesses by judging others for what I was really recognizing as a strength of theirs that wasn't of mine—and here's where the work started for me, the work of putting the focus on who I was, what I wanted, and what I needed to heal to get to the exceptional person that lives in me. I have no desire for seeing the world through no one's eyes but my own, so the only person I care to analyze is me, and I choose to do that from a place of love and with the confidence to be better.

The Accident That Tested My Body and My Faith

Affirmation: I am capable of shifting when life tests me the hardest.

Brace yourself for an experience that has truly tested the core of my soul at a time when I should have been preparing for retirement. At 45, marked by achievements in sports, education, and building a foundation around becoming an established entrepreneur. I've been through hell and back, like many living through highs and lows, emerging victorious in the face of life's trials and tribulations. Only to get to a pivotal point in my life when both my body and my faith were put to the ultimate test. Everything I've been through up until now became an arsenal in confronting the adversity that unexpectedly came my way.

A typical week in my life consisted of a full-time career as a basketball coach/teacher, organizing sports events, refereeing basketball games, and partaking in sports camps across various schools throughout NYC. But then, my life took yet another unexpected turn. On October 29, 2018, I went from an active life to one of sudden limitations in a matter of weeks. The shift was quick and unforeseen, catching me off guard mentally and physically. On this particular day, I was working at a relatively new position with a charter school in Brooklyn. I was excited about this day because it marked my return to coaching girls' basketball-and a pursuit I cherished but haven't done since my assistant coaching position at CUNY York College. Despite my preference for coaching at the college or professional levels, I was genuinely enthusiastic about taking on the Basketball Coaching position at the junior high school level. Prior to this job, I had been eyeing the prospect of investing a laundromat and delving deeper into business ownership. After holding positions as a Beacon Director for years and understanding that continuing to work for a check wasn't going to bring the wealth I sought, I had no intentions of going back to work for someone else. However, a colleague of mine saw potential in my contribution to the organization and encouraged me to apply. I went through the application and interview process, ultimately securing the position. While I had initially hoped for a school in Queens, I was assigned to a location in Brooklyn. Upon starting in August of 2018, I had the opportunity to meet the department's team of directors and coaches, and it got me excited about bringing my skills to another borough of NY.

My responsibilities extended beyond coaching the girls' basketball team; I was also tasked with overseeing the girls' division across Brooklyn—a responsibility that really excited me. I've always been drawn to opportunities that allow for a broad scope of work and embrace diversity, a sentiment that aligns with my passion for organizing and running sports events. However, the demanding hours that came with the position caught me by surprise. We were required to report at 7:30 am, and our workdays concluded at 5 pm. On days that involved meetings, scheduled tryouts, and eventually practices, my start times shifted by two hours. Commuting from Queens, I would leave home at 6:30 am and often wouldn't return until 8 pm on a regular workday or even later on alternating days. I didn't have two consecutive days off at a time, and this meant many of my other hobbies like refereeing and doing basketball clinics would come to a halt. These extended hours weren't what I had initially anticipated, especially at this stage of my career when I had hoped for a lighter workload to accommodate my involvement in other ventures. Despite the unexpected nature of the workload, I had willingly signed up for it, and I was committed to seeing it through. It was definitely different amounts of work that grew each day, which had me second guessing if this was the right position for me. But the excitement of the girls within the school who really wanted to learn to play basketball and be on the team more than made up for second guessing my choice.

On the 29th, shortly after concluding my first after-school practice with the girls, I slipped and fell on some liquid that had been left on the stairwell. The impact was hard and awkward, initially not appearing overly serious until I began to struggle during the journey back home. Upon reaching home, I resorted to taking Tylenol to alleviate the pain and then retired to bed. However, when I woke up, I was met with excruciating pain and noticeable swelling. My right knee had swollen to twice its usual size, I could barely apply full pressure when walking, and a throbbing ache extended the entire right side of my body from my neck down to my lower back. I contacted both the Principal and her advising I speak to the Human Resources Director to share what had happened, I found myself on the way to the emergency room. My initial visit to CityMD resulted in a thorough examination, a temporary leave from work, the placement of my arm in a sling, the provision of a cane, prescription pain medication, and an immediate referral to an orthopedic doctor. At this point, a Workers Compensation claim was initiated by HR, which initiated a process I had to navigate. Already in a lot of pain, I found myself returning to the emergency clinic upon reviewing the doctor's notes, realizing she left out medical notes that were important to recording my injuries. This necessitated a second examination, where a different doctor conducted a comprehensive examination, documented thorough notes, and delivered a diagnosis. This doctor underscored the seriousness of my injuries, placing me on indefinite leave from work and expediting an appointment with an orthopedic specialist by personally making the appointment himself. The outcome of the orthopedics examination revealed the need for surgery on both my left knee and right shoulder with tears and damage to both. While the extent of the procedures depended on X-rays and MRI test results, the pain had become unbearable, compounded by the stabbing sensations, limited mobility, and stiffness on my entire right side.

It took several weeks before Workers Compensation granted approval for the required tests and several months before approving surgery as a result, significant damage: rotator cuff tears in my shoulder, and a torn meniscus in my knee. The authorization covered only these procedures, leaving my neck and back concerns for later, even though the X-rays suggested their need for immediate attention. Six months passed before I obtained approval for my first surgery, focusing on the shoulder, which took place in April 2019. Following the surgical healing and clearance to begin physical therapy, my second surgery—to repair my left knee tear—took place in July 2020. Meanwhile the injuries to my neck and back were getting worse. While still treating my shoulder and knee, I had to pause on those treatments to deal with the pain I was having with my neck. After additional testing and evaluations, the outcome of those tests resulted in anterior cervical fusion on my spine in November of 2020, followed by second left knee surgery in December 2022 due to the short duration of physical therapy caused by the urgency of the spinal fusion surgery. Subsequently, a microdiscectomy was performed on my cervical spine in March of 2023 due to the emergence of symptoms of loss of sensation, numbness, pain, and weakness in my right shoulder, arm, and hand.

Unquestionably, right from the outset of these injuries, I faced limitations that forced me to take a step back. Every physical activity that had become second nature to me was abruptly halted. I made a concerted effort in the first year to push myself during physical therapy, hoping for a swift recovery, much like how I handled injuries during my athletic career. However, these injuries took unsettling control over my body. I never appreciated my ability to do the little things in life the way I was now. You don't see how good you have it until it doesn't come so easy anymore. If someone had told me as I left work that night that in 2023, I'd be engaged in conversations with my doctors about potential permanent disabilities, I wouldn't have believed them. Among these injuries, the most concerning was the distress I suffered every day on the right side from my neck to my foot. My back was afflicted by multiple herniated and bulging discs, which have compelled me to rely on a cane for over two years. Simple everyday activities such as sleeping, sitting, standing, walking, kneeling, and bending are plagued by persistent pain that prompts me to resort to medication for even a modicum of relief. This medication might last two or three hours, enough to try and fall asleep until the cycle of pain repeats itself all over again.

Over the first two and a half years following the accident, my endurance was tested not only physically, but also in terms of my faith. Through a succession of injuries and surgeries, I held onto hope for relief and the return to a semblance of normalcy. Yet, nearly five years later, I'm still yearning for healing. My aspiration is to reclaim the activities I cherish and to venture into the vast expanse of life that remains ahead of me. While I've tried so hard to keep myself occupied around my house to avoid descending into the dark place I experienced in the first two years, I must admit that I did fall into that abyss initially. The mental toll I endured nearly led me to surrendering to the belief that peace would remain elusive in this situation. The reluctance to face questions about my health, the constant pain I have, and why I was walking with a cane, led me to isolate myself. I often downplayed the extent of my injuries, wishing to appear stronger than I actually felt. The circumstances seemed to have me trapped, and the simple act of taking a walk came accompanied by pain and a sense of defeat that was difficult to grapple with. Only those who have shared in a similar anguish truly understand the battles and challenges from this entire process.

I joined social media groups with people dealing with work related injuries and these stories had me leaning more and more on my faith every day. Listening to people losing their homes, will to live, and families, had me looking for ways to keep from going down that rabbit hole. I too felt like giving up and dealt with the loss of people who didn't know how to put their own selfish needs to the side and try to understand a fraction of what I was dealing with. Nothing ever prepares us for tragedies like this, but when I realized this was a battle I had to lean in on my strength to get through is when I discovered the need to talk into recorders and release the beast that was forming inside me. People always reveal themselves at your darkest times, and I got to experience this first hand. However, separating myself from them got me closer to my faith and remembering exactly who I should be leaning on first and foremost, and always. I could have desired anything and everything besides the medication to numb the pain, but my past showed me that making life-changing decisions while at my weakest moments often brings more problems, and I wasn't willing to walk that road again. Although the battle is nowhere near over, what I refuse to do is let the devil win. For me, this was about healing and living another day to use these moments as courage to help others.

Beyond the injury itself, other dimensions involve dealing with the insurance company, waiting on their decisions, addressing income concerns, and questioning what my life looks like if these injuries are permanent in my life. How can I chart the course toward building my businesses to the heights I aspire to with all these limitations? The real challenges come when explaining to their doctors that little things like trying to sit for more than fifteen minutes at a time triggers so much pain that I become scared to get up, only for them to document that as something I should be able to deal with. Hello, that is not normal! It is a scary and unethical process that no one should have to experience.

The impact of the COVID pandemic was less pronounced on me, as I was already in a state of isolation. The most painful aspect of that period was witnessing the loss of so many lives and not being able to pay proper respects. In tandem with my own healing journey, I bear the responsibility of caring for my mother. This isn't solely about me anymore. I've had to communicate with my brothers about sharing the load of looking after her. Observing my 83-year-old mother in need of my assistance more than ever, particularly when my own body often confines me, is an upsetting experience.

The Quest of Intentional Living

Life is filled with emotional rollercoasters. We all experience them. We all go through periods when life is incredibly rewarding, as well as stretches of adversity that appear endless. There is no way around it. That's just life.

I got to a point in life when I feared celebrating wins because they always seemed so short-lived—having that championship feeling filled with high adrenaline, thinking I'm on top of the world and nothing can stop me... and then, the bombs drop, and I go from high octane to stressed the hell out.

Have you ever had that experience of an unexpected financial blessing, and at the same time, unexpected expenses appear, and you go from celebrating a win to mourning the loss? To the inexperienced mind, the first emotion is to get pissed off and start questioning why you can't live in the moment of goodness, to questioning why a generous moment turns negative so quickly. This is the "I can't win for losing" moment.

Then I learned to pause from the victimized thinking that things were happening *to* me and not *for* me. It was when I began viewing situations from a fresh perspective that these experiences finally started to unfold with clarity. The shift in my perception transformed moments of confusion into hidden blessings. I altered my mindset, reaching a place of understanding and gratitude. For instance, one day I was packing up some boxes and moving out of my mother's apartment into my new one. As I was going through clothes I was keeping and giving away, I checked the pockets of a pair of old jeans. In these jeans, I found $700. The biggest smile came across my face. I didn't remember where it came from or how long it was there. I had a habit of stashing money in different places as a way of storing and forgetting it. These jeans was a gift from an old girlfriend that I hadn't worn since we broke up the year prior. I thanked God and felt like I was having a lucky day. I continued packing and then took a break to eat and check the mailbox. In the mail was a statement from one of the credit card companies I thought I had paid off in full the previous month. It turned out that when I sent off the payment, I didn't include a recent purchase I made with it. I sent what was on the statement before the purchase. So now I was looking at a statement with a balance of $550.

My immediate instincts had me pissed as I thought about how fast I went from excitement of finding $700 in some old jeans to anger of having $550 of it gone in a matter of two hours. The Michelle of today understands how blessings work. I was blessed with the $700 because God already knew about that $550. The young me, the one who felt like life was, once again, stealing my joy, saw it negatively. I failed to recognize that my prayers for divine guidance in managing my finances and achieving freedom from debt were indeed being answered. I had asked for something, but I wasn't prepared for the manner in which it manifested. While I perceived the gift as a punishment, God saw the expense and provided a solution. Answered prayers have a way of coming at times when we need them, even if they are not always in the manner we anticipate. Nevertheless, it is still a timely provision, whether in the form I desired or not. That money arrived right on time with $150 to spare. Perspective!

To take it a step further, it served as a valuable lesson concerning my energy when it came to money, as I allowed it to have control over my emotions. I acquired the knowledge of celebrating gifts by accepting them as how I intended the reward. I realized that money is a tool that serves, and when I possess authority over its rightful significance of it in my life, I lose the ability to retain it with gratitude whether it is coming in or going out. This applies to all areas of life. As they say, wisdom comes from experiences. Looking back, I was so clueless about so much of what life was and is. That thinking is attributed to years of training and understanding purpose. Every day, I aim to live my life thinking and acting intentionally by appreciating the sequences of events and my ability to choose how to respond to them. For numerous years, I mistakenly attributed my experiences to mere misfortune, unaware that circumstances were actually unfolding in my favor. I lacked the mental clarity necessary to comprehend the positive occurrences transpiring in my life. It doesn't mean every situation has great endings, but what it has taught me is the power of my thought - how I have control of how the outcomes translates.

Living intentionally holds significant importance for me, and I understand the sentiment. Life, much like happiness, emerges as invaluable lessons learned. Perspective, put in its rightful place, are mere tools that we can use to better our lives and see the world in a realistic view. The reward is to live a limitless life and see how things are actually happening for our benefit. Rather than adopting the mindset of a victim, I choose to embrace the perspective of a victor. Irrespective of the influence of external factors, everything starts and ends with me. I recognize that I am the ultimate driving force behind what impacts me. I firmly believe that my choices, actions, views, and mindset shapes my path. I reclaim my autonomy and realize that the outcomes I see are within my reach. I embrace that the beginning and the end of my journey lie within me and that's my intentional living.

The Value of Presence
Claim Your Seat at the Table

"Don't just be in spaces with people who like you. Create and dwell in spaces with people who thrive like you."
Michelle Reed

I trust myself enough to believe that things happen just the way they are supposed to whether they work out or not. I know that regardless of which way the pendulum swings, it will ultimately swing in my favor. I hope you acknowledge this about yourself, too.

A friend of mine who is a public figure and frequent among many A-listers and prestigious businessmen and women for years invited me to be a speaker on panels among some of these great people, and for years, I declined for no other reason except I was afraid and lacked the confidence. I felt I wasn't at the level of these speakers, and they wouldn't care what I had to say. I unfairly judged myself by fixating on what I lacked when comparing myself to them. I put these people on pedestals and demoted myself. Repeatedly, I reinforced the notion that I was less than them, and I persuaded myself that the number of commas in my bank account was insufficient and that I had not attained an adequate level of success.

I decreased my own value, which was a grave mistake. It wasn't about me lacking the ability to speak before an audience. I just didn't believe that I had reached a level of success in my career to talk about.

What Happens After The Game

In my mind, my attention and connection were directed toward an audience of student-athletes, that I can be more of an asset to them. Sitting at tables with esteemed executives, high-level politicians, affluent individuals with vast wealth, and other well-known professionals who were household names did not feel like my rightful place. I really downplayed my own accomplishments and suppressed my inner radiance. Talking about not loving oneself.

This platform provided me with the opportunity to share my experiences from a standpoint of excellence, highlighting the remarkable journey of a young Black girl who emerged from challenging circumstances in the projects and rose to the heights of her professional basketball career in the WNBA. It was an extraordinary feat—one that few individuals who started in similar neighborhoods can claim to have accomplished at that specific time. And it's not merely the journey of reaching professional basketball status that deserves recognition, but also the multitude of achievements I garnered along the way—the championships, accolades, scholarships, global travel, inclusion in the esteemed book of genius records, and a plethora of other accomplishments that define my extraordinary path.

It took me years to embrace the notion of selflessness and began sharing my story. This transformative journey also led me to start healing within myself , realizing that my pursuit of what I am passionate about had nothing to do with the amount of money in my bank account. It became more about how I can inspire and help others. It was about delivering a message that people can relate to and being willing to be vulnerable enough to tell it. Reaching that level, which allows me to be transparent, is the reason why a little girl or boy goes after their dreams, gives back to the community, and believes that they too can live and be the best version of themselves with unlimiting beliefs.

I silenced my voice at a time when someone needed to hear me. I also silenced that voice in me that needed to share. I sold my achievements short because I was looking for outside voices to validate me. I was looking for my value to be weighed by how much wealth in money I had and not by the wealth of knowledge I could provide. I listened to the noise instead of listening to my heart. This experience also highlighted the importance of my personal journey toward cultivating self-love.

At this juncture in my life, it matters little to me who occupies the table. As long as it is the right table, I firmly believe that I deserve to be present. What truly matters to me is that the panels I participate in are dedicated to sharing authentic and uplifting experiences for every listener. I value the opportunity to both learn as a humble student from exceptional teachers and impart knowledge as a teacher in return. I welcome the butterflies that form in my stomach when meeting some of the greatest minds in the game. I am proud of the fear it creates because I now know that the fear I feel is a reminder that I am in new waters and that it's ok to feel uncomfortable and be confident enough to know I am deserving of my place. The fear I experience serves as a sign that my faith is about to ignite, propelling me toward the realization of my greatness.

I will never silence myself again. I am living intentionally. I am committed to the process. My story is just as important as anyone else's, and yours is, too. Do not dim your light for anyone. One can never truly know who is listening and who may be in need of motivation through our words. There is power in the tongue. Refuse to let anything or anyone silence you, especially not YOU.

"Some people are never going to clap for you. Win anyway."
Steve Harvey

346

Free the Past

Don't wait for life to happen for you. Get up and make it happen because it's for you. I remind myself of this as often as it takes to sink in. Personally, I can't speak for anyone, but it's quite common to hear people say, "Ask and you shall receive." This phrase serves as an encouraging reminder I hold onto. However, it's important to recognize that the process doesn't end there; it requires taking action. To actively bring about the things I desire, I am learning to embrace the concept of repetitive manifestation, whereby I vocalize my intentions and continually reinforce them through practice. Just imagine if we had the power to will things into our lives just by asking for it. What a life. I don't know about you, but I would be living a worry-free life.

Much of what we ask for depends on where our mindset is at the time we are asking for it. The outer world doesn't change our mindset; our mindset changes when we make up our minds to change it. It starts with the thoughts we keep. Our thoughts are the vocabulary that rules our brains and are triggered by a bunch of wants, needs, and must-haves. Do we have the capability of manifesting things from our thoughts? I believe so; I believe in those vibrations. Just like we can attract good, we can attract bad.

How we think and feel determines our state of being and where we are in our lives. Are we living a life with forward thinking or are we focused on remembering the past? The problem with living in the past is that it keeps us from seeing the possibilities the future holds. We cannot solve the problems that have already happened in our past, especially the ones that hold us there. The focus starts on what we can control right now in the moment and bringing happiness into those moments. How has living in the past made life easier for you? Especially traumatic experiences. It is natural and understandable to engage in reflection, as it is a part of human nature. However, it is important to know that dwelling on the traumas of the past often leads to one outcome: the emergence of bitterness. Why in our right mind would we want to live there? Drawing up the past forces us to stay in those routines and blocks us from creating new ones. The vision we should focus on creating is what we want the future to look and feel like, and we can begin to do this by living as if those visions are already happening.

I learned this when I sat down one day and meditated wondering why I don't enjoy celebrating Christmas as I did as a child. I love watching Christmas movies. The moment they start playing on the Lifetime Network in October, I can watch them for hours. These movies to me aren't about the gifts but they embody the essence of family, love, and selfless giving. What truly captivates me is how each storyline beautifully culminates in a joyful and fulfilling conclusion. The last time I found joy in Christmas was when I was maybe 10 or 11 years old. That was the last Christmas my whole family gathered around our traditional boxed tree together and shared time and space in one room together. My mother always showered us with gifts until my brothers felt they were too busy for the gatherings. Year after year, my mother did her best to make Christmas homey pulling out the same boxed tree and the new decorations for it, but one or two of my brothers always had other plans. I still had the excitement of finding the gifts my mother tried to hide until she stopped because I always found them before she wrapped them. Because I always found them, the wrapping part turned into something she and I did together just to keep the spirit of Christmas going. As one year turned into two, two into three, and so on, all of the Christmas spirit was shared with just me and my mother. As I got older and was able to share in gift-giving with my family, I lost the will because my mother and I bought gifts out of love, but our family was lacking love-sharing. My brothers found the streets more appealing than home, and by this time, they were having families of their own, and we gathered mainly around times when people thought they were going to get something, like the holidays. Watching Christmas movies put me in that fantasy world of what love should feel like but didn't exist for the Reed family.

I always had to adjust when I got into relationships because the majority of the relationships I was in were with people with strong or thriving family elements. I guess in some sort of way I was attracting what I longed for. In celebrating with them, it felt uneasy at first blending in, trying not to show my inadequacies, and not reveal my inner sadness of how much I wish it was my own family living those moments together. The older I got the more I realized, I needed to let go of dwelling on the past. It became clear that clinging to bygone moments was hindering my ability to forge new, significant memories that I have the power to shape and cherish. I promised myself to mold my present and future into a reflection of my desires, rather than being confined by what had been. I took steps to shape my reality, ensuring that it aligned with how I envisioned my life to be—both in appearance and in the emotions it evoked. I set a goal of making the future of Christmas worth looking forward to. The incredible part is that I hold the power to shape this transformation, and it doesn't require any monetary expenditure. It simply required a shift in my mindset, an investment of time, and dedicated effort. It struck me that I had become more attached to my past than to the possibilities of my future. Consequently, I embarked on a journey to detach my emotions, consciously flicking off that switch of attachment, knowing that remarkable experiences and adventures awaited me.

This is a prime example of how our thoughts can rob us blind of our true happiness. Sometimes, we don't know we are doing it until the habitual routine creates dark spaces where light is supposed to shine. Now, I concentrate on creating thoughts around being grateful for what is and looking forward to what will be. Nothing I've been through will continue to block where I'm headed. This is the path I'm choosing, and I know the universe will align just the right coordinates to make that happen.

I'm no victim of these experiences. It was what it was. I know I am becoming a better person from it because now what seemed like a holiday of gift-giving taught me to give additional love to myself and others without gift-giving. Gift-giving is a bonus, not a requirement. Love is the requirement.

I don't need permission to believe and want better experiences. I just needed to recognize how powerful having positive thoughts can and will keep me from visiting a past that cannot be managed. The way I perceive and experience life is deeply influenced by my thoughts and emotions. Therefore, I consciously choose to ignite positive emotions that fuel my aspirations. It requires a diligent and habitual practice of mindfulness to skillfully manage the influence negative thoughts can have when they surface, but recognizing them, feeling them, and moving past them is my way of growing through them. I hold no resentment within. Instead, I choose to fill myself up with extra love whenever I feel myself needing it.

Do the work. Let the past go and take your power back. For me, it was Christmas. For you, it is something else, but the same rules apply. I learned that these struggles was teaching me what I was meaningful to me. Let's take this journey together. It's constant, it's daily, it's lifelong, and it's doable. Let's draw from places that fuel our positivity and greatness and keep living the people we are and not what we've been through. Don't let things get really bad before making changes.

Let's set clear intentions. Life feels really good when we are the reason why it's good. Make a habit of making new and meaningful moments that bring peace, forgiveness, freedom, and happiness into our lives. Let's trust our future and free our pasts. It's happening right now, are you ready? Don't lose sight of the joy of life. If ever detoured, remember that it's never too late to refocus and get back on track.

Wish Fulfillment

A wish is a desire, something we aspire to become reality. We all have wished for something, and the best wishes are those we can fulfill, but what does it take to bring such wishes to fruition? There is a popular phrase that warns us: *Be careful what you wish for because you just may get it*. Making wishes is a universal phenomenon. We use them to try to manifest things we want associated with excitement and anticipation. Wishes can be very complex, often resulting in unexpected outcomes. I like to use wishing as a way to motivate myself to take action. I've wished for jobs, love, money, friendships, opportunities, clarity, you name it. All achievable things, but how they materialize is the unforeseen challenge.

For example, here I was a retired professional basketball player, I had achieved a good amount of success throughout my career. Despite my achievements on the court, I yearned for a fulfilling romantic relationship. I wanted a partner who understood my shift from a demanding basketball schedule and the passion I still had for the game and provided emotional support during those challenging times when I struggled with finding my new outlook professionally away from the game. My wish seemed to come true when I met Nique, who was a basketball enthusiast and a supportive person. We quickly formed a connection after meeting during New York Pride. She had a bubbly personality, was spontaneous, and was someone who understood the intricacies of her life in law enforcement and mine stepping into this new world. She was nine years older than I and had a way of showing me something different about myself and life that I liked. We always had something to talk about, and we supported each other's careers. She came from a close-knit family and took family vacations with her mother to visit various family members throughout the year. She developed a great relationship with my mother, which made our family outings that much more special. We had fun together, talked about just about everything, and fought fairly. We disagreed to be heard and not to cause pain, which I found refreshing. It made out disagreements short lived and easy to move past. Besides my mother in the stands at my pick-up games or tournaments I played in, she was my loudest and biggest fan. The two of them together in the stands was hilarious. We were very close and did just about everything together.

As our relationship progressed over three years, I discovered that we spent a lot of time and money traveling, going to casinos because she loved gamble, and shopping, but making solid plans investing in our future together wasn't happening. I would often bring it up being that I still lived at home with my mother, and she shared an apartment with hers. I felt we both were in positions to build upon a place of our own. It was something we spoke about but gained no traction on her end. She seemed comfortable with the flow of our relationship, and I wanted to share a space beyond her just spending time at my house. I would go to her apartment to pick her up or drop her off but had never been inside. She told me her mother wasn't all that happy about her being a lesbian, so she didn't entertain at her house. I respected that, but after being together over three years, there was no need for us to remain in that kind of situation, especially when we could afford to have our own place. It was something important to me and her, but again when it came to her taking action, it was always a pause. I was getting to a point where us spending our time and money on material things and ventures weren't the only memories I wanted to have within our union. Even some of her friends would question when we were going to make the move together, and she would always say soon. One evening, I asked her about her pause to live together, and she kept saying she didn't have any. She just wanted to make sure her mother was ok when she moved. I took it as an excuse but left it alone. The conversation got put on hold because of the tragic events on 9-11. Of course, the world was in an uproar, faced with fear, and because she worked in law enforcement, she was mandated to report to the scene. Things shifted quickly because I became more concerned about her safety and the poor conditions she was subject to working in Manhattan. At that point, nothing mattered but her safety and eventually her health.

So, a year went by, and the reality of her career's constant demand took a toll on her health. Like many, inhaling all those fumes started creating breathing problems for her. I prayed constantly for her health to improve, along with the thousands of workers on the scene for months. It got so bad for her that she ended up retiring earlier than expected. She only had three years left, so with her health becoming a concern, she was able to get her full retirement. This was a relief, and I prayed for her to get out of that situation.

Like I mentioned earlier, it's important to be careful what you wish for because of how that wish will manifest itself. Her retirement changed our relationship. She had more time on her hands and started engaging in gambling even more. So much so she started being deceitful about her whereabouts. I never had a problem trusting her or her lying to me. We were always upfront and honest with each other. Until one weekend when, upon her return from a trip to visit her family in the South, I found a receipt from a ATM dated that Saturday from a casino. The very Saturday she was supposed to be visiting family. Of course, when I asked her about the weekend, she lied, until I showed her the receipts that fell out of luggage. I gave her a whole hour to tell me the truth, and she was committed to the lie. That's when my heart sank and realized the person I was looking at had a gambling addiction. It was her money, so there was no need to lie, but it explained why her commitment to us building a home together was so hard for her. She'd rather feed her addiction than our future. That wasn't a deal breaker for me, but a series of actions continued after that caused me to feel uncomfortable in the relationship. I ultimately began losing interest in the relationship and decided to end things because I wasn't in a position to sacrifice my happiness for dishonesty.

Through the ups and downs, I realized that our life was going in different directions. I wanted our relationship to flourish, I prayed and wished on it, but I didn't expect my wish to play out like this. My wish came true for her safety and for her to retire before the job killed her from its demands, but I wasn't mentally prepared for the reality of us ending an almost five-year relationship that was built on so much love but evolved into disappointment.

As I pondered the situation, a question arose within me: What I do with this unexpected outcome? How could a seemingly harmless wish result in such disappointment? I'm not sure. But what I do know is when I pray or wish for something, I try to be as specific as I can in my words. I also know that I must be prepared with how it shows up. It may not be the way I want it, but it may show up exactly how it needs to be.

Customizing Information for Personal Growth

With each passing day, my comprehension deepens, and I observe my unique ability to seek clarity in every piece of knowledge molded in me. This process of growth is truly invigorating. Today, a college degree is no longer necessary for financial prosperity. Instead, all it takes is a brilliant idea and the knack for effectively addressing people's needs and solving their problems, even the ones they don't know they have. Clearly defining the objective and ultimate goal is of utmost importance. In recognizing this, my pursuit of knowledge encompasses both personal and professional development, and it entails nurturing new habits.

Developing these new habits is not without its challenges. It demands redefining what I learn and how I apply what I learn in striving for excellence. In doing so, there are certain aspects of my previous belief system that needs to become obsolete, as my newfound perspective requires a transition from old ways of thinking, doing, and being. The vision I hold for my future has expanded significantly, cultivated by new disciplines, mindsets, concentration, passions, and strengths. As I embark on this transformative journey, who I become along the way is just as crucial as the visions I aspire to achieve. I am prepared to invest as much effort as necessary to shape my thoughts, emotions, and actions, and this undertaking demands a level of focus unlike any I have experienced before—something I eagerly anticipate.

What Happens After The Game

All the knowledge I have acquired thus far has been shaped by the beliefs and teachings of those who, themselves, learned from others. Initially, I was taught to apply these teachings without questioning their veracity, except when it concerned the education of my people's history—a conversation unto itself. During my early academic years, determining the accuracy of what I was taught proved challenging unless I delved deeper into the topics that interested me, assessing how uniquely they applied to my life and the direction I wished to pursue. As my thirst for knowledge grew, I came to understand that what works for others may not necessarily work for me. Thus, I receive information with an open mind while simultaneously questioning, "Does it align with my own truth?" Some teachings stem from outdated beliefs that were effective at that time, but with the world evolving and advancing rapidly, one must question the relevance of what is being taught in relation to one's own perspective.

I have learned to receive information but challenge and mold it to fit my specific needs and interests. By refraining from blind acceptance, I avoid relying on others' opinions as the sole basis for my success. For instance, when my mother shares her understandings about money, I gain insight into her beliefs, yet I recognize that we don't see money the same. What worked for her does not necessarily work for me. While her perspectives are valid, her notion of working diligently for a company and retiring with a pension and social security, although fascinating and successful for her, may not hold true in 2023, particularly in our country. Pensions, 401(k)s, and social security have become uncertain prospects, prompting me to shift my principles toward ownership, profitable investments, and robust savings—creating a secure future independent of any company or job.

The challenge I currently embrace involves reevaluating the information I receive and aligning it with my beliefs and visions. My definition of success extends across all areas of life. The society we knew before the arrival of cell phones differs vastly from the past. Previously, making connections with others required effort, memorizing phone numbers, using beepers, calling from house phones, and speaking face to face. Today, cell phones simplify this process but diminishes genuine human connection. I highlight this shift to emphasize how swiftly times change and how societal operations evolve. Adjusting from what one was taught to what is currently unfolding proved challenging for individuals like my mother. She learned to type on a typewriter, while I gained experience on both typewriters and computers. Computers challenge her as does the use of a cell phone. Which speaks to how our worlds differ so vastly. What emerges from our two worlds is growth, as this cycle continues, my principles will seem extinct for those behind me. That's why how we learn is just as important as what we learn. However, real transformation occurs during the execution, and that is when life happens.

Looking Back

Being able to look back and see how much of life I wasn't prepared for is scary. Life at every level comes with important responsibilities. How and if we are taught these intricacies is vital. It would be unfair of me to put the blame on anyone for the poor choices I made. It would be me playing the victim role in the way my life played out. That would also mean I did not take responsibility for my actions, and that is the farthest thing from the truth. As miserable as those experiences were to live through, they were some of the best things that needed to happen in my life. I waited for the life lessons I thought school was supposed to provide, but they never happened. I realized that life's challenges happen during good times and, oftentimes, come with conflict and countless adventures. Those experiences developed my ability to examine subsequent situations through a sharper lens. Usually, the lessons weren't learned right away, but with maturity and understanding, life started to expose why each thing happened and why it had to play out the way it did. For me, learning my levels of strength and potential to become better versions of myself happened not just when things were going great in my life but when I was challenged the most. I was forced to either give up on myself or fight through and discover greater parts of myself that had to feel uncomfortable in order for me to advance to a higher level.

The ending is never the ending until life is over. Until then, every start comes without limits, and what we convince ourselves is an ending is just a new beginning to another level of growth and advancement. Not until I started changing how I perceived the world did I start protecting myself from the stinking thinking that tainted my vision to see my full potential. My potential isn't defined by my mistakes. My potential is developed from my mistakes, enabling me to improve interactions with my imperfect self. I had to let go of the stories I told myself, even in the moments I was writing this book, to review, shape, and protect my values and maintain them. I refuse to believe what I am not. I am not my mistakes, and I am not my past. I could not change living back there. In this time and space, I am learning and rebuilding myself. I am free from holding myself back due to the fears created in my childhood and carried over into my adulthood. I could always wonder if I would have done things differently in each situation that I consider setbacks, but what good would that do? What would it change now? How would it deny me of my past? No matter how I play back my experiences, it does not take away from the rising star in me that will uncover my genius. Instead of me measuring myself by my youth, I rather use this time to manifest some grandiose life I am creating filled with spectacular talent, my attractive demeanor, and my ability to help others in order to leave a legacy that outlives me.

In order for change to happen, I had to be wrong about some things. Those wrongs taught me the most meaningful lessons that I carry with me to this day. Being able to look back and see my growth and being able to evaluate each phase is life changing. It was necessary in order for me to grow. I am humbled more than ever because of my past ignorance, and rather than consider myself a failure, I approve of my screw-ups. I am thankful for the chance after chance I received to get it right. I had to fail in order to move forward and succeed. Hitting rock bottom means something different for everyone, but for me, it means GROWTH. If everything I did failed, it wouldn't go on record that I didn't try. At some point, because I will keep going, I will get it right. My value is not about money. My value is rooted in doing purposeful and meaningful work that makes me feel great inside. I can now live up to my values, and regardless of how others perceive me, my self-worth is all about my happiness and achieving what I set out to do in my life. I still have work to do to be better and more responsible. I still live with the pain and triggers that often peek through, but my greatest advantage is knowing how to control it all and having a clear perspective of where it comes from.

About the Author

Michelle Reed is a retired professional basketball player, educator, mentor, entrepreneur, author, and speaker from Queens, NY. She has a bachelor's in interdisciplinary studies from Western Kentucky University and an Associate of Science in business management from Sullivan College. For the past 18 years, she has passionately served as program director, basketball coach, consultant and referee, and community liaison.

Michelle is a former pro basketball player with the WNBA Los Angeles Sparks; FIBA Tapiolan Honka in Espoo, Finland; and Drava Visual in Croatia, Europe. She is a NYC P.S.A.L. High School City and State Champion and All-American, JC/CC Kodak Women's All-American, Junior College Most Valuable Player, NCAA Sun Belt Conference Champion, participated in NCAA Sweet 16, USA Olympic Festival Gold Medalist, and two-time Basketball Scholarship Recipient.

Being the well-rounded person that she is, Michelle naturally loves to help others and watch them win. When Michelle is not engaged in her true passion of sports, she enjoys sharing her inspiring journey, hoping her exciting career ignites a spark of motivation in others to find their place in the world, own it, and become a true force of positivity. Michelle's passion for writing blossomed from her love for reading. As an avid reader, she realized the power of authenticity and vulnerability in connecting with readers who share similar interests and passions. Embracing her true self became the very essence of her storytelling, unlocking the pages of years of journaling to share her captivating narrative.

Follow Michelle at **Facebook** [/whathappensafterthegame] and **Instagram** [@WHATG23]!